IRISH TRAVELLERS:
RACISM AND THE POLITICS OF CULTURE

Irish Travellers

Racism and the
Politics of Culture

JANE HELLEINER

UNIVERSITY OF TORONTO PRESS
Toronto Buffalo London

© University of Toronto Press 2000
   Toronto Buffalo London
   Printed in Canada

ISBN 0-8020-4843-9

Printed on acid-free paper

Canadian Cataloguing in Publication Data

Helleiner, Jane Leslie, 1961–
   Irish Travellers : racism and the politics of culture

   (Anthropological horizons)
   Includes bibliographical references and index.
   ISBN 0-8020-4843-9

   1. Irish Travellers (Nomadic people).   2. Ireland – Ethnic relations.
   3. Racism – Ireland.   I. Title.   II. Series.

   DX217.H44 2000   305.891'4970417   CX00-931986-7

University of Toronto Press acknowledges the financial assistance to its
publishing program of the Canada Council for the Arts and the Ontario Arts
Council.

University of Toronto Press acknowledges the financial support for its
publishing activities of the Government of Canada through the Book
Publishing Industry Development Program (BPIDP).

Contents

Acknowledgments

This book has been many years in the making and would not have been possible without a wide network of support. My primary debt is to the many Travellers who were willing to share part of their lives with me. As promised, I do not identify individuals for reasons of confidentiality, but here I would like to thank all those involved and express particular gratitude to my camp neighbours, who offered months of warm hospitality and companionship to a Canadian stranger.

My in-laws, Betty Szuchewicz, Ursula and Ulick Murtagh, and Frank Murtagh, facilitated the research by providing a home away from home and ongoing support throughout the course of the project. I am also indebted to Ciaran and Grace Doyle, who offered both friendship and office space at a critical time. Others who facilitated my work in Galway City include Jane Newman, Ned Crosbie, and Chris Curtin. In the post-fieldwork years I was fortunate to benefit from feedback provided by the late John O'Connell, Stasia Crickley, Máirín Kenny, Brid O'Brien, and the Cultural Heritage Group of Pavee Point. A period of writing at Trinity College, Dublin, facilitated by Ronit Lentin, was critical to the completion of the manuscript. I am keenly aware that not all of those who have supported this project will share the views found here and I emphasize that I alone remain responsible for the arguments developed and any errors of fact and/or misinterpretation of archival or fieldwork material. It is my hope, however, that my material and arguments will serve to spur increased research on these topics in Ireland.

As a graduate student in the Department of Anthropology at the University of Toronto I benefited from the guidance and support of Shuichi Nagata, Peter Carstens, Krys Sieciechowicz, Michael Levin, Stuart Philpott, Gavin Smith, my cohort of graduate students, and especially fellow members of the feminist caucus. Other scholars who offered direction during doctoral research included Sharon Gmelch, the late Mimi Kaprow, Judith Okely, and Marilyn Silverman. In my present academic home at Brock University I have enjoyed the multidisciplinary collegiality of colleagues in the Department of Child and Youth Studies, the Department of Sociology, and the Women's Studies program.

The Social Sciences and Humanities Research Council provided funding for my doctoral fieldwork, and at Brock University I have received support from the Office of the Dean of Social Sciences, a President's Fund for the Advancement of Scholarship Release Time Research Award, and internal General Research Grant funding from the Social Sciences and Humanities Research Council. Undergraduate research assistants Angela Barclay, Sonja Justensen, Joy Stewart-Riffle, Neil Runnalls, and Michelle Webber have also made contributions to this project. Reviewers for the University of Toronto Press provided valuable feedback on the manuscript, while Margaret Burgess and Anne Forte did excellent work in copyediting. I am indebted to photographer Derek Speirs for permission to use his photos.

My parents, Georgia and Gerry, whose commitment to social justice continues to be an inspiration, have been steadfast in their support of my academic career. My children, Kieran and Tomas, have ensured that my life is well balanced and full of joy, and Bohdan, who has been at my side from the inception of this project to its completion, has replenished me with love, patience, and humour. To all of them I offer my loving thanks.

IRISH TRAVELLERS

Introduction

On the second night after moving into a trailer in a Traveller camp in Galway City, Ireland, I was feeling relaxed and optimistic about the prospects for my research. The day had been spent getting to know many of my new neighbours in the camp and I was delighted with the warm reception that I had received. Generous offers of advice and assistance had begun to partially mitigate the challenges of adjusting to camping in a trailer without electricity, running water, toilet, or rubbish facilities.

While enjoying the heat provided by the pressed peat 'briquettes' that a neighbour had brought for our stove, my husband and I decided to turn on our newly hooked-up truck battery-fed television. When the late night national news appeared, however, our sense of well-being was shaken by a breaking news item – there had been a violent attack on a Traveller camp in Galway City. An anxious glance outside confirmed it was one of the other camps in the city that had been targeted and that our own camp was peaceful, but a new sense of vulnerability made for an uneasy night.

The vigilante assault by non-Travellers was described the following day in a national newspaper report:

> The Mayor of Galway yesterday appealed for calm and patience by both sides in the wake of Thursday night's attack on an itinerant encampment in the Rahoon area, by a crowd of up to 100 ... Five caravans belonging to itinerant families were towed by tractors out of a field ... into which they had moved, in the early hours of Thursday morning. They had been served with a court order to leave a nearby site, and insist a Corporation official suggested they move to the field. (*Irish Independent*, 27 September 1986: 5)

I knew from my reading of the existing literature and my own archival research that this attack was only the latest in a series of such incidents in the city. I also knew that such vigilante attacks represented the more extreme end of a continuum of exclusionary actions affecting Travellers in the city, region, and Ireland as a whole. The events in Rahoon clarified in a particularly stark fashion the crux of my research project, which would combine a documentation and analysis of the history of anti-Traveller racism both locally and nationally with an ethnographic analysis of the ways in which Travellers forged a distinct identity and way of life within its shadow.

While the comparative literature on ethnicity and racism includes important analyses of anti-Irish racism in the context of colonialism and migration, as well as discussion of racism and ethnicized divisions within Northern Ireland, the phenomena of ethnicity and racism within the Irish Republic have received relatively little attention (Allen 1994; Brewer 1992; Hainsworth 1998; Hickman 1998; Poole 1997).

Largely neglected by mainstream scholarship, the issues of ethnicity and racism in Ireland have, however, been tackled by activist scholars concerned with anti-racism at both national and European levels, and their work has begun to challenge long-standing official and popular perceptions of Southern Ireland as an ethnically homogeneous, mono-cultural, and non-racist state. (Crowley and MacLaughlin 1997; Lentin and McVeigh forthcoming; Tannan, Smith, and Flood 1998).[1] Some of this work has begun to locate the 'specificity of Irish racism' within Southern Ireland's history of colonialism, post-colonial nation-building, and semi-peripheral position within the larger world system (McVeigh 1992, 1996).

Some of the first challenges to a model of Southern Ireland as ethnically homogeneous and free of racism came from activists concerned with the status of Travelling People (see Dublin Travellers Education and Development Group 1992; Gmelch 1989; McCann, Ó Síocháin, and Ruane 1994). The identification of Travellers as an ethnic group has been a central premise of the human rights and community development work of Traveller advocacy organizations from at least the 1980s, and these groups by naming the discrimination and exclusion experienced by Travellers as a form of Irish racism have been influential in injecting the term into Irish political discourse (McVeigh 1996: 9).

Along with their efforts aimed at improving the position of Travellers in Ireland, advocacy groups such as Pavee Point, the Irish Traveller Movement, National Traveller Women's Forum, and a variety of regional

Traveller support groups have also provided leadership and organizational capacity for the broader anti-racist coalition of the 1990s, which mobilized to challenge an upsurge of right-wing xenophobic and racist activity that accompanied the economic growth of the Irish 'Celtic Tiger.'

Despite the high profile of Traveller organizations within the contemporary politics of anti-racism in Ireland, concrete progress toward recognition of economic, political or cultural rights of Travellers has been limited. Southern Ireland has yet to ratify the UN International Convention on the Elimination of All Forms of Racial Discrimination and Travellers continue to be targeted by racist discourse and exclusionary practices ranging from violent conflicts such as the attack in Galway, to being 'barred' from a wide variety of commercial establishments, to structural neglect in the areas of accommodation, education, health, and social services. The effects of such practices are evident in the disproportionate levels of poverty, low life expectancy, and high neonatal and child mortality within the Traveller population (Task Force on the Travelling Community 1995).

I became interested in Travellers during my first trip to Ireland in 1983–4. During this initial year-long visit my Canadian gaze was captured by the highly visible Traveller trailers or caravans strung out along roadside verges or clustered in 'wasteland' areas on the outskirts of towns and cities. Intrigued by the romantically distinctive 'camping' and appalled at the evident lack of basic services, I began to make inquiries about the Travellers and their location within Irish society. Many of the non-Travellers replying to my questions constructed a negative picture of a population that was dirty, dangerous, and best avoided.

While living in Galway City, I made contact with some non-Traveller service providers who were involved in working among Travellers. Some of them had rather different views insofar as they emphasized the poverty and deprivation of Travellers as evidence of the need for state and voluntary sector intervention. As a result of my interest I was invited by some of these workers to a number of programs and events (e.g., literacy class, women's club, pilgrimage) where I was able to meet many Travellers. These initial encounters encouraged me to think about returning to conduct anthropological fieldwork as part of my anticipated graduate research and I spent much of the remainder of my year-long stay reviewing the existing scholarly and policy literature and compiling a file of Traveller-related press reports from back issues of the provincial newspaper.

In 1986–7 I was back in Galway City as a doctoral student ready to conduct research more formally. My goal was to better understand both the history of anti-Traveller racism and how Travellers engaged with and struggled against racism in their everyday lives while working to create and recreate a distinct identity and way of life.

During this second visit my husband and I spent ten months in the city, nine months of which were spent living in a trailer parked in a camp among a shifting number of Traveller families. From this location I conducted ethnographic participant-observation, augmenting this with interviewing and additional archival research. While this experience provided the bulk of the ethnographic material for this book, several shorter research trips in 1994, 1995, 1997, and 1999 allowed for further archival work.

Racism and Ethnicity in Ireland

As anthropological work continues to demonstrate, despite predictions of an increasingly globalized world where social inequality and cultural difference are erased, these phenomena are not disappearing but rather being created and/or reproduced in the course of economic and political change. Writers such as Wolf (1982) and Roseberry (1989) have worked to firmly locate anthropological subjects within changing and unequally structured regional, national, and global political economies.

Theorists of ethnicity and 'race' working from this perspective have emphasized how ethnic and racial boundaries and identities are actively constructed within shifting political economies and relations of power linked, for example, to state and nationalist projects (e.g., Williams 1989; Greenhouse 1998).

The larger project of documenting and analysing the links between Southern Ireland's political economy and processes of racism and ethnic formation remains to be done, but a number of the necessary pieces are emerging. For example, there is growing documentation of the processes of post-1922 nation-building wherein the male members of the Catholic propertied classes who gained power with independence self-consciously worked to create a unified Catholic, Gaelic, and capitalist state (Foster 1988: 518–19, 533–5). A body of work now addresses the way in which a nationalist myth of homogeneity obscured the diverse experiences and unequal positioning of different classes, men and women, and various religious and ethnic groups (e.g., Curtin, Donnan, and Wilson 1993; Curtin, Jackson, and O'Connor 1987; Curtin and Wilson 1989).

Within the limited literature on racism and ethnicity in Ireland some attention has been paid to the experiences of religious minorities – for example, Protestants and Jews. This focus has reflected the significance of religion as a marker of ethnic boundaries and inequality in Ireland. Following centuries of colonial domination during which Catholicism signified grounds for subordination, Catholic nationalism emerged as dominant in the struggle for independence. The importance of Catholicism in the self-definition of the new state was increased with the 1921 Treaty that partitioned the island and was codified in the 1937 Constitution that clearly articulated the ethos of a Catholic state. As the Irish nation was equated with Catholicism, non-Catholicism became a fundamental marker of 'Otherness' (Lentin 1998).

The importance of post-colonial nation-building projects for processes of ethnicization is also well-illustrated through reference to the Gaelic-speaking minority. In Ireland, this spatially concentrated and linguistically and culturally distinct population has experienced both economic marginalization and targeted state intervention, but remains unethnicized. The non-ethnic status of this population can be attributed to a process of Irish nation-building that equated the Gaelic language with the core of the nation despite its minority status. The political projects that peripheralized non-Catholics as ethnicized 'Others' simultaneously worked against ethnicization of the distinctive Gaelic-speaking population.

Within the emerging anti-racist scholarship the experiences of Jews and Travellers have been featured as examples of long-standing 'organic' or 'endogenous' Irish racisms which pre-date the more recent rise in anti-immigrant and refugee racism (McVeigh 1992; 1996). While highlighting the existence of a history of Irish racism, the phrase 'organic racism' needs to be used with care, as it may uncritically reproduce naturalized constructions of 'insiders' and 'outsiders' of the nation rather than interrogating how such distinctions have been historically produced and reproduced within wider processes of colonialism, nation-building, and capitalist development. In this study I attempt to provide an account of some of these dynamics.

The Specificity of Anti-Traveller Racism

The Irish Travellers have attracted scholarly attention since the late nineteenth century and have been referred to by a variety of terms, including 'gypsies,' 'tinkers,' and 'itinerants.'[2] The first systematic documentation of their living conditions, however, was the government sponsored 1963

Report of the Commission on Itinerancy, whose major purpose was to outline a comprehensive settlement program for this population.

While this pioneering report denied ethnic status to Travellers, the identification of Travellers as an ethnic group who experience racism in Ireland has been a central premise of Traveller advocacy organizations from the 1980s (see McCann, Ó Síocháin, and Ruane 1994). The attribution of ethnicity as well as the use of the term 'racism' to refer to anti-Traveller discourse and action, however, continues to be contested in both official and popular discourse.

In contrast to dominant constructions of many 'Gypsy'/Roma populations elsewhere in Europe, Travellers in Southern Ireland are constructed as an indigenous Irish minority and constructions of 'racial' difference in terms of such signifiers as colour, physiognomy, genes, or 'blood' have been largely absent from Traveller-related discussion. Much more common has been a dominant construction of Travellers as a population distinguished, not by 'race,' but rather by a negatively evaluated 'way of life,' exemplified by specific features including itinerancy, trailer-living, particular occupations, and poverty (e.g., Mac Gréil 1996: 328–9).[3]

For some activist-scholars, then, anti-Travellerism is understood as a form of 'racism without race' – i.e., a form of inferiorized difference that does not invoke biological inferiority, but rather notions of undesirable cultural difference (see Anthias citing Balibar 1995: 294). This position follows theoretical work that has argued that a newer 'neo-racism' or 'culturalist racism' often replaces the discourse of racial and/or biological inferiority with invocations of cultural identity or national boundaries.

Those examining such forms of culturalist racism have called for a rejection of analytical distinctions between categories and ideologies of dominance based on signified physical/biological features (race, racism), and those based on signified cultural features (ethnicity, ethnicism), arguing that when culture is constructed in essentialist terms – as a form of natural difference that is invoked as a basis for inferiorization and exclusion – there is little difference from forms of exclusion based on putative 'race' (e.g., Anthias and Yuval-Davis 1992: 12; van Dijk 1993: 22–3).

My analysis here follows both the activist scholarship and the theoretical literature discussed above in labelling anti-Travellerism as one of a plurality of Irish racisms. The construction of Travellers as simultaneously 'Irish' and 'white' – a construction that distinguishes them from some of the other populations in Ireland that also experience racism – coexists with their construction as inferiorized Others. This construction in turn reflects their particular historical relationship to – and economic, political, and ideological location within – the Irish state and imagined nation.

This study takes as a major goal the illumination of the historical specificity of anti-Travellerism in Ireland with the purpose of de-naturalizing this form of Irish racism and pointing to its articulation with other forms of social inequality. It is my hope that attention to the history and experience of Travellers will also facilitate broader comparative discussion of the position of other populations suffering from racism in Ireland. Discussion of parallels and differences between Travellers and other groups can, I believe, contribute to a strengthened anti-racist coalition.

An in-depth focus on anti-Traveller racism in Ireland can also make a contribution to the expanding literature on anti-Traveller/'Gypsy'/Roma racism in Europe as a whole. There are important and growing links between Irish Traveller advocacy groups and their equivalents in other European states and scholarship that documents the histories and experiences of racism in particular regions can be useful to such alliances. While I do not pursue a comparative discussion of different forms of Irish racism or of anti-Traveller/'Gypsy'/Roma racisms in Europe here, it is my hope that this work can be used to facilitate such projects in the future.

Racism and the Politics of Class, Gender, and Generation

My discussion of the history and experience of anti-Traveller racism in Ireland works to locate these phenomena within a changing Irish political economy. As mentioned, this involves placing anti-Travellerism within the context of macro-processes such as nation-building and capitalist development. In my discussion of these processes I am particularly interested in exploring how anti-Traveller racism has articulated with wider constructions and social relations of class, gender, and generation.

The articulation of anti-Traveller racism with class has been noted by some writers (Mac Laughlin 1995, 1996; McVeigh 1992, 1996), and in this study I explore in some depth the links between early constructions of Travellers and the changing agrarian relations of the late nineteenth century. Likewise, I argue that there are important connections between anti-Travellerism and the bourgeois nationalism of the early twentieth century. In a discussion of the history of Traveller experience in Galway City in particular I point to the ways in which the interests of the propertied were reflected in often exclusionary actions, while class/ neighbourhood-based divisions, exacerbated in the context of economic development, came to the fore in struggles over the implementation of a Traveller settlement policy.

Drawing upon existing feminist work on Irish nation-building and economic development (Curtin, Jackson, and O'Connor 1987; Smythe 1993; Mahon 1995), as well as writing on the articulation of racism and gender (e.g., Anthias and Yuval-Davis 1992; Yuval-Davis 1997), I bring a gendered analysis to the history of anti-Traveller racism through a discussion of how early anti-Traveller discourse obscured Traveller women by emphasizing the threat posed by a masculinized population and how the later settlement program targeted women as primary agents of assimilation and integration. In both cases I argue that the gendered construction of Travellers supported both anti-Traveller racism and hegemonic gender relations within the wider population.

Finally, I link anti-Traveller racism to a larger project of constructing childhood in Ireland. Here I draw on interdisciplinary work in childhood studies that has pointed to the sacralization of 'the child' in modern Western societies, and described how politicians and others have maximized the rhetorical power derived from constructing various social problems as 'dangerous' to children (Best 1994; Jenks 1996). I link this discussion to the politics of anti-Traveller racism by analysing how 'child saving' became a central justification and legitimation of anti-Traveller action in Ireland, and how through such constructions generational as well as gender- and class-based inequities were both reinforced and reinscribed.

The Politics of Identity and Culture

The goals of this study include the documentation and analysis of anti-Traveller racism and an examination of how Travellers have forged a distinctive identity and way of life within its constraints. Anthropological work has emphasized how ethnic and racial boundaries and identities are not the result of primordial or objective cultural difference, but rather are actively constructed through history within political economies and relations of power.

Such a perspective challenges more essentialist constructions of identity and culture as an attribute or possession of individuals or groups. Ethnicity relates to processes and politics of boundary-making between 'us' and 'them,' and, as Yuval-Davis writes, 'cultural stuff,' 'rather than being a fixed and homogeneous body of tradition and custom ... needs to be described as a rich resource, usually full of internal contradictions, which is used selectively by different social agents in various social projects within specific power relations and political discourse' (Yuval-Davis 1997: 43).

While emphasizing how identity and culture are forged within relations of power, it is also important to recognize the agency of subjects within these constraints. Indeed, this is an area to which ethnographic work has a great deal to contribute. Ethnography can document the ways in which differently and often unequally positioned individuals and groups actively create and recreate social relations and cultural meanings in everyday life.

My discussion and analysis of Traveller identity and culture, like my discussion of anti-Traveller racism, pays particular attention to differentiations of class, gender, and generation. Relations of class among Travellers have often been noted in outsiders' constructions but rarely analysed. Here I point to some of the dynamics behind economic differentiation and emphasize the significance of class disparities for an understanding of Traveller economic activities as well as political capacity.

Following feminist-inspired ethnography I also examine closely the relationship between gendered social relations and inequality through an examination of women's lived relations and agency in such areas as work, residence, kinship, marriage, and sexuality (Bell, Caplan and Karim 1993; Moore 1988; Wolf 1996). My goal is to emphasize the complexity of Traveller women's locations with a gendered politics of culture.

My analysis has also benefited from a renewed ethnography of childhood that has emphasized both how childhood and children are central sites of cultural contestation and how children are themselves active players in such struggles (Scheper-Hughes and Sargent 1998; Stephens 1995). Attention to both gender and generation forces recognition of how wider social processes articulate with more intimate forms of diversity and inequality. Ethnography, with its serious attention to the richness of lived experience, is uniquely positioned to illuminate these connections, and ultimately to challenge constructions of homogeneous and static identities that support problematically essentialist models of cultural difference and determinism.

The analytical perspective taken in this study reflects the theoretical currents of the 1990s and differs in a number of ways from earlier scholarship among Travellers in Ireland. Early sociological work (involving participant observation in a camp on the outskirts of Galway City) supported by the Dublin and Galway voluntary itinerant settlement committees, for example, attributed to the Travellers a 'subculture of poverty.' This label was, however, rejected by other activists and by Sharon Gmelch and George Gmelch, whose ethnographic fieldwork in Dublin in the early 1970s led them to conclude that the Travellers constituted an ethnic group (Gmelch and Gmelch 1976) – a status that had been explicitly denied in the Report of the Commission on Itinerancy (1963: 37).[4] The 'subculture of poverty' label was subsequently retracted by the original researcher (McCarthy 1994; Walsh 1971).

The extensive work of the Gmelches described Traveller culture as characterized by 'a flexible system of adaptive responses,' but much of their work also emphasized how urbanization had led to what they saw as a cultural breakdown resulting in a number of 'dysfunctional' and 'maladaptive' features (e.g., G. Gmelch 1977: 160). The pessimistic analysis of Travellers' lives in Dublin emphasized the internal conflicts and tensions of class, gender, and sometimes generation among Travellers and, by linking these to cultural breakdown, often appeared to lend support to an assimilationist state settlement project even when this was not the intention of the authors. Ironically, the portrayal of Traveller ethnicity and culture was reminiscent of the 'culture of poverty' model that it had replaced.

More palatable to some Traveller advocates in the 1980s and 1990s was the analysis of anthropologist Judith Okely, who conducted fieldwork in the 1970s among a population that she labelled 'Traveller-Gypsies' in England (1983). In contrast to the Gmelches, Okely focused on the resilience of Traveller-Gypsy ethnicity and culture in the face of ongoing interaction with non-Gypsies or Gorgios and argued that the 'absence of autonomy [from non-Gypsies] should not preclude the understanding that the group's beliefs and practices have coherence and form a meaningful whole' (1983: 33–4).

Okely's more optimistic and even celebratory assessment of Traveller-Gypsy strength and adaptability in the context of unequal relations with powerful non-Gypsies offered an important challenge to recurrent predictions by outsiders of an imminent disappearance of Traveller-Gypsy populations. To Okeley's important emphasis on the flexibility and adaptability of Traveller-Gypsy identity and culture within the context of oppression, I have added greater attention to class, gender, and generational tensions and inequalities within and across an ethnicized Traveller/non-Traveller boundary. The latter allows for recognition of some of the phenomena described by the Gmelches without interpreting these as evidence of cultural breakdown from a putative past of cultural homogeneity and harmony. Such divisions, I argue, are integral to the dynamics of both racism and cultural production and reproduction in an unequal society and structure both the wider Irish social formation and Travellers' social relations. The perspective used here views racism, identity, and culture as actively forged within unequal structures and relations of state and class as well as gender and generation.

Constructing the Field

While my theoretical guideposts are eclectic, they share a grounding in a critical perspective that requires anthropological work, conventionally understood as in-depth participant observation, to be broadened considerably.

Anthropology has for some time recognized the constructed and contingent nature of 'the field' in time and space (Gupta and Ferguson 1997). The 'ethnographic present' is increasingly located in a specific history, while the 'ethnographic place' is situated within wider national and global geographies. In such a context ostensibly bounded fieldwork sites are problematized, as is the (agrarian/sedentarist) discourse and methodology of 'fieldwork.' The limitations of conventional ethnography have been particularly evident in the discussion and analyses of the 'travelling cultures' seen as characteristic of late or post-modernity (Clifford 1992).

The limitations of traditional anthropology have been noted for some time within Irish anthropology, where Arensberg and Kimball's influential *Family and Community in Ireland* (1961) was criticized for having created a 'trail of mystification' for later researchers by not paying sufficient attention to historical and spatial processes of colonialism, uneven capitalist development, and contested state formation (Gibbon 1973; Peace 1989). One result of such critiques has been that anthropologists of Ireland now engage constructively with the wealth of Irish historiography (e.g., Silverman and Gulliver 1992).

In the case of the Irish Travellers, however, detailed historical analyses are lacking despite some demonstrations from elsewhere in Europe of how archival work can be used to reconstruct the history of anti-Traveller/Gypsy racism as well as aspects of everyday experience (Lucassen, Willems, and Cottaar 1998; Mayall 1988). In the absence of such work in

Ireland Irish Travellers continue to be portrayed as people with (contested) origins but without history (Okely 1983; Trumpener 1992).

In this study I make use of archival research as well as existing biographies and autobiographies to reconstruct aspects of the history of anti-Traveller racism and Travellers' lived experience from the turn of the century to the period of fieldwork.[5] My use of archival sources has been influenced by critical discourse theorists writing on European racism. The work of van Dijk (1993, 1997) in particular suggested how much of my material – notably newspaper reports, government minutes, and parliamentary debates – could be analysed as examples of élite discourse that constructed Travellers in racist ways and through such constructions legitimated anti-Traveller action.

The 'field' of anthropological study has been increasingly reconceptualized to encompass deeper histories and broader geographies, but one of the hallmarks of anthropological work remains the richness of 'localized' ethnography and most anthropologists continue to conduct research, especially participant observation, in a particular place or places.

In my case, the process of conducting 'fieldwork' among Travellers occurred in a fixed time and space and involved primary reliance (at least conceptually) upon the spatially bound units of both 'the camp' and Galway City, while my archival research broadened this to the surrounding region and to the Irish state. Although I recognized that camp, city, regional, and national boundaries were continually transgressed by Traveller mobility (and that a 'travelling' anthropologist would have produced a different study), these boundaries were none the less significant insofar as they corresponded with political and administrative borders that shaped and constrained Traveller experience. The spatially bound units of the camp, Galway City, and the Republic of Ireland, then, remained important for the purposes of data collection even while I recognized the limitations of such boundaries in the lived experience of Travellers, and the fact that these 'fields' were in turn shaped by wider global forces.

Galway City and Travellers

My decision to return to Galway City was prompted by my earlier archival research there and by the presence of my husband's close relatives who, despite some doubts and scepticism regarding my research interests, offered substantial logistical support, including a small office space where I could set up my computer and enter my fieldnotes at regular intervals.

At the time of my fieldwork Galway City had a population of 47,000, making it the fifth largest city in the Republic of Ireland (*Galway Advertiser*, 9 October 1986). Located on the west coast of Ireland, Galway City began as an early settlement around a castle built for the King of Connacht in 1124. The town was of sufficient importance to receive its royal charter in 1484, and by the sixteenth century it was the most cosmopolitan town in Ireland, maintaining strong links of trade and settlement with Portugal and Andalusia (Foster 1988: 18).[6] In the mid-nineteenth century Galway was firmly established as the administrative, service, and commercial centre for western and northern Connacht, with a county jail, courthouse, university, and many shops. At about the same time improved roads and the development of a rail service from Dublin consolidated its importance as a tourist centre due to its proximity to the seaside resort of Salthill and the rural areas of Connemara (Ó Tuathaigh 1972: 130, 135).

In the early 1950s the central government promoted internationally financed industrial development in the Galway region, and by the mid-1960s the city was specifically targeted for investment and provided with an industrial estate (Ó Cearbhaill and Cawley 1984: 258–9). The result was an increase in employment and the city's population and boundaries expanded rapidly. Galway City has continued to see tremendous economic, demographic, and spatial growth associated with international investment in industry and service sectors and a vigorous tourist trade. Throughout the 1990s the city was in the forefront of the 'Celtic Tiger' economic boom. As in other parts of Ireland, however, this growth has been uneven and inequalities have deepened.

Galway City and the surrounding region has had a high national profile in the area of Traveller–state relations. There is a history of recorded Traveller presence from the turn of the century and official counts of 'vagrants' made from the 1940s to 1960s revealed that County Galway had more Travellers than any other county in Ireland during this period (Commission on Itinerancy 1963: 115). Even after the extensive migration of Travellers to the Dublin region in the 1960s and 1970s, County Galway continued to have the second highest proportion of the approximately 30,000 Travellers in the country during the 1990s.[7]

Counts of Travellers within Galway City itself have been conducted since the mid-1970s. The 1986 Traveller count which occurred during my fieldwork recorded 125 Traveller families (i.e., co-residential units) with a total of 843 persons. Two-thirds of these were living in some form of housing while the remaining one-third were living in semi-official or unofficial camps. Although the definition of who constituted a 'Traveller' for the purposes of this count was constructed by city officials, this provides a rough sense of the population living within the urban boundaries during my most intensive research period.[8]

Galway City has a history of highly publicized and politicized confrontations between Travellers and non-Travellers as well as attempts at political mobilization by Travellers and non-Traveller advocates. It has also been the site of several projects directed at Travellers, including group housing, training centres, and, since the fieldwork period, the construction of both temporary and permanent serviced sites (known as 'hardstands,' 'halting sites,' or simply 'sites') for Travellers. The circumstances of the fieldwork period described here, then, are already part of the historical rather than contemporary reality of Travellers in the city.

Camping and Participant Observation

Although I was aware from an early point that the majority of the Travellers in Galway (similar to many other centres, with the exception of Dublin City) were in fact living in houses and flats, I was keen to combine my archival research with 'participant observation' conducted from the position of residence within a Traveller camp. I felt that living in a trailer on a site would more easily facilitate the kind of in-depth participation in daily life that my anthropological training had emphasized and was encouraged by the similar methodology of earlier researchers in Ireland (i.e., Gmelch and Gmelch; Walsh) and Britain (Okely). Fortunately for me my proposal also resonated locally because some of the clergy working among Travellers had taken up residence in trailers.

My return to Galway City in the summer of 1986 corresponded with vacation time for many of the service providers that I had met previously, and without access to these 'gatekeepers' I was initially left to my own devices. Some attempts to meet with Travellers living in camps involved literally walking up and striking up conversations – usually prefaced by mentioning the names of the absent service providers who were all well known to the Travellers. These early conversations were, tellingly, facilitated by external political and legal pressures. When I arrived the Travellers parked in two camps in the city were facing court proceedings aimed at their removal. Faced with eviction, Travellers in both of these locations, after listening to my research goals, welcomed me to camp along side of them, perhaps in the hope of additional support. The precarious position of these camps, their political visibility, and my lack of any transport with which to move a trailer in the case of eviction, however, made me wary about responding to these offers. Instead I focused my attention on other more secure prospects.

Progress toward my goal of entering a more secure camp came later when a returned service worker advised me to attend one of the youth training centres that was offering programming in horticulture and 'life-skills' – i.e., cooking, music, and physical education – to Travellers. With the support of the non-Traveller director I spent half-days for a month in an ambiguous role (neither trainee nor staff member) that facilitated invitations to visit Travellers in houses and various camps.

By this time my desire to buy a trailer and move into a camp was generally known, and during one visit the husband of the woman that I was visiting offered to sell me the empty trailer that was parked beside them. Uncertain of its quality I declined, but on a second visit, when he offered me the fourteen-foot trailer that he and his wife were actually living in, I decided to accept. By this time I recognized that my priority was not so much to find a trailer as to find a parking space for a trailer that was not under any immediate threat of eviction – a much scarcer resource. The fact that this trailer was 'in situ' in a relatively secure camp made it especially valuable, and because the trailer was already being used, I reasoned, it must be livable.

In the course of negotiating the trailer purchase, I explained my research goals again and indicated that I wished to remain in the camp for a couple of months. Concerned about my reception by other residents, I asked to be introduced to the sellers' elderly father, who lived next door. When I went to his trailer I found a number of the other adults of the camp visiting there and I took the opportunity to publicly ask for permission to live in the camp for research purposes.

While I was assured of my welcome, Travellers' lack of ownership of camping land, together with the absence of a local protocol to ensure research accountability, limited their ability to accept or reject my presence and to exert any formal control over my subsequent activities. As with earlier invitations to other camps, it is also likely that the initial welcome extended to me was premised upon a hope that the presence of an outsider associated with key service providers might have the result of reversing years of official neglect. Certainly those camping in this location had long-standing complaints about the lack of basic services provided, and, after years of demanding action from the authorities, described themselves as 'ashamed' and frustrated by their living conditions.

The following day when my husband and I moved in I was relieved that the rather stressful experiences of walking into campsites in search of conversations would now be replaced with more 'natural' interactions of everyday life. While my plans were not firm when I entered, we remained in this location for the rest of the research year – a total of nine months.[9]

During this period the composition and spatial organization of the camp shifted, but over the nine months that I stayed in the camp fourteen families defined as co-residential units, containing eighty-one people, spent time residing there. Seven of these families remained parked in the camp for the entire nine-month period while the other seven arrived and/or departed over the course of my own stay.

In addition to the camp residents there were regular visitors, including those living elsewhere in the city, as well those who were passing through on their way to and from other parts of the Republic, Northern Ireland, and England. Living in the camp, then, provided me with the opportunity to meet a wide range of Travellers beyond those who were actually parked there.

While residence in the camp provided in-depth access to resident and non-resident Travellers, it also meant that I was associated with the particular kinship-based groupings represented there and conversely was less involved with other groupings elsewhere in the city and region. The degree of social distance and in some cases potential or actual tension between different kin-based clusters was apparent whenever I talked about the possibility of moving to another camp. When I broached this subject I was invariably advised against it by my neighbours, who volunteered stories of how other Travellers were prone to violence and might steal our possessions. Some Travellers living elsewhere in the city made similarly critical comments about my neighbours and expressed surprise that I had not moved out of the camp. One family living in a house told me that they had agreed to talk to me out of concern that I meet more than just the 'dirty ones.' Such comments, which echoed the inferiorizing discourses of non-Travellers, pointed to significant divisions between Travellers.

As anticipated, camp life lent itself to the traditional anthropological method of participant observation. From my trailer I could see and be seen by everyone who came in and out of the camp. It was also possible to observe the outside activities of men and children and to overhear louder conversations and arguments. By living in the camp I was drawn into its daily activities and found it much easier to ask questions about what I was experiencing. Through what turned out to be a particularly cold winter, stretches of relative quiet and sometimes boredom were punctuated by bursts of intense socializing associated with events such as births, christenings, match-making, weddings, illness, death, and the arrival of visitors from other parts of Ireland and Great Britain. The continual making and unmaking of plans to change accommodation and/or travel outside of the city also injected interest and excitement into daily camp life.

In the camp the trailers were parked lengthwise in a rough circle with their doors facing inward. A small chimney poked through the roof of each trailer or larger mobile home. Some households also had makeshift TV antennae. By the doorway of most dwellings was a collection of items, including a bucket, a mop, and a small stand with bowls or 'vessels' placed on top. Each trailer or mobile had a gas canister outside which provided the fuel for cooking. Some had milk tankards for storing water. In front of each doorway was a piece of carpet or cardboard intended to reduce the amount of 'muck' being tracked inside the trailers. The premium on camping space in the city was evident in the presence of a couple of empty mobiles left in the camp by their owners: by leaving a mobile in the camp Travellers who were living elsewhere attempted to reserve a spot in case they wished to return later.

The central area of the camp was often muddy from continual rainfall and was zig-zagged by the tracks of the cars and vans driven in and out during the day. Scattered around on the ground were car and truck batteries, bicycles, pram springs, pieces of wood and cardboard, and rags. Here and there were piles of scrap metal, coal bags full of copper wire, and an overturned car or two. A couple of dogs were usually scrounging around for scraps of food. Almost all of the people who entered the camp were either residents or close relations paying visits from other camps or houses; the few non-Travellers who came in were drivers who had taken a wrong turn, visiting service workers, or city workmen or officials.

The following description can provide some sense of the rhythm of camp life. Before 9:00 in the morning some of the children who were going to school, and those young people who attended a training centre, would be picked up by their respective buses. Shortly afterward, some of the adult men would gather in one of the larger mobiles of the camp, where they were often joined by others who had arrived from elsewhere in the city. While some ate breakfast there, others just had a cup of tea while they discussed their plans for the day. After breakfast most of the men (some with their wives) would drive off in their cars or vans to collect scrap and other recyclable items, engage in door-to-door selling, trade in cars or car parts, meet with service workers, visit other Travellers, or go to the ball alley or pub. They returned frequently throughout the day to eat meals, work on cars, sort scrap metal, or visit with others while watching television or listening to the radio.

While some married women joined their husbands in activities outside the camp, many others spent much of the day engaged in cooking, cleaning, and child care inside their own dwellings. This work was often broken by short trips to other women's trailers to borrow items or to have a brief chat. Later in the day, work was frequently interrupted for longer visits with Travellers who had arrived from outside the camp. Unlike the married men, who drove in and out of the camp all day, married women rarely left the camp on their own. None of the women in the camp drove a car or van.

By early evening, more visitors often arrived in the camp. During the long nights of the winter many of the men would form a group in one mobile home to play cards and watch television, but in the summer they often chatted outside, occasionally around a blazing fire. The women also would go 'rambling,' and some would gather together in another trailer or mobile where they could talk and watch television. Visiting would last from 7:00 p.m. until sometime between 10:00 p.m. and midnight. On weekends there was usually an intensification of visiting and trips to the pub, and some Travellers would go to mass on Sundays.

I usually left the camp in the mid-morning to write up my notes from the previous evening at the home of my partner's relatives close to the city centre. From this base I would sometimes go to the city offices or county library to continue my archival work. I also conducted interviews and did some shopping or other errands during this time.

Returning to the camp at the same time as school ended, I was invariably visited by groups of children who would sit and watch my activities and engage in conversation. Sometimes teenagers or adults would also drop in for a chat. Following our evening meal, I would usually join a group of women who had gathered for the evening in one of the larger trailers in the camp. My presence in such gatherings was generally encouraged and I enjoyed the offered tea and bread or biscuits along with other visitors. Because I was unable to take a turn hosting larger gatherings in my own small trailer I tried to reciprocate the generosity of my regular hostesses through occasional gifts of food and clothing, and when requested, by taking photos of family members. Some of the women with limited literacy skills also asked me to write letters and assist with forms. Following my return to my own trailer I would jot down brief notes on the evening's events and conversations, and these provided the basis of the expanded fieldnotes which were entered into the computer the following day.

As mentioned previously, my neighbours continually expressed their frustration at the abject living conditions created by a lack of basic services, but they also emphasized what they saw as the inherent value of a camping way of life. Both of these views were significant in shaping their response to my trailer residence. Travellers in the camp and other Travellers that I met outside the camp invariably expressed surprise that I had chosen to live in the difficult conditions of the camp, but even those in houses reinforced the decision by emphasizing that through living in a camp I was experiencing the 'real' Traveller life and would know what to write about in my book. Those introducing me to other Travellers always mentioned that I was living in a trailer, and this fact alone seemed to partially compensate for the many ways in which I was not integrated into a Traveller way of life (i.e., through kinship, marriage, work activities, and so on). I was regularly asked how I liked the camp and Travellers enjoyed hearing me extol its virtues, such as the communal feeling and relative lack of expense. Some warned me that I would be 'lonely' for the camp when I returned to a house and would find readjusting difficult.

Since the introduction of a settlement policy in the early 1960s, the construction of Traveller life as inherently deprived, primitive, and harsh has been largely accepted by non-Traveller service providers, and for these individuals my decision to live 'on the road' was positively received as evidence of a moral commitment to the Traveller cause. The reaction of settled people with an active anti-Traveller stance, however, was to suggest that as a non-Irish outsider I could not possibly know what Travellers were *really* like regardless of my living arrangements. For many of these, I remained a naive 'Yank' (a label to which Canadians are well accustomed) who was being 'codded' by the Travellers.

Living in the camp facilitated participant observation and even semi-structured interviewing, but it dramatically curtailed more formal research methods. Prior to moving into the camp I had had some success conducting taped interviews with Travellers who were living in houses, although concerns had been expressed about revealing this fact to any other Travellers. In the camp setting, however, I received more overt refusals to requests for taped interviews and anxiety was voiced when I tried to write down information. While I was able to take genealogies from individuals if these were conducted privately, I had only limited success with my attempts to compile family budgets and did not press where there was resistance.

As had been the case in the earlier interviews, the most commonly voiced concern was the possibility that any information shared with me might, if passed on to other Travellers, incite or exacerbate tensions and conflicts within and between family groupings. Particular fears were expressed about the possibility of anything that I had written down falling into the wrong hands. Much of the ethnographic information presented here, then, comes from reconstructed daily observations and informal conversation rather than formal recorded interviews or note-taking. The sense of vulnerability expressed by my interlocutors also led me to be as discreet and circumspect as possible in my inquiries and to keep all written notes secure. The responses of Travellers to my research activities not only shaped the production of 'data' but have directed my subsequent writing as I have grappled with ethical and political issues of representation.

The Politics of Research and Representation

Anthropologists are increasingly reflexive about the politics of the re-search conditions in which their 'data' is produced, as well as the politics of representation involved in the 'writing up' process. In the early 1980s there was critical discussion of both methodology and ethics in Irish anthropology, and there has been specific criticism of past practice in Traveller-related research (M. McDonagh 1994; Collins 1994). Traveller activist Nan Joyce, for example, has written about how 'you get foreign-ers coming and writing books about us: some of those books are very hurtful – the people who write them should be sued' (Joyce and Farmar 1985: 116).

There are a number of aspects of my research and writing that warrant comment in this regard, including my involvement in the local politics of Traveller-related issues in Galway City.

I have already described the attack suffered by some camping Travel-lers on the second day of my own trailer residence. The affected families had been resisting court proceedings aimed at their eviction, and acting upon what they claimed were the instructions of the city, had moved their trailers out of the original camp and into a nearby field where they had been assured security. In the new location they were attacked by a group of non-Travellers who dragged their trailers out from the field and on to the roadside.

The incident served to focus attention on the 'problem' of roadside Traveller families and became the catalyst for a number of events, including the formation of a Travellers' committee and the candidacy of its spokesperson Margaret Sweeney in the spring national election on the platform of Traveller rights.[10]

Having been in contact with some of the affected Travellers before this event I was able to follow the subsequent developments quite closely. Following the attack, for example, I attended and taped an angry residents and tenants meeting on the subject of Traveller accommodation and, upon request, I let some Travellers listen to it. What they heard contributed to their decision to attend the next meeting. It also led to a request from some Travellers that I be the secretary of the newly formed Traveller Committee. Uncomfortable with such a formal role I offered instead to tape the Traveller Committee meetings and to provide transcripts that could serve as minutes to the members. This allowed me to attend meetings but in a relatively passive capacity. My participation in the Committee did, however, include attendance at and participation in organized demonstrations and other activities. The involvement with the Traveller Committee extended my contacts with Travellers, and renewed my commitment to combining camp-based ethnography with a critical analysis of political discourse and practice in the area of Traveller policy-making and implementation.

Along with the issues raised by my participation in some of the more formal political events of the year, I was also very conscious of the initial wariness expressed by my Traveller neighbours about my researcher status. In the early days of my research I was often referred by Travellers to various settled people who they declared were 'experts' on Travellers and/or had books in their possession that had everything about Travellers already in them. When I persisted in my research some complained that I was writing a book from which I would make a lot of money. The ambivalence toward books about Travellers written by outsiders was clear in the case of one middle-aged Traveller woman who treasured a volume about Travellers that she owned because it contained photos of a relative but who also told me that other photos reproduced in the book made many Travellers feel ashamed.

Changing attitudes toward written accounts of Traveller life were, however, evident among younger literate Travellers. When I let it be known that I had purchased the biography of Traveller woman Nan Donohoe (Gmelch 1986), several younger Travellers borrowed it from me and older Travellers asked me to read out loud particular passages relating to Galway City. At the same time, magazines produced by Traveller youth in the training centres were passed around among families and read with great interest and pride.

While the struggle to ensure space for Travellers' voices is ongoing, the 1990s have seen a growing body of writing by Travellers that combines autobiography with analyses of anti-Traveller racism and policy recommendation (i.e., Collins 1994; McCann and Joyce forthcoming; M. McDonagh 1993, 1994; R. McDonagh 1999). It is important to emphasize that this study by a non-Irish and non-Traveller outsider is necessarily differently located from, and therefore not a proxy for, Travellers' own voices.

With the very existence of anti-Traveller racism and the value of Traveller culture still deeply and unequally debated in Ireland, writing about these issues as an outsider remains a fraught project. One of my strategies of responding to this was a deliberate decision to direct much of my attention to the history of anti-Traveller discourses and actions of non-Travellers. This decision was reinforced by directives that I received from younger, more literate Travellers, who explicitly asked me to address anti-Traveller discrimination in my work.

Of course, 'studying up' was not without its own challenges and sensitivities. The ability of Galway City politicians to delete their own views and actions from the public record, for example, was apparent when, during the 1980s, the Galway city council increasingly conducted debates on Traveller accommodation issues 'in committee,' which meant that there were no minutes available for examination. Likewise, a key city official made his most revealing anti-Traveller remarks to me when he was 'off the record.'

The powerful also have a greater ability than the powerless to silence criticism. Early in my fieldwork, for example, when the biography of Nan Donohoe was published, her account of how her family and other Travellers were attacked by stone-throwing youths in Galway City was publicly challenged by a city politician who demanded that a retraction be printed in the book because of its alleged slandering of the city's image. The fact that the views of this politician received local press coverage, while the contents of the book itself did not, reveals how the powerful can more easily control dominant discourse. Despite the challenges, I have offered here a documentation and analysis of the history of anti-Traveller racism both nationally and in Galway City. Such a documentation and analysis, while partial, is intended to challenge the pervasive denial of this aspect of the Irish past.

While attention to anti-Traveller racism challenges the powerful, my use of ethnography to discuss the production and politics of Traveller culture is potentially more problematic. During fieldwork, as I have indicated, there was wariness and sensitivity about my recording aspects of daily life – and being 'off the record' was, of course, less of a possibility for the Travellers who shared their lives with me in the more public camp setting. This consideration shaped my writing trajectory as I delayed publishing some of my ethnographic material out of concerns about privacy. With the location of my fieldwork now transformed, and the shifting political context of Traveller-related discussion, I can offer this study, with the important reminder to the reader that much of the ethnographic material now relates to a historical rather than contemporary reality.

Ethnographic description, however, remains open to the criticism that it engages in a 'voyeuristic' approach to Travellers lives. It is important to clarify here that my use of ethnography is intended, through reference to lived experience, to emphasize the agency, creativity, and personhood of those who are oppressed, and to deepen analyses of the complexities of culture under these conditions. In a context where the very existence of Traveller culture is still contested, however, discussion of its complexity may appear dangerously premature in so far as such discussion may be used to support the denial of rights or contribute to further inferiorization. Given the ongoing struggle for recognition of Traveller ethnicity and culture as a basis for basic human rights, my description of Travellers' lives runs the risk of being 'misread' by those who would deny the claims of Travellers for equality within Irish society. It is important to note that this would constitute a serious misreading of this study. Life among Travellers forced upon me an awareness of both the depth of anti-Traveller racism in official and popular discourse and practice and the ways in which my neighbours involuntarily but none the less courageously engaged with this as they forged lives of complexity and resilience. In this text it is this reality that I try to convey with the goal of ultimately contributing to more effective anti-racist and cultural projects.

Chapter Organization

Chapter 1 begins to locate Irish Travellers and anti-Traveller racism within the political economies of colonialism, nation-building, and dependent economic development through a reconstruction of the competing and shifting constructions of Traveller origins from the late nineteenth century to the 1960s. These stories of origin are analysed as narratives that reveal how Travellers have been ideologically and concretely located in imperial, nationalist, and capitalist projects by others.

Using local government records, the provincial press, and the debates of the Irish parliament, chapter 2 examines more closely the history of local and national anti-Traveller discourse and practice in the independent Irish state. The archival sources demonstrate the existence of anti-Traveller racism from an early period while also revealing how anti-Traveller racism was linked to the legitimation and reproduction of other social inequalities, including those of class, gender, and generation in the new state.

Next I focus on the dramatic developments of the 1960s, with particular attention being paid to the development of a comprehensive national Traveller settlement policy within the context of a broader political project of economic and social 'modernization.' The struggle over the implementation of this new policy in Galway City from 1960 through to the fieldwork period of 1986–7 is documented along with the ways in which the policy of Traveller settlement and 'absorption' articulated with anti-Traveller racism and the urban geography of class.

Travellers' lived experiences of racism and the struggle to forge a distinct way of life and identity are the subjects of chapters 4 through 7. In these chapters I draw upon archival, biographical, and ethnographic participant observation to explore the social relations of such phenomena as travelling, work, gender, and childhood among Travellers. I emphasize how these arenas of daily life were both shaped by the oppressive forces of racism, and served as important sites for the production and reproduction of Traveller identity and culture. In each of these areas there are shown to be identifiably distinctive Traveller social relations and cultural ideologies that produce and reproduce a collectively-felt identity, but also deep divisions and various forms of inequality. These phenomena are explored within the context of increasingly politicized struggles for Traveller culture at both local and national levels.

In chapter 4 I demonstrate how trailer-living and camping were invoked as central to Traveller identity, even when a majority of Travellers in Galway City lived in some form of housing. Camping was linked to intense experiences of struggle and deprivation, and therefore was a source of ambivalence as well as pride. Travellers' patterns of mobility and accommodation, I argue, complicated dominant discourse and practice that equated housing with 'settlement' and camping with mobility. This same complexity both facilitated and impeded pan-Traveller political mobilization around the issue of official camping sites in Galway City in the late 1980s.

A discussion of the Traveller economy and forms of work in chapter 5 addresses outsiders' contradictory images by focusing on the different forms and social relations of work found among Travellers. The resilience of Travellers' forms of work within advanced capitalism, as well as the ways in which relations of exchange structured class-based inequalities, is emphasized. The production of an ideology of self-sufficiency and the significance of this for impeding and facilitating collective identity and political action is discussed.

Feminist anthropological literature on forms of women's work and position within family and community relations is used in chapter 6 to explore the connections between the organization of work, residence patterns, marriage and sexuality, and the positioning of Traveller women within ethnicized and gendered boundaries and identities.

Chapter 7 focuses on the relationship between the constructions of Traveller childhood and youth in dominant discourse and the organization of childhood and youth in daily life. Of particular interest is the way in which aspects of settlement policy both challenged and reproduced a distinctive life course. Children remained economically active even when schooling created a 'double day,' and reforms in the area of marriage created a newly significant and deeply gendered category of 'youth.'

Some post-fieldwork developments are examined in the concluding chapter. These include an analysis of the parliamentary debates over the 1989 Prohibition of Incitement to Hatred Act, and the contents of the 1995 Task Force on the Travelling Community. Both texts are located within broader currents of greater European integration and uneven economic growth of the 1990s that accompanied both continuity and change in the politics of racism and culture in Ireland.

Chapter 1

Origins, Histories, and Anti-Traveller Racism

Some of my ancestors went on the road in the Famine but more of them have been travelling for hundreds of years – we're not drop-outs like some people think. The Travellers have been in Ireland since St Patrick's time, there's a lot of history behind them though there's not much written down – it's what you get from your grandfather and what he got from his grandfather.

Nan Joyce, Traveller activist and author (Joyce and Farmar 1985: 1)

In the wider literature of 'Gypsy studies' a tendency to invoke Traveller/ Gypsy/ Roma origins as 'explanations' for contemporary identities and experience has often resulted in the construction of such populations as (following Eric Wolf's phrasing) people with (contested) origins but without history (Lucassen, Willems, and Cottaar 1998; Okely 1983; Trumpener 1992).[1] While some scholars eschew serious engagement with such accounts others have recognized their significance, not as statements of historical facts, but as socially constructed narratives that are produced by and in turn legitimate and/or contest particular identities and boundaries (Okely 1983).

Unlike many 'Gypsy,' Roma, and other Travellers in Europe who are attributed with collective origins outside of their respective 'host' nations, Travellers in Ireland have been constructed, and have constructed themselves, as an indigenous minority. Attributions of origin have emphasized the essential 'Irishness' of Travellers and, in contrast to colonized indigenous populations elsewhere, Travellers have not been constructed as racially 'Other.' While the imputed origins of Travellers are largely free of a discourse of 'race,' attributed origins have none the less often been deeply stigmatizing and have been used to legitimate anti-Traveller action. They have thus, I argue, often been central to the reproduction of anti-Traveller racism.

The origin stories told about and by Travellers in Ireland have focused not on 'where' they are from so much as on 'when' and 'why' they emerged as a distinct group within Ireland. The origin account that emerged in the 1950s and achieved dominance from the 1960s to the 1980s portrayed Irish Travellers as the descendants of peasants forced into landlessness and mobility by the evictions and famines suffered by the Irish during the centuries of British domination. This particular account of Traveller origins was effectively used as part of the justification of a state settlement program introduced in the 1960s. According to this understanding of Traveller origins, for example, the settlement program was promoted as the action of a benevolent state motivated by a national duty to 're-settle' victims of colonialism.

The ascription of colonial origins, however, is not only relatively recent but is also challenged by Traveller advocates. Activists such as Nan Joyce (cited above), who have been involved in resisting aspects of the state settlement program, have pointed to earlier theories that traced Traveller origins to a much older pre-colonial Ireland (Dublin Travellers Education and Development Group 1992; Joyce and Farmar 1985:1; Ní Shúinéar 1994; M. McDonagh 1993). As the debate makes clear such origin stories, whether colonial or pre-colonial, are profoundly linked to relations of power and resistance. Claims of pre-colonial and colonial origins, made in the context of struggles for the recognition of Travellers as authentic Irish citizens, are part of larger post-colonial nationalist discourses in which Irish citizenship, identity, and culture are opposed to the colonial past. Not only are Traveller origin stories contested, but the focus on origins to the exclusion of a dynamic history has obscured the processes that have produced and reproduced Travellers through time – thereby naturalizing rather than historicizing Traveller experience. As in the present, so, too, earlier representations of Traveller origins were both contested and linked to wider social relations. Through documentation and analysis of the history of various origin stories, I challenge the use of such stories as 'explanations' of the position of Travellers in Ireland, and redirect attention instead towards the economic and political processes and relations of power that produced them.

I begin with a brief history of mobility in Ireland in the context of British colonialism. I then describe and locate the discourses of British Gypsylorists, Anglo-Irish Celtic Literary Revivalists, and the folklore of the Irish peasantry within the context of British imperialism, Irish cultural nationalism, and agrarian class relations respectively. Finally, I look at some of the changing constructions of Traveller origins in the post-colonial period.

Colonialism and Mobility in Ireland

Okely has for some time drawn attention to the fact that Irish and Scottish Travellers have commonly been constructed as indigenous to their respective regions, whereas 'Gypsies' in England and Wales have frequently been constructed as exotic outsiders (i.e., migrants from India) (1983). Along with challenging the historical truth of the latter ascription she has suggested that these contrasting origin stories should be contextualized within the history of internal colonialism within the British Isles (1994).

Following her work, I begin with the location of Irish mobility within the context of pre-conquest Ireland and then British colonialism. Gaelic Ireland was based on pastoralism rather than agriculture and had a decentralized political system. Pre-conquest Ireland was divided into many small political units called lordships or 'tuaths' within which lords, chieftains, freemen, and serfs were linked to one another through ties of clientage (Foster 1988: 9–10). The pastoral mode of subsistence, the movement of clients between lordships, and the existence of many itinerant occupational groups (including learned classes such as poets, bards, and doctors, as well as lower status groups such as jesters, gamblers, musicians, merchants, and craftsmen) created a mobile society (Quinn 1966: 18).

Ireland had been nominally under English control since the twelfth century, but the Tudor 're-conquest' that began in the mid-sixteenth century firmly established it as an English colony. The Gaelic periphery and English core of the single colonial system were, however, characterized by differing political economies. The mobility of Gaelic society had been noted in the twelfth-century writings of Giraldus Cambrensis, but it was only in the sixteenth century that it was taken (along with religious, kinship, and political practices) as evidence of 'barbarism' and used to justify the colonial enterprise (Canny 1976: 126–8). English colonial discourse and practice from the second half of the sixteenth century often equated the 'civilizing' of the Irish with a suppression of mobility.

During the Tudor re-conquest of Ireland, English administrators viewed Irish wanderers with apprehension, seeing them as potential leaders or followers for the armies of lords and chieftains resisting domination. As a result, wanderers were treated harshly by the colonial administration.[2]

In spite of oppressive policies, however, there continued to be large numbers of wandering persons. This mobile population represented in part a continuation of the Gaelic way of life in spite of a policy of 'Anglicization' (i.e., the introduction of English law and land tenure), but was also increasingly the result of colonization itself. For example, many Irish landowners were displaced through the system of plantation which resulted in the removal of Catholics and their replacement with Protestant settlers.

There is evidence of continuing attempts on the part of the state to control itinerancy during the eighteenth century. For example, it was resolved by the Irish Parliament in 1710 'that the strict execution of the laws in force against sturdy beggars and vagrants and confining the poor to their respective parishes, would be a public and seasonable service to this kingdom' (1710 111: 780; Index 1763). That this resolution was not effective is apparent in descriptions of rural life during this period, which make reference to the itinerant hawkers, showmen, musicians, beggars, mountebanks, and whiskey sellers who could be found at religious patterns and fairs (Maxwell 1949: 160, 157).

The 1800 Act of Union, which abolished the Irish parliament and made Ireland and Britain into a free trade area, was followed by the collapse of household-based industries that provided supplemental income to small cultivators. The loss of these income-generating activities, combined with other developments such as population growth, pressures toward consolidation of land, less labour-intensive pasturage in agriculture, and a series of potato famines, forced many more rural Irish into vagrancy and/or emigration (Foster 1988: 319–25).

While it is clear that there is a history of wandering people in pre-colonial and colonial Ireland, it is difficult to come to any conclusion regarding the relationship between these wanderers and the 'tinkers' who would attract scholarly study by the end of the nineteenth-century. There is, for example, an intriguing seventeenth-century reference to 'plain tinkers' described as 'divers gravers in gold and silver ... who make their chalices, harps, buttons for their sleeves, crucifixes, and such-like' (Quinn 1966: 167), but it is not clear whether these were sedentary or itinerant or whether they were single craftspersons or formed of family groups. Brian Merriman's satirical poem *The Midnight Court* (Kennelly 1970), written in 1780, also refers to 'tinkers' but only hints that they comprised an endogamous population of mobile family units engaged in metal work and begging.

There is clearly more archival work to be done, but the available evidence suggests that 'tinkers' were not particularly visible (at least to the élite) within the larger itinerant population prior to the nineteenth century. By the 1830s, however, references uncovered by Sharon Gmelch suggest that 'tinkers' were sometimes distinguished as a 'class' distinct from other wanderers. As she notes, *The Commission on the Condition of the Poorer Classes* (1835), one of many commissions set up in response to widespread poverty in Ireland and alarm in England over Irish immigration, included the following statement made by a resident of County Longford: 'Ordinary beggars do not become a separate class of the community, but wandering tinkers, families who always beg, do. Three generations of them have been seen begging together' (1835: 574 qtd. in S. Gmelch 1975: 10). Another submission to the same Commission from a resident of County Mayo stated that: 'The wives and families accompany the tinker while he strolls about in search of work, and always beg. They intermarry with one another, and form a distinct class' (1835: 495 ibid.). Both of these passages identified the 'tinkers' as forming a 'class' that was distinguished by particular economic activities (e.g., tinkering or begging) as well as distinctive social relations – notably, mobile family-based units, linked by ties of kinship and affinity to one another. Evidence for a distinctive population is also suggested by the presence of Irish Travellers in the southern United States who claim that their ancestors emigrated from Ireland during the famine period (Harper 1971: 18).

While 'tinkers' may have been distinguished by the general populace from other wanderers during this period, there is at present no evidence to suggest that this was a significant distinction for the British authorities in Ireland at the time.

Vagrants, Gypsies, and 'Tinkers' in England

The lack of apparent official concern on the part of British authorities vis-à-vis Irish Travellers stands in contrast with the situation in England, where different economic and political processes had resulted in an earlier emergence of 'Gypsies' and other travellers as a 'problem' for the state. A brief outline of the history of English itinerancy and its relationship to 'Gypsies' and 'tinkers' is important because it was in England, not Ireland, that the Irish 'tinkers' first attracted sustained official attention as a distinct category of mobile peoples.

The larger body of work on the historical phenomenon of 'masterless men' in England reveals that the colonial policies to suppress mobility in Ireland from the mid-sixteenth century onwards coincided with increased state activity against 'vagrancy' at home. In the case of Ireland, the state was concerned with imposing a new colonial order, but in the case of England, the goal was the maintenance of control in a context of rapid internal change.

Widespread itinerancy in England was linked to the breakdown of the existing agriculturally based feudal order. The decline of the manorial system and the commercialization of agriculture resulted in growing landlessness and insecure wage labour, which combined with rapid population growth to create a large population of wandering poor who were perceived as a social and political danger to society (Beier 1985: 21).

According to some commentators, 'Gypsies' were identified as a distinct population within the larger category of vagrants of this period. A number of statutes were passed specifically targeting 'Egipcions,' including a 1530 Act which banned their immigration to England and declared that those presently in the country should leave (Mayall 1988: 189). Beier (1985: 59–61) argues that the 'Egyptians' were culturally and racially distinct from other vagabonds but others, citing legislation aimed at persons 'p'tending themselves to be Egipcyans' and 'counterfayte Egipcians' (see Mayall 1988: 189–90) have suggested that these 'Egyptians' may have been indigenous vagrants who adopted and then reproduced a lucrative exotic identity (Okely 1983: 13–15).

The larger vagrant population in England included some of those who had left Ireland during periods of famine, war, or rebellion. A survey of beggars in England published in 1567 noted that 'there be many Irishmen that go about with counterfeit [begging] licenses' and that over one hundred Irish men and women had arrived in the past two years to wander and beg (Quinn 1966: 147). Beier suggests that the Irish vagrants, like the 'Egyptians,' tended to travel in larger kinship-based groups, and that Irish vagrants were viewed as threatening to the social and political order by the authorities because they were associated with rebellion and Catholicism. In 1572 a vagrancy statute ordered Irish vagabonds and beggars to be sent home after punishment (Beier 1985: 62–4).

The term 'tynker' was known as a trade name in England by 1175 and as a surname by 1265 (OED), and this fact is frequently cited in support of claims that the presence of Irish Travellers can be dated from this much earlier period. The extent to which the term referred to a distinct category of people is, however, unclear. Further complicating the picture is the finding that the term 'tinker,' currently sometimes used to refer to Irish Travellers in England, has not always had a specifically Irish referent within the United Kingdom (Acton 1974: 77).

What is clear is that by the sixteenth century, those labelled as 'tynkers' were part of the larger mobile population of concern to the English state. In 1551–2, 'tynkers,' along with peddlers and other vagrant persons, were forbidden to travel within England without licence from the justices (Mayall 1988: 189). By 1596 all 'tynkers wandering abroade,' as well as 'p'sons ... wandering and p'tending themselves to be Egipcyans or wandering in the Habite Forme or Attyre of counterfayte Egipcians,' were declared rogues and vagabonds under one Poor Law Act (Mayall 1988: 189). Any differences or similarities between the 'Eygptians' and the 'tynkers' are not only difficult to determine from these references, but appear to have been irrelevant in the eyes of the state.

While the early history of 'tynkers' and 'Egipcians' in England remains the subject of a great deal of speculation, Mayall has described how, by the nineteenth century, those for whom travelling was a way of life (he refers to these collectively as 'Gypsy-Travellers') could be distinguished from other mobile persons 'who travelled in order to obtain employment but otherwise adopted and conformed to a sedentary way of life' (1988: 14). Unlike in Ireland, where a similar distinction existed but did not become salient in official discourse and practice, in England 'Gypsies' were problematized and targeted for intervention.

Early in the nineteenth century 'Gypsies' were the focus of attempts at their spiritual 'reclamation' by evangelical Protestant missionaries, while the latter half of the century was marked by efforts at settlement and the promotion of wage labour on the part of the state. On the legislative front anti-'Gypsy' agitation culminated in the introduction, between 1885 and 1894, of a number of Moveable Dwellings Bills aimed at ensuring registration of all 'Gypsy' dwellings, compulsory school attendance, settlement, and ultimate absorption (Mayall 1988: 138).

British Gypsiology and the Racialization of 'Gypsies' and 'Tinkers'

The increasing efforts at intervention and control of 'Gypsies' that marked the end of the nineteenth century in England were paralleled by the growth of scholarship that was centred within the Gypsy Lore Society founded in 1888.

The British Gypsiology movement of the late nineteenth century was one of many movements that reacted to the processes of industrialization and urbanization with a study of the 'folk.' Drawing from the emerging fields of linguistics, anthropology, and folklore, its members collected information on the linguistic and cultural practices of 'Gypsydom' out of a concern to record 'a decaying language and culture' before it inevitably disappeared in the face of 'progress' (Mayall 1988: 5).

Central to the Gypsy lore literature was the concept of 'race,' which was used to distinguish between the 'true Gypsies' and other wanderers (ibid., 4). At this time, European explanations of difference in terms of environmentalism and religion were largely replaced by a racialization of the world's population (Miles 1989: 30–7). The scholarly project of racialization provided substantial ideological support for the political and economic project of colonization in Ireland and other parts of the world, and for the processes of nation-building and national competition within Europe (ibid., 114–15). Within European nations, notions of race were further invoked in discussions of minorities, including the Jews, the Irish (within England), and the 'Gypsies.'

By the late nineteenth century, at the height of British imperialism, British scholarship had racialized the 'Gypsies' of England as non-Anglo-Saxon as well as non-European. It was generally believed by the Gypsiologists that the comparative philology of Grellman in the eighteenth century had conclusively demonstrated a Gypsy origin in India.[3] The discourses of Gypsiology were then linked to the colonial discourses of Orientalism as scholars searched for congruences between the racial, linguistic, and cultural attributes of Gypsies on the one hand, and various populations of India on the other. Like the dominated colonial subjects outside of England, the Gypsies within England were simultaneously exoticized and degraded. Gypsies were described as proud, independent, driven by wanderlust and sexual passion, while at the same time being animalistic, criminal, treacherous, idle, parasitical, and heathen (Mayall 1988: 76, 80–1).

The same political, economic, and discursive processses that racialized the Gypsies within England also racialized the Irish. While the early Norman and later Tudor conquest of Ireland had been justified on the basis of alleged cultural inferiority with a particular emphasis on religion, the eighteenth and nineteenth century saw a shift toward an emphasis on racial inferiority as the Irish were increasingly constructed as a distinct Celtic race in opposition to the Anglo-Saxons (Curtis 1984). The racialization of the Irish coincided with nationalist challenges to British imperialism within Ireland, and with substantial Irish labour migration to England. Anti-Irish racism was then pervasive in British élite and popular discourse of the nineteenth century (Miles 1982: 121–50).

I now want to turn to consider more specifically the significance of this wider context for constructions of Irish Travellers. While never a major topic of interest, the Irish 'tinkers' did briefly emerge as a sub-area of interest in the early issues of the Journal of the Gypsy Lore Society because they (along with Scottish 'tinkers,' 'tinklers,' or 'gypsies') were believed to have some bearing upon one of the central preoccupations of the Gypsylorists – that is, the timing of the entry of Gypsies into Western Europe.

Despite general agreement on the Indian provenance of Gypsies, there was considerable debate over both the precise location of their origins and the timing of their migration to Europe. The 1888 preface to the first issue of the *Journal of the Gypsy Lore Society* outlined three major hypotheses: (1) that the Gypsies had entered Europe in 1417 shortly after leaving India, (2) that the Gypsies had left Persia in approximately A.D. 430 and had entered Western Europe at a later period, or (3) that the Gypsies had been in Europe for two thousand years as metal workers.

The latter 'prehistoric theory' postulated that the first undisputed British reference to 'Egyptians' in 1505 (actually recorded in Scotland), did not, as was usually argued, indicate a recent arrival of Gypsies in Britain. A much longer 'Gypsy' presence in Britain was, it was suggested, demonstrated by earlier references to 'tinkers.' The suggestion of a link between the 'tinkers' of the Middle Ages and the 'Egyptians' of the sixteenth century led to an interest in the possible connections between contemporary 'tinkers' and 'Gypsies.' Interest in the Scottish and Irish 'tinkers' then emerged as a by-product of the debate over the origins of the 'Gypsies' in Britain.

For the British scholars, there were three possible origins of the Irish and Scottish 'tinkers': (1) that they were 'Gypsies,' (2) that they were an indigenous nomadic group, or (3) that they were a mixture of indigenous nomads and 'Gypsies.' Uncertainty regarding the status of Irish and Scottish Travellers was evident in the many editorial changes made to articles and references from other sources that were reprinted in the *Journal of the Gypsy Lore Society*. Such changes also make it apparent that terms such as 'Gypsy' and 'tinker' were often used interchangeably in the popular discourse of the late nineteenth and early twentieth centuries.

Just as linguistic study of Romany was thought to have revealed the origins and history of the 'Gypsies,' it was claimed that linguistic research into the language of the 'tinkers' (referred to as Shelta in the Gypsiology literature) could provide the key to their origins. Gypsiologists attributed the discovery of a tinker's 'cant' to the current president of the Gypsy Lore Society, Charles Leland, who claimed to have first recognized it in 1876. The topic of Shelta and the status of its speakers was taken up by David MacRitchie, whose primary area of interest was the Scottish 'Gypsies.' In articles on Irish 'tinkers,' however, MacRitchie argued that the latter's language was a compound of English, Romanes, and Gaelic (1889: 353) and that cultural and archival evidence supported the view that 'the tinker caste in Ireland is ... Gypsy to some extent' (ibid., 351).

The claim that the Irish 'tinkers' were at least 'semi-Gypsies' (ibid., 352; see also MacRitchie 1890) would, however, be challenged by another Gypsiologist and scholar of Gaelic, John Sampson. Sampson had collected vocabulary from an Ulster 'tinker' living in Liverpool, and concluded from his study of this vocabulary that Shelta was a dialect or jargon 'exclusively of Celtic origin' (Sampson 1890: 209). He went further to suggest that Shelta was originally derived from a 'prehistoric Celtic' although many of the words were of more recent origin, created through various modifications of modern Gaelic (ibid., 207–8). On the basis of this linguistic research, Sampson asserted the independent origins of the Irish 'tinkers' and English Gypsies despite 'the many striking coincidences of life which link the Celtic to the Romani vagrant' (ibid., 204).

Based on the material collected by Sampson, another Celticist, Kuno Meyer, concurred that Shelta was of Irish origin and added that it was a secret language of great antiquity, probably formed prior to the eleventh century (1891: 260). He suggested that 'though now confined to tinkers, its knowledge was once possessed by Irish poets and scholars, who, probably, were its original framers' (ibid., 258).

The dating of the 'tinker's' cant to a period prior to the eleventh century, however, did not ensure a similar dating of 'tinker' origins. This was because, following Meyer's argument, it was assumed that Shelta could not have been fashioned by illiterate 'tinkers.' In an admission of the independent variation of language and blood, the 'tinkers' were reduced to the status of mere carriers of a linguistic link to Gaelic Ireland. Charles Leland would later summarize the new orthodoxy: '[Shelta] appears to have been an artificial, secret, or Ogham tongue, used by the bards, and transferred by them, in all probability, to the bronze workers and jewellers – a learned and important body – from whom it descended to the tinkers' (Leland 1892: 195). The irony of this demotion of the Irish 'tinkers' was that a similar argument was not applied to the Gypsies. If it had been, the fallacy of the linguistic basis for the Indian origin theory, as Okely (1983) has pointed out, would have had to have been acknowledged.[4]

Once it was concluded that the linguistic evidence indicated a Celtic rather than Indian origin, the Irish 'tinkers' were slotted into the racial hierarchy of Travellers created by British Gypsiology. At the top of the ladder were the allegedly pure-blooded 'true Gypsies,' who alone were worthy objects of ethnological study. Below the Gypsies were the Scottish Travellers, whose status was uncertain (i.e., either Celts or mixed Gypsy and Celt), and below them were the allegedly Celtic Irish 'tinkers.'

While the Irish 'tinkers' were ranked below the 'true' Romani Gypsies, they were distinguished by Sampson from the allegedly inferior non-Gypsy English vagrants for whom the Gypsiologists had nothing but contempt. While Sampson acknowledged that Shelta was spoken by English wanderers, he was at pains to distinguish the Celtic 'tinker' from 'his less reputable English connections – the grinder and street hawker' (1890: 204). Sampson did this by alleging that the Shelta spoken by the 'knife grinder, street hawker, and other shady characters' was 'corrupt,' and that 'scarcely a tithe of the words in daily use by the Irish 'tinker' are intelligible to his English half-breed cousin' (ibid., 208). Thus, in the hierarchy established by the Gypsiologists, the Irish 'tinkers' were located below the Gypsies and, less clearly, the Scottish Travellers, but above the 'half-bloods' (i.e., Gypsy and Anglo-Saxon) and, those at the very bottom of the hierarchy, the English vagrants (see Mayall 1988: 78–9).

This hierarchy reflected the obsession with 'race' and racial purity characteristic of colonialism, but also the significance of class. In the Gypsiology schema, the English lumpenproletariat was placed *below* the racialized and colonized 'Other,' whether Gypsy (i.e., Indian) or Irish 'tinker' (i.e., Celt). According to the racial logic of the literature, the small minority of true Gypsies were acceptable because their lifestyle was racially determined, but the majority of Travellers, whose itinerancy was not deemed to be racially based, invited nothing but condemnation of their alleged degeneracy (Mayall 1988: 80). The legitimacy of the Celtic Travellers was in between these two extremes.

The racialization of Irish 'tinkers' as Celts led to their occupying a marginal position at the intersection of Gypsiology and another scholarly discourse, that of Celticism. Just as the Gypsy Lore Society had glorified the minority of 'true' Gypsies at a time when Traveller-Gypsies were being harshly repressed, (and Orientalism celebrated aspects of the colonized East), so, too, the scholarly subfield of Celtic antiquarianism glorified an ancient Gaelic Irish past while ignoring the historical present of colonial domination.

Celticists were intrigued, not with the present circumstances of Irish 'tinkers' in England or Ireland, but rather with their possible links to an ancient Irish past. One of the key figures who spanned Gypsiology and Celticism was John Sampson, who clearly indicated that his major concern was to record the linguistic and cultural traits of Irish 'tinkers' before their extinction: 'Preserved in his life, as in his language, are many archaisms, which one would fain see placed on record, before Time with his harsh breathing aspirates them out of existence' (Sampson 1890: 221). The Celticist Kuno Meyer was even more candid about the nature of his interest in this tinker 'jargon': 'I would scarcely have taken much interest in Shelta, if it were nothing but tinkers' cant, fabricated from Irish in modern times, of a kind not superior to the backslang of costers and cabmen. It was the fact of there being evidence to the great antiquity of Shelta that made me want to know more about it' (1891: 261).

The Celticists' interest in Shelta provided the Irish 'tinker' with a certain status in scholarly circles that would be augmented by their incorporation into the Anglo-Irish literature of the Celtic Literary Revival. In this literature Irish wanderers, including 'tinkers,' would, unlike the English vagrants, be portrayed, not as degenerates, but rather as symbols of nationalist aspirations.

The Celtic Literary Revival, Cultural Nationalism, and the 'Tinkers'

While British scholarship constructed Gypsies and tinkers as racialized 'Others,' this same attribution meant that they were largely unracialized in Ireland – rather they were part of the racial 'Self.' Within the very different economic and political processes of Ireland at this time, they were symbolically available for use in expressions of cultural nationalism.

In Ireland, colonialism had led to resistance that took many forms, but by the end of the nineteenth century the political situation was moving toward an intensified nationalist struggle against British domination that would end with independence in 1922. Renewed nationalism in Ireland was marked by the competing claims for leadership by the Protestant Anglo-Irish ascendancy and the emerging Catholic bourgeoisie. The former were represented in a cultural nationalism that looked to pre-colonial Ireland for inspiration. This cultural nationalism was artistically expressed in the Celtic Literary Revival, a literary outgrowth of the scholarly currents of Celticism that had, in turn, intersected with the Gypsiology literature. Given the preoccupations of the Anglo-Irish Celtic Revivalists it seems likely that the conclusions drawn by Kuno Meyer concerning the antiquity of Shelta would have generated interest, and it is therefore perhaps not surprising to find that wanderers and 'tinkers,' in particular figure rather prominently in their writing.

Along with the fact that a number of Gypsiologists had personal connections to Ireland (including John Sampson and Kuno Meyer), there is evidence of cross-fertilization between them and the Celtic Revivalists. Douglas Hyde, a prominent member of the Revival (co-founder and first president of the Gaelic League in 1893 and later the first president of Ireland) wrote a play entitled *The Tinker and the Fairy* which was first performed in Dublin in 1900. Hyde is quoted in the *Journal of the Gypsy Lore Society* as saying that he had not met a tinker who knew Shelta (Anon. 1908: 130). Another Revivalist, John M. Synge, author of the play *The Tinker's Wedding* (1924; first published in 1904), also indicated a familiarity with the Gypsy Lore literature when he wrote that the vagrants' life was a pageant 'not less grand than Loti's or George Borrow's' (Synge 1966: 196).

Wanderers, including 'tinkers,' appear in the literature of the Celtic Revival in part because they, along with the peasantry, especially in the west of Ireland, were seen as embodiments of the pre-colonial past. In a haunting description of a 'tinkers'' camp, Synge suggested that the 'tinkers' were outside modern history. He wrote that: 'People like these ... are a possession for any country. They console us, one moment at least, for the manifold and beautiful life we have all missed who have been born in modern Europe' (ibid., 199).

In the literature of the Celtic Literary Revival the figure of the 'tinker' or wanderer was also sometimes used to critique the post-famine peasantry, which had allegedly departed from its Gaelic roots. Indeed, it has been suggested that for Yeats and his contemporaries, the 'tinkers and beggars and the unregarded poor, were the true heirs of the Ireland of the kings and the bards' (Raine 1981: 21).

The use of the wanderer to represent the antithesis of what was considered to be the materialism, stultifying Catholicism, and repressed sexuality of post-famine Ireland was explicit in Lady Gregory's play *The Travelling Man* (Gregory 1970: 21–8), where Christ in the guise of a tramp was refused shelter and food by a rural woman. Similarly, in Synge's play *The Tinker's Wedding*, the tale of a Tinker woman's desire for a respectable Church wedding mocks the values of the post-famine peasantry. Likewise a peasant woman chooses to leave her repressive marriage for a life on the road in his *The Shadow of the Glen* (1924; first published in 1910).

Unlike the Gypsiologists in England, however, the artists of the Celtic Literary Revival had little interest in distinguishing between 'tinkers' and other wanderers on either linguistic or racial grounds. Wanderers, including 'tinkers,' were celebrated for their allegedly Celtic origins, but also for their putative cultural features of mobility, freedom from wage labour, and uninhibited sexuality. The wanderer figures of the Celtic Literary Revival symbolized the position claimed by the Anglo-Irish artists – that is, to serve as 'bards' for the Irish nation.[5] Such claims, however, denied the intervening colonial period of domination and the position of the Anglo-Irish as contemporary representatives of this domination. The attempt by the Celtic Literary Revival to appropriate a pre-colonial Celtic Ireland as the basis for a new cultural nationalism was challenged by alternative understandings of history among the dominated Catholic population. Alternative understandings of the history of the nation, and the particular place of 'tinkers' within this history, are revealed in the folklore of the post-famine peasantry.

Irish Agrarian Class Relations and the 'Tinkers'

Rapid industrialization and urbanization characterized England at the end of the nineteenth century, but uneven and dependent development in Ireland as a result of colonization had resulted in processes of de-industrialization and a predominantly rural population. Within this context wanderers, including 'tinkers,' who served as links between urban and rural centres as well as between more and less commodified regions of the country, did not attract missionary or state efforts at control. At the same time, however, the constructions of 'tinkers' found among the rural population reflect tensions engendered by changes in rural Ireland in the post-famine period.

The numbers of landless and mobile persons were increasing in the early decades of the nineteenth century before the deadly effects of the series of crop failures in the mid-nineteenth century that came to be known collectively as the Famine dramatically altered the class composition of rural Ireland. During the Famine (1845–9) Ireland's population was halved, and those who died of starvation and disease or emigrated were, disproportionately, the rural poor – for example, labourers, smallholders, and cottiers. Prior to the Famine these groups formed the majority of the rural population, but in the post-Famine period the proportion of middle and larger farmers was greatly increased (Foster 1988: 340). The effects of the Famine, combined with the land legislation of 1881 and 1882, which provided ownership to many tenant farmers, resulted in a general if uneven process of 'rural embourgeoisement' throughout the island (ibid., 439).

The particular experience of the 'tinkers' during the dramatic transformation of Ireland during the nineteenth century awaits more systematic archival research. Census material, however, suggests that the occupational category of 'tinker' suffered a disproportionate decline during the critical period of 1831 to 1851, followed by a numerical increase in the later part of the century.[6] Nevertheless, it is difficult to be certain of the relationship between the occupationally defined 'tinkers' recorded in these early censuses and the 'tinkers' described, for instance, by John Sampson in 1890. The latter were characterized by a multi-occupational family-based work strategy and could have been recorded under a variety of other occupations in the census.

In spite of a paucity of evidence there is reason to believe that 'tinkers,' while perhaps reduced in numbers, were a more distinct and visible category of the population in post-famine rural Ireland. They were by this time part of a much smaller landless and mobile population whose family economies were substantially different from the numerically dominant landed peasantry. It is into this context of a changing rural economy and society that we need to place the 'tinker discourse' of the late-nineteenth-century rural folk.

Folklore and the 'Tinkers'

While discussion of the relationship between the rural embourgeoisement of the late nineteenth century and increasing anti-Traveller racism remains speculative (Mac Laughlin 1995, 1996; McVeigh 1992) some insight can be gained from the poetry, plays, and prose of the Celtic Literary Revival, which contained reworked versions of stories gathered from the rural Irish who were thought to provide a link to the Gaelic past. Some of this material has been published in a more direct form and through this some access to the 'popular' discourse concerning the 'tinkers' of the period can be gained. In these accounts 'tinkers' are attributed Irish provenance, but are clearly portrayed as outside of, and inferior to, the 'moral community' (Scott 1976).

What is striking about this material is the consistently negative image of the 'tinkers.' Indeed, Sampson suggested that the 'tinkers' were at this time uniquely 'tabooed and dreaded' (Sampson 1890: 204) by country people, and Lady Gregory commented that the 'country people – who are so kind to one another, and to tramps and beggars ... speak of a visit of the tinkers as of frost in spring or blight in harvest' (Gregory 1974: 94). The Oxford English Dictionary entry of 1896 noted that 'tinker' was at this time an abusive term in Ireland.

In origin accounts collected by Lady Gregory at the turn of the century in the West of Ireland, the rural peasantry linked the mobility and outcast status of the 'tinkers' to alleged moral and religious transgressions. For example, she was told a story in which a 'tinker' told St Patrick that a lump of gold or silver was worthless while a smith told him its true value. St Patrick punished the tinker's deception by 'put[ting] a curse on the tinkers that they might be for ever with every man's face against them, and their face against every man; and that they should get no rest for ever but to travel the world' (Gregory 1974: 96). In a similar vein, another tale told of how a 'tinker' refused to make a vessel for Christ: 'I often heard it said that our Lord asked a tinker one time to make Him some vessel He wanted, and he refused Him. He then went to a smith, and he did what was wanted. And from that time the tinkers have been wandering on the roads' (ibid., 197). In a third account it was said that the 'tinkers' were the only ones who would agree to drive the nails into the hands and feet of Christ and 'that is why they have to walk the world' (ibid., 96).

In these accounts, rural folk in the West portrayed the nomadism of the 'tinkers' as punishment for unethical practices associated with their particular way of making a living. For such breaches they were transformed from sedentary artisans into a 'wandering tribe.' As many of the tales emphasize, 'tinkers' were distinguished by their alleged immorality as well as by geographical mobility, which made them permanent outsiders and distinguished them from sedentary artisans such as smiths and carpenters with whom they shared similar relations of work.[7]

It is not surprising that the 'tinkers,' outsiders who served as economic links to a wider market economy, were received with ambivalence by some farmers. Indeed, the portrayal of 'tinkers' as those who would exploit Christ and St Patrick for economic advantage can be read as a displaced critique of capitalist morality by farmers experiencing the vicissitudes of partial incorporation through petty commodity production. An association of 'tinkers' with capitalist relations might also explain the apparent success of some 'tinkers' in defrauding farmers through the claim to make money out of money ('coining'). Of course the deeper source of farmers' challenges lay in wider structures and processes of colonial governance and economic underdevelopment, not in their relations with Travellers.

The attributed immorality of the Travellers went beyond accusations of religious and economic transgression to the arena of gender relations and sexuality. Synge, for example, based his play *The Tinker's Wedding* on what he was told about 'tinkers' by country people in the East of Ireland.

One man had told him of a 'tinker' couple who had never been married (Synge 1980: 53), while another gave him an eye-witness account of how the 'tinkers' swapped wives 'with as much talk as if you'd be selling a cow' (ibid., 31). Similar accounts were collected by Lady Gregory in the West of Ireland during the same time period. One country person told her: '[the tinkers] sell their wives to one another; I've seen that myself ... [and that] as to marriage, some used to say they lepped [leaped] the budget [bag of tinsmiths tools], but it's more likely they have no marriage at all' (Gregory 1974: 94).

The suggestion of informal liaisons among Irish Travellers had found its way into scholarly sources a decade earlier. In the *Journal of the Gypsy Lore Society*, MacRitchie reproduced an account from a 'lady resident in Limerick' which included a second-hand description of 'tinker' wife-swapping at a fair and the suggestion of 'budget-leaping' weddings (MacRitchie 1889: 352). John Sampson repeated the alleged 'facts' of wife exchange and lack of Church weddings among Irish Travellers, and added the additional feature of close-kin marriage. He wrote: '[tinkers] intermarry among themselves, often with but slight regard for the rites of the Church, or the table of prohibited degrees. Their exchange of wives, moreover, is a civility extended only to members of the clan' (Sampson 1890: 204).

Farmers' views of 'tinker' marriage reflected class differences in modes of social and cultural reproduction. In the pre-famine period a large proportion of the rural population, notably the cottiers and landless labourers, had practised early marriage with little match-making or property transfer. By the 1880s, however, the process of rural embourgeoisement was accompanied by a very different system of late and arranged marriages centred upon impartible male inheritance and female dowries (Fitzpatrick 1983; Gibbon and Curtin 1978).

For the 'tinkers,' in contrast, survival depended primarily on the labour of family members rather than the transfer of property such as land and dowry. Marriage and child-bearing for them were prerequisites for economic survival, and both occurred at a young age. For propertied farmers, however, the young marriages of the 'tinkers' represented sexuality loosened from economic considerations of landed-class reproduction and Church regulations.

Anxiety about the potential threat posed by 'tinkers' to class relations between households, and also to patriarchal control over gendered and generational relations within farming families, was apparent in the preoccupation with the possibility of inappropriate liaisons with them. This preoccupation is suggested in a number of literary works that explore the putative attractions and dangers of marriage to a male 'tinker.' A poem from this period by the nationalist Thomas McDonagh entitled *John John* describes how a country woman fell in love with and married a Traveller but failed in her attempts to domesticate him and was eventually abandoned (Kennelly 1970: 292–3). A similar theme is found in a later poem called *The Ballad of the Tinker's Wife* by Sigerson Clifford (Kennelly 1970: 359).

In the work of J.S. Synge, female characters such as Nora and Pegeen in *The Shadow of the Glen* and *Playboy of the Western World* of course expressed their autonomy in part through their attraction to male wanderers, but this work prompted outrage among conservative Catholic nationalists, who saw the portrayal of such attractions as an insult to the ideally domesticated, asexual mothers of the nation (Cairns and Richards, 1987; O'Brien Johnson and Cairns, 1991).[8] The imagery, however, can be placed in the context of late nineteenth and early twentieth century changes in gender relations. Rural women in propertied farming families were experiencing a shift away from productive labour to full-time housewifery that weakened their economic autonomy and increased their domestication within the household (Bourke 1993). This process co-existed with a dramatic migration of young unmarried women away from rural areas – which left behind increasing numbers of aging bachelors.

The literary images of (usually failed) liaisons between male Travellers and female members of the propertied classes expressed but also reinforced ethnic, class, and gender tensions and inequalities between Travellers and non-Travellers, propertied and propertyless, men and women at this time.

Irish Independence and the 'Tinkers'

By the early twentieth century, Irish politics were radicalized through opposition to involvement in the Boer War and later the First World War (Foster 1988: 456). Part of this radicalization involved the replacement of a pre-existing cultural nationalism with a separatist revolutionary nationalism among Irish Catholics. The result was the Easter Rising of 1916, and the acceptance of the Anglo-Irish Treaty in 1921, which established Ireland's Dominion status within the British Empire. The new state emerged as one dominated by a new class – a Catholic bourgeoisie which managed to marginalize earlier socialist, labour, and feminist elements within the nationalist movement (ibid., 515). It was this bourgeoisie that would direct the new ideologies and practices of nation-building.

The 'rise of bourgeois nationalism' (Mac Laughlin 1996: 49) has been identified as significant for understanding the trajectory of anti-Traveller racism and is examined in more detail in chapter 2, but here I explore the implications of independent state development for the limited scholarship on Travellers written during this period.

Foster suggests that the preoccupation of the new state was self-definition against Britain – both political and cultural (1988: 516). Accordingly, the scholars of independent Ireland were engaged in a revision of the Anglo-Irish view of Irish history. This new history downplayed the role of the Anglo-Irish in Irish cultural development in favour of a continuity of Gaelic society and culture up until the nineteenth century.

The nationalist historian Eoin MacNeill in his important *Phases of Irish History* (1920) argued for the existence of an early pre-colonial Irish civilization and nation. In a description of ranked pre-Celtic 'occupation – castes' he speculated that: 'the tinker-clans of recent times in Ireland and Scotland may well be survivals of some of these ancient industrial communities' (1920: 82), thereby identifying Travellers as unequivocally Irish and providing an 'explanation' of their contemporary occupations and lower social status through reference to an ancient social order.

Another major scholar of this historical revisionism was Daniel Corkery, whose first work was entitled *The Hidden Ireland* (1967; first published 1924). In this work he argued that 'despite conquests, plantations, confiscations, and famines, eighteenth-century Ireland had witnessed the survival of the essentials of Gaelic culture which had been partially preserved in the few remaining *Catholic* gentry houses and the peasants' hovels' (quoted in Cairns and Richards 1988: 125). Significantly, Corkery saw the core of Irish culture as having been preserved by the Gaelic aristocracy, and disseminated to other classes by the wandering bardic schools which had operated up to the end of the eighteenth century (Foster 1988: 195).

Although Corkery made no explicit link between 'tinkers' and the eighteenth century Gaelic bards, such a connection was implied in the 1930s writing of MacGréine (1931, 1932, 1934), the first folklorist to collect information directly from the 'tinkers' or 'travellers' (as he acknowledged they called themselves). MacGréine called for more study of the 'traveller-folk,' arguing that: 'These "travellers," the *bacaigh* of an earlier time, the poor scholars – the Irish *scolares vagantes* – have been the medium for the spread of folk tales and all manner of traditions' (MacGréine 1931: 185–6). For MacGréine the 'tinkers' were important repositories of Irish tradition, and he protested what he saw as a growing anti-Travellerism in the 1920s and 1930s using a romanticized primitivist discourse:

> To those people who would seek to 'civilise' [the tinkers] ... who refer to them as a 'national problem'; 'a nuisance to farmers'; and so on, I would say: Leave us our wandering tinkers. House them and they pine; they have no outlet for their restlessness. Why cage a bird? Why civilise a tinker? (MacGréine 1931: 177)

MacGréine's views supported the Irish Folklore Commission's later issuing of a 'tinker questionnaire' to its folklore collectors in the early 1950s. At that time the Folklore Commission stated that it wished to compile documentation on the 'tinkers'' way of life 'before it is too late' (Irish Folklore Commission 1952 [henceforth IFC]: 5), and described the 'tinkers' as 'one of the oldest classes of Irish society' and as probable repositories of Irish tradition (ibid., 5).

This identification of Travellers with a disappearing 'traditional' Ireland had links to the work of the Celtic Literary Revivalists, and indeed continues as a minor theme in more contemporary writing on Travellers. Such nostalgic harnessing of Travellers as symbols of a 'national' tradition on the wane, however, made them the subject of a form of salvage scholarship, and offered little space in a self-consciously modernizing nation.

Respondents to the 1952 'tinker questionnaire' (not Travellers themselves but outside observers) were asked among other things to record 'anything known about who the tinkers really are in origin, or how it has happened that they took up the nomadic life?' The responses to this question from non-Travellers were various, although most attributed an Irish origin to the 'tinkers.' Focusing upon the responses of those in the western counties alone, we find attributions of pre-colonial origins, for example, that they were of pre-Christian origin (IFC 1255: 31), and that they were the pure Irish race (IFC 1256: 146), but also attributions of colonial origins, for example, that they descended from dispossessed noble lords (IFC 1255: 283). More uncommon were accounts of non-indigenous origins, for example, that they were descendants of the lost children of Israel or from Egypt (ibid., 233, 439).

It was not until the 1960s that the various discourses concerning the 'tinkers' became codified into one dominant explanation of their origins. An important precursor of the new paradigm was the writing of folklore collector Sean McGrath. In a discussion of origin accounts collected from

Travellers themselves, to be discussed below, McGrath stated that 'genuine' tinkers were of interest because they were 'symbolic of an older Ireland' (1955: 19), and then offered his own conclusion that many of the Travellers were of colonial origin, the descendants of small landowners who were victims of Cromwell's 'to hell or to Connacht' policy or of those who were dispossessed during the Famine (1955: 28). This construction of a colonial origin for the 'tinkers' would become the new orthodoxy after its reproduction in the 1963 Report of the Commission on Itinerancy.

McGrath was also notable for his statement that while 'genuine' tinkers might have historical significance, these constituted only a minority of those presently on the roads. Like many politicians of the period, he challenged the authenticity of the majority of the Travellers in his region:

> Unfortunately in the last ten years, the bands of travellers who visit this area of West Clare, are not of the *true Traveller class*, and the outrages they instigated, have somewhat marred the rating of the *real traveller*. (1955: 23–4)

> Despite the apparent increase in the tinker population, the older type steadily seems to disappear ... there are vagrants on the Irish roads today, and they are a shame and a disgrace to the *genuine tinkers* of the country. (1955: 8) [my emphasis]

McGrath's argument that most Travellers were not, in fact, heirs to an 'older Ireland' allowed him to disregard the earlier scholarly, literary, and folklorist tradition that had asserted their historical significance. It also allowed him to countenance the calls for the state to take action against them at a time of severe economic crisis.

Both MacGréine and McGrath recorded various origin accounts from Travellers themselves. Some of the stories were concerned with the origins of particular families. For example, two families told McGrath that they had pre-colonial origins (descent from the smiths of Brian Boru's army, and descent from plough-makers employed by the High King of Ireland, respectively), while colonial origins were claimed by others who said that they had been thrown off their land by Cromwell (McGrath 1955: 7).

Along with family accounts, however, there were other stories that asserted a more collective 'tinker' identity. While some of the stories collected by MacGréine were similar to those told by the rural folk, for instance, 'that it was a red haired tinker who made the nails with which Christ was crucified, and that on this account tinkers must be wanderers forever' (1931: 177; see also Court 1985: 88–9), others inverted these dominant versions.

MacGréine, for example, was told by a Traveller that because a 'tinker' stole one of the four nails that were forged to crucify Christ, there was one day of the year on which all 'tinkers' could steal without sinning.[9] He was also told that 'a tinker once blinded the Devil, and on this account a tinker will never go to hell' (1931: 176–7). A similar inversion of the St Patrick story is found in a Traveller autobiography from the 1970s:

> At the time of St Patrick, there were many travellers in Ireland. Indeed it was they who helped St Patrick when he was a boy slave. They smuggled him away from his cruel master, because the travellers hated any form of slavery or being tied down to settled life. (Maher 1972: 63)

Such stories, told to non-Traveller collectors, reveal simultaneous acceptance of the dominant themes of Irish nationalism and Catholicism, and active rejection of stigmatization of the Traveller way of life.

MacGréine interpreted an apparent lack of consistency in Traveller accounts as evidence that Travellers lacked a 'clear tradition' regarding their origins. None the less, insofar as these stories can be read as attempts to claim a place *as Travellers* within the moral community of independent Ireland, they provide evidence of a collectivized historical consciousness.

As this chapter has made clear, however, constructions of Travellers have been dominated by outsiders who have attempted to 'explain' Travellers in terms of various origin stories. While there has been general consensus on the Irishness of Travellers (a construction that has resulted in the absence of 'race' in the construction of difference), attributions of degraded origin, for example, of moral transgression and/or British oppression, have served to naturalize and inferiorize Traveller identity and have justified anti-Traveller action in racist ways. The centrality of such origin stories to the construction of ethnic boundaries and to the reproduction of anti-Traveller racism has ensured that these stories continue to be a site of contestation in contemporary Ireland.

Chapter 2

'Menace to the Social Order': Anti-Traveller Racism, 1922–59

In the previous chapter I discussed how contested stories of origin told about Travellers in Ireland have served to naturalize Traveller identity and anti-Travellerism by removing these phenomena from history.[1] Despite some attempts to locate Travellers and anti-Traveller racism within the context of changing class relations of the late nineteenth century and the emergence of bourgeois nationalism in the early twentieth century (e.g., Mac Laughlin 1995; McVeigh 1992), little original historical research has been conducted – a striking omission given the well-developed historical scholarship on Ireland and examples of such research on 'Gypsies' or Roma in other parts of Europe.

Along with the absence of in-depth historical work, there are repeated popular and political claims that tensions between Travellers and non-Travellers are a relatively recent phenomenon. An example of this appeared in a recent exchange in the Irish parliament, when one politician stated that the 'serious rift' between 'the travelling and settled communities' was relatively recent because 'Twenty or 30 years ago travellers were welcomed into communities' (Dáil, Neville, 4 February 1999: 1464), an assertion echoed by another speaker who also recalled 'very happy relationships between the travelling and settled communities' but agreed that relations had deteriorated 'over the past 30 years or so' (Dáil, O'Donoghue, 4 February 1999: 1465).

The suggestion that tension between Travellers and non-Travellers emerged during the lifetime of the speaker (in this instance in the late 1960s) is an example of what Gibbons (citing historian Oliver MacDonagh) has called the 'contemporaneity of the past' in Irish political culture (1996: 82). In discussions of Travellers the 'tendency to collapse the past into an ever receding present' obscures a history of anti-Travellerism that, as we have seen, can be traced at least as far back as the late nineteenth century. The continuing denial of this longer history has supported dominant models of an anti-racist and homogeneous post-colonial Irish nation.

In this chapter I begin to document a history of anti-Traveller racism at both the local and national levels from the formation of the new Irish state in 1922 to the establishment of the Commission on Itinerancy in 1960. The discussion begins with a tracing of anti-Traveller discourse and exclusionary action in Galway City and its immediate region – the area of my later fieldwork. Using the Galway provincial press and the Galway city council minutes I document anti-Travellerism in this region and then link this to national developments through an examination of anti-Travellerism in the parliamentary (Dáil) debates.

Material from the Dáil debates is used to explore the particular characteristics of anti-Traveller discourse, notably the construction of Travellers as fellow Irish on the one hand and as inferiorized threats to community and nation on the other. Particular attention is paid to the links between anti-Traveller racism, the interests of the propertied classes, and ideologies and practices of gender and generation in the new state.

Anti-Traveller Racism in Galway City, 1922–59

There are identifiable references in the provincial press to Travellers in nearby towns from at least 1908, but the first reports on Travellers in Galway City itself appeared in the summer of 1922, when tense relations between pro- and anti-Treaty forces in Ireland were dissolving into civil war.[2] The provincial paper, the *Connacht Tribune*, and the Galway Urban District Council minutes recorded the urban council's decision to request that the police remove some 'gipsies' who were the target of a complaint by a property owner (*Connacht Tribune* [henceforth *CT*], 3 June 1922: 5; Galway Urban District Council [henceforth GUDC], 1 June 1922).

A week later, there was a more general order to the police to remove 'gipsies ... from the district' (GUDC, 8 June 1922: 106), but the following month there were still concerns that 'gipsies' were 'camping all over the district and are a great annoyance to the public' (GUDC, 24 July 1922: 126). Council members expressed frustration with the inability of the police and military authorities to eliminate the problem. One council member asked: 'How is it that in Tuam [another town in the county] all these gipsies were done away with and put out of town? I think we should be able to do the same.' The chairman of the Galway city council was reported to have replied laughingly: 'If you have no objection we will arm the Urban Council with sticks, and I will put you in charge' (*CT*, 9 September 1922: 5).

Despite the flurry of concern during 1922, the issue of Travellers' camps does not reappear in the recorded minutes of Galway council until the mid-1930s. In the local press, however, evidence of continued pressure on the local government and police to act against the 'gipsies' continues through the 1920s. In 1923, for instance, a group of private home-owners lobbied the city council, claiming that there was danger of an epidemic breaking out if a nearby camp of 'gipsies' were not removed (*CT*, 10 March 1923: 5). This was followed by a letter to the editor again criticizing the failure of the police to 'clear the gypsies out' (*CT*, 31 March 1923: 2). The reference to 'an epidemic' utilized a discourse of pollution associated not only with marginalized groups and Travellers and 'Gypsies' but with the social geography of class and racism more generally (Okely 1983; Sibley 1981, 1995).

In this case the language also dove-tailed with the official discourse of the 1925 Local Government Act, section 20, which allowed sanitary authorities to declare 'A tent, van, shed or similar structure used for human habitation' either a nuisance or injurious to health under the public health act. Although Travellers were not mentioned in the parliamentary debate on the contents of the 1925 Act, two decades later, in the course of updating the legislation, the relevant Minister stated that the 1925 regulations had in fact been 'framed primarily ... to apply to those itinerants who are in the habit of dwelling temporarily on road margins' (Dáil, MacEntee, 4 July 1947: 1013; see also Seanad, Childers, 19 December, 1947: 1894). There is certainly sufficient evidence of anti-Travellerism at the local level to support this retroactive claim.

By 1925, the Galway Chamber of Commerce was also arguing that Travellers posed a threat to the city's economic health, notably its already internationalized tourist industry. The Chamber moved unanimously that:

The attention of the responsible authorities be directed to the encampment of vagrants all around Galway ... These vagrants as beggars are a perfect nuisance. In shops they worry customers to an intolerable extent. In the coming season we are expecting a large influx of tourists, and if these vagrants are around to receive them, you may expect, to the injury of our town, caricature articles will be published in British and American newspapers descriptive of beggar life in Galway. (*CT*, 18 April 1925: 5)

From the mid-1920s onward there are fewer references to Travellers within Galway City itself, but their presence in the surrounding region continues to be mentioned in press reports. A 1926 letter to the editor from a reader living in a village just outside Galway referred to the 'alarming growth of the tinker and tramp pests' and added a description of their putative activities:

> Securing no quarters within the town areas large parties of those tribes move on into the country districts far away from the supervision of the Guards. A laneway in Barna is continually inhabited by every tinker and tramp from Dublin to Galway. There they settle down, and from morning to night they are a source of annoyance to the people of the district – coming begging for all their necessaries of life from door to door. To add to all of this discomfort they keep a number of wicked, half-starved dogs, a danger to all passers-by. On returning from Galway, where they sell their tins and rags, they make merry, and on Saturday nights they keep up a great hullabaloo quarrelling and using most filthy and obscene language. (*CT*, 4 December 1926: 7)

The issue of Traveller camps *within* the city re-emerged in the minutes in 1935, when the council decided to get legal advice 'with regard to camping of itinerants in the area' (GUDC, 11 October 1935: 386). This marks the beginning of a period in which additional legislation was sought to keep Travellers out of Galway. In 1937 the Town Clerk instructed solicitors to prepare by-laws (under the 1925 Act) 'to put itinerants out of the area' (GUDC, 3 June 1937: 269), and two years later by-laws against 'tents, vans, sheds and similar structures used for human habitation' in the urban area were approved by the council (Galway Borough Council [henceforth GBC] 10 October 1939: 181). It would be another four years until these were confirmed by the central government, and in the meantime there was continuing pressure from private home-owners and farmers on the county and local government to act (GBC, 9 June 1939; *CT*, 17 June 1939: 4). A letter to the editor from a resident of Portumna, for example, complained about the tinker 'nuisance' in both rural and urban areas:

> Every farmer knows what it is to have hay and straw pulled out of his sheepcocks by these free and easy gentry for feed and bedding, to find horses and asses have been turned into his fields at night, to have relays of the vagrant family besieging his door for a whole catalogue of food and

clothing, till his naturally charitable traditions are badly strained, and, when the plague has passed on, to see the whole roadside strewn with rags, boots, bottles, half-burned sticks, bits of paper, feathers, – in fact, with every kind of filth and mess imaginable ... on the fair day afternoons in the towns, the shopkeepers have to suffer from the pest ... scenes of brawling and obscene language have often disgraced our towns on these occassions (*CT*, 2 April 1938: 10).

In 1938 when the Galway city council attempted to prosecute one group of Travellers under the Public Health Act, the Sanitary Inspector found that the 'gypsy' camp in question was clean and expressed doubt that the Act could be used against them (GBC, 10 November 1938: 55). The finding, however, did not stop complaints from residents about nearby 'encampments' and 'undesirable people in caravans' (*CT*, 17 June 1939: 4; *CT*, 22 June 1940: 7).

By 1941 the council was attempting to enlist the help of the Department of Agriculture in getting 'gypsies' excluded from the city on the grounds that their horses were allegedly spreading foot and mouth disease (GBC, 11 March 1941: 375) – a theme also pursued by a number of speakers in the national parliament. The Minister for Local Government responded by assuring the city council that arrangements had been made with the police to restrict the movement of Travellers 'as far as possible' (*CT*, 26 April 1941: 4).

In 1943 the by-laws made in 1939 against tents, vans, and so on were confirmed by the central government, and their efficacy is suggested by the reduced discussion of camping Travellers within the city. Apart from a single directive from the council to the police to 'curb the activities of beggars and tinkers in the city and suburbs' (*CT*, 15 September 1945: 5), Travellers disappeared from the city council agenda for the rest of the decade. Again, however, the continued presence of Travellers in the city as well as in the surrounding region is clear from press reports.

There is also evidence to suggest that some Travellers were living in houses in the city at this time. George Gmelch (1977: 137–8) has noted that the nation-wide slum clearances of the 1930s affected many Traveller families already in urban areas who were rehoused in new estates along with other Irish, but significantly often in separate terraces. This appears to have been the case in Galway, where the city minutes include a reference to an 'itinerant' living in a tenement (GUDC, 29 April 1937: 250–1), and there is a report of 'Gipsy vans' at one of the newly constructed housing terraces (GUDC, 28 May 1936: 105).

Clearly identifying individuals in houses as 'Travellers,' however, is not always straightforward. Some squatters evicted from 'shacks' in 1931, for example, had common Traveller names, and one was quoted as saying that 'he had nowhere to go except the side of the road,' but they were not explicitly identified as 'itinerants' or 'tinkers' (CT, 7 November 1931: 7). Others with common Traveller names listed as living in tenements and condemned houses were also not explicitly distinguished from other residents in the records (GUDC, 25 October 1933: 82). It is possible that some of the families living in housing experienced externally and internally imposed identities not easily fit into current either/ or categorizations of 'Travellers' and 'non-Travellers.'

An ambiguous identity could in fact be useful in the context of systemic anti-Traveller racism. Files from the 1940s and 1950s reveal that few Traveller families made it onto the housing lists submitted by city officials to the council, and those that did were rarely appointed as tenants even when they were classed by health officials as priority cases. One family, for example, only managed to get onto the 'priority' housing list because they were allegedly not 'strictly itinerant':

> The ＿＿ family who live in a tent were formerly deleted from the Priority list *on the basis that the* [Galway] *Borough Council were not prepared to house families of the itinerant class.* Ald. ＿＿ made a strong submission for the return of this family to the Priority List and maintained that they were *not strictly itinerant class* as they had been resident in Galway for a considerable period and were enduring extreme hardship.
>
> The Council agreed to the return of the ＿＿ family to the Priority List subject to their being housed at ＿＿ should a vacancy occur there and that the house *was not suitable for any other applicant on the list.* (GBC, 20 January 1958: 280) [my emphasis]

This example reveals that there was a policy in Galway City to refuse tenancies to 'itinerants' as late as 1958, and that even those described as not 'strictly itinerant' were accorded lowest priority. The order to house this family in a particular location where there were already a number of other Traveller families living in houses also demonstrates that politicians contributed to the spatial ghettoization of Travellers.

The city's allocation practices meant that particular areas of council housing became associated with Traveller families prior to the settlement program of the 1960s. The evidence available from the housing files reveals that these houses were occupied by a fluctuating number of

Travellers, often without a change in legal tenancy. Married children, siblings, or elderly parents, for example, often joined those who had houses for short periods, either living with them or in a caravan parked outside.

It was, however, the camping Travellers who preoccupied local politicians, and by the 1950s there were increased efforts aimed at their removal from the city. In the autumn of 1951 the city council passed an Order for the Control of Temporary Dwellings under section 31 of the new Local Government (Sanitary Services) Act, 1948, and Travellers camping in Galway were successfully prosecuted despite the arguments advanced by one solicitor that 'the well-fitted caravan belonging to [the individual being charged], who was a horse dealer and who was born in one of the caravans, could hardly be described as a temporary dwelling as it was the permanent abode of ... his family' (CT, 29 March 1952: 5).

In the spring of 1953 the city council prohibited 'temporary dwellings' from seventeen roads in the city, and later the same year directed the attention of the police 'to the influx of begging gypsies who were making a very bad impression on visitors' (GBC, 5 August 1953: 362). In 1955, the police were again asked by local politicians to visit camps regularly and 'endeavour to keep the tinkers on the move' (GBC, 17 February 1955: 479). Travellers still living in the city in the 1980s recalled how camping within the city boundaries at this time risked constant summons and fines by the 'sanitary man.'

Local press reports referring to Travellers increased dramatically during the 1950s, and in 1955 (the peak of reporting for the decade) the city council began to intensify pressure on the national government to produce new legislation 'for the control of itinerants' (GBC, 1 September 1955: 27). A vigilante attack on a Traveller camp by farmers in the Galway City area in 1956, far from generating concern for the Travellers, led a Galway politician to demand 'immediate action' against 'itinerants' from the Minister for Justice (Dáil, Coogan, 20 June 1956: 636), a call which would be repeated in following years. In 1959 the Municipal Authorities Association conference, held in Galway City, supported a Galway City resolution calling on the Minister for Justice to set up a commission 'to consider the problem of itinerants from all aspects' (GBC, 20 August 1959: 429; CT, 19 September 1959: 9). The following year the national Commission on Itinerancy was formed.

It is apparent from these archival sources that Travellers were actively excluded from Galway City through evictions, prosecutions, and the denial of housing. These measures were taken at the urging of the propertied classes – for example, the land owners, the Chamber of Commerce, and private homeowners – and justified in terms of protecting the 'public health' and/or the economic interests of the city.

While the historical record reveals the existence of an anti-Traveller stance among the local élites much less is known about relations between Travellers and other groups such as the urban working class and/or poorer farmers or labourers. Such relations may have been characterized by the more mutually beneficial and harmonious co-existence described by the politicians at the beginning of this chapter, but clearly such relations were forged within the context of a more dominant ideology and practice of anti-Traveller racism. The degree to which Galway City was representative of other jurisdictions in the pre-1960 period requires additional research, but the regional press reveals that anti-Travellerism was salient in local politics of several of the smaller towns of the region (i.e., Tuam, Ballinasloe, and Athenry) during the decades that followed independence. It was also part of political discourse at the national level from the late 1930s.

Anti-Traveller Racism in Parliamentary Discourse, 1939–59

As discussed earlier, the 1925 Local Government Act was retroactively described as legislation that dealt with 'itinerants' but there appears to have been no parliamentary discussion of the Traveller issue at the time that it was first introduced.[3] The first reference to Travellers that I located in the national debates came later during war-time (known as the Emergency in neutral Ireland) in 1939 when James Dillon, representing County Monaghan and a member of the main opposition party Fine Gael, rose in the Dáil to address 'a matter that [he did] not think was raised before ... the question of itinerancy on the roads.' Itinerancy, the representative went on to claim, had become a situation of 'acute difficulty in rural Ireland' (Dáil, Dillon, 16 March 1939: 2107–8).[4] This first reference was followed by claims from Patrick Cogan, a Wicklow farmer activist, that an increasing number of camping 'hawkers, tinkers, and vagrants' were 'causing great inconvenience and annoyance to rural dwellers' (Dáil, Cogan, 2 October 1940: 39).[5]

The Minister for Justice questioned the suggestion of increasing numbers but responded by asking the police for a report on the issue (Dáil, Boland, 2 October 1940: 40). The following year speakers linked Travellers to the spread of foot-and-mouth disease (as had been asserted in Galway), with one deputy calling for emergency powers of internment to be used against them (Dáil, Meaney, 4 June 1941: 1444–5; see also Dáil, Cogan, 4 June 1941: 1434). The suggestion was an ominous one in the context of the Nazi genocide against 'Gypsies'/Roma on the continent.

Links between the emergence of anti-Traveller rhetoric in the Dáil and anti-Semitic and fascist currents of the World War II period require additional research but are suggested by the fact that Eoin O'Duffy, leader of the fascist-inspired and anti-Semitic Blueshirts in the early 1930s and a co-founder with James Dillon of Fine Gael, had spoken against Travellers, describing them as an 'unworthy class' at a Longford County Council meeting (Gmelch 1986: 53).

The timing of Dillon's statement in the Dáil and his reference to 'itinerancy' as an issue for 'rural' Ireland coincided with a dramatic mobilization of farmer's groups in Ireland and it is possible that the introduction of the Traveller issue by both James Dillon and Patrick Cogan was in response to concerns voiced by these organizations. A link between the farmers' organizations and anti-Travellerism is further suggested by the later anti-Traveller discourse of some members (including Patrick Cogan) of the 'farmers' party,' or Clann na Talmhan, which emerged in the early 1940s. This party, with its populist appeal to a class-stratified agricultural population experiencing economic crisis, threatened the political base of the major opposition party Fine Gael, which courted the large farmer constituency and the governing Fianna Fáil government, which drew part of its support from small farmers.[6]

In his review of the evolution of Clann na Talmhan, Varley does not mention anti-Travellerism, but he notes that some of the farm leadership believed that agricultural interests were being thwarted by an 'unproductive' strata of political élites, commercial middlemen, and in some cases Jewish and Freemason usurers (Varley 1996: 592). That there may have been parallels between such views and anti-Travellerism is suggested by the fact that some members of the Clann elected to the Dáil in 1943 consistently spoke against Travellers (e.g., Patrick Cogan of Wicklow and Francis O'Donnell of Tipperary). Anti-Traveller statements, however, were also part of the discourse of other parties, including the governing Fianna Fáil, which instituted the first census of 'vagrants camping out' in 1944.

This first census was carried out by the police and produced a figure of 5,151. A second count conducted in 1952 recorded 6, 275 persons. In both cases urban districts were excluded from the census, perhaps reflecting the perception of the Traveller problem as exclusively rural.[7] It is important to recall, however, that the presence of Travellers in urban districts was addressed by the 1948 Local Government (Sanitary Services) Act, which gave local authorities the power to make by-laws regulating and prohibiting 'temporary dwellings.'

Although the significance of the 1948 Act for Travellers was initially downplayed by the Fianna Fáil government minister introducing the legislation (who insisted that the relevant sections were primarily designed to improve the regulation of holiday camping), when pressed on the issue by Patrick Cogan he acknowledged that the new Act could indeed be used against camping Travellers (Dáil, MacEntee, 4 July 1947: 1013, Dáil, Cogan, 4 July 1947: 1022; Dáil, Cogan, 10 December 1947: 710, Dáil, Childers, 10 December 1947: 710). As we have seen, in Galway City the Act was employed for this purpose.

In 1948 Fianna Fáil was replaced by a coalition government consisting of both right-wing (Fine Gael and Clann na Talmhan) and left-wing (Labour, National Labour, and Clann na Poblachta) parties. The coalition government, while occasionally reproducing anti-Traveller statements, did not introduce any new anti-Traveller legislation. The lack of any co-ordinated action was in contrast to the situation in Northern Ireland, where a 'Committee on Gypsies and Like Itinerants' had issued a report in 1948 and where in 1950 a Gypsies Bill aimed at curtailing itinerancy was introduced (although then unexpectedly withdrawn) in the Stormont Senate (Noonan 1998).[8]

In the South when the Minister for Justice was asked by a deputy from South Kerry to regulate Traveller camps, he suggested that his lack of action was due to legal obstacles: 'I appreciate these bands of vagrants are a great nuisance and if I could see any satisfactory way of dealing with them I should not hesitate to introduce proposals for legislation' (Dáil, MacEoin, 21 July 1949: 1572). The following year, however, the same Minister took a different tack when he rejected a Clann na Talmhan member's call for increased control over Travellers with a much stronger (and unusual) defence of the 'rights' of the Travellers, who were described as 'persons whose people have been on the roads for centuries ... [and who] have a prescriptive right to be on the roads' (Dáil, MacEoin, 22 November 1950: 1067).

A Fianna Fáil government re-elected in 1951 came under pressure from opposition members as well as some politicians from its own party, to act against the Travellers (Dáil, Cogan, 12 July 1951: 1495–6; 18 July 1951: 1830–1; Dáil, Dillon, 18 July 1951: 1831; Dáil, Maguire, 31 October 1951: 211), and during the tenure of a second coalition government (1954–7) the Traveller 'problem' became firmly established as an urban issue.

By this time Ireland's post-war participation in the Marshall Plan was beginning to have an effect on the domestic economy. O'Hearn has described how, under pressure from the U.S. to dismantle earlier policies aimed at the development and protection of indigenous industry, the government began to encourage export industries and foreign investment. He has also pointed out that these reforms were accompanied by 'austerity budgets' that cut food subsidies and social services and limited wage gains in the early 1950s. By 1955 industrial and agricultural production were down, unemployment was up, and the population was declining (O'Hearn 1998: 38). This was the context for an intensification of anti-Traveller discourse in the parliament.

While the Minister for Justice had been asked to remove the 'itinerants' camped in and around Dublin as early as 1949 (Dáil, Belton, 9 March 1949: 994), in 1955 and 1956 a series of deputies complained about Travellers' horses and camps in and near the cities of Galway, Cork, Limerick, Waterford, and Dublin (Dáil, O'Malley, 13 July 1955: 726–7; Dáil, Manley, 13 July 1955: 736; Dáil, Burke, 13 July 1955: 737–8; Dáil, Coogan, 20 June 1956: 636; Dáil, Lynch, 11 July 1956: 665). Reflecting this new focus the 1956 official count of Travellers included the urban districts in its purview for the first time. When Fianna Fáil returned with a majority government in 1957 deputies representing urban areas took up the Traveller issue with unprecedented intensity. Although rural concerns continued to be articulated (Dáil, Dillon, 9 April 1959: 308–9; Dáil, Lynch, 15 April 1959: 484) the 'problem' was described as particularly pressing in built-up areas, and specifically in the new housing estates of the city of Dublin. One Dublin representative expressed the views of several of his colleagues when he called for the Travellers to be 'put ... off the roads' altogether (Dáil, Burke, 16 April 1958: 189–90).

It appears that the late 1950s marked a shift in Fianna Fáil thinking about Travellers. In 1957 when a deputy from Dublin asked for legislation to deal with 'tinkers and their encampments' in the city (Dáil, Belton, 1 May 1957: 466), the Minister for Justice responded that his department and others were studying the matter (Dáil, Traynor, 1 May 1957: 467). After two more years of frequent questioning on the issue, the Minister for Justice indicated that the parliamentary secretary Charles Haughey was 'actively engaged in a study of the problem of itinerants in all its aspects with a view to making proposals' (Dáil, Traynor, 18 May 1960: 1478). Shortly after this the Commission on Itinerancy was formed. Its report, published in 1963, outlined a wide-ranging settlement program, key principles of which were adopted as government policy in 1964.

The above outline reveals that anti-Traveller discourse has a longer history at the national level than is generally recognized and that in the war and post-war period most anti-Traveller discourse came from the political right (while the infrequent defences of Travellers, as I discuss below, tended to come from members of the left-wing parties of Labour and later Clann na Poblachta). That anti-Travellerism was motivated by class interests – specifically the interests of the propertied – was, however, obscured by political rhetoric that identified Travellers as a threat to non-class based categories, for example, 'rural' or 'urban' dwellers, or, as we shall see, 'women and children.' They were also identified more broadly as dangerous to the nation's public health, economy, and 'social order.'

The construction of the Travellers as a collective 'danger' to the nation had political uses for the powerful during a period of economic weakness (by post-war European standards), growing class disparities, and considerable political turmoil. A deepening of anti-Traveller sentiment fostered by local and national politicians allowed for a partial deflection of social unrest as Travellers were identified as one of the causes of the failed promises of the post-colonial state. Closer examination of the anti-Traveller discourse of the Dáil debates reveals links between anti-Traveller racism and class-based divisions as well as those of gender and generation.

Constructing Inferiorized Others

Anti-Traveller discourse in the war-time and post-war parliament included implicit references to an ethnicized (although Irish) identity. Sometimes such references took the form of allusions to the alleged origins of the Travellers as a descent-based collectivity. One politician, for example, repeated the claims of some earlier nationalist scholars when he described Travellers as the descendants of high-ranking Irish clans dispossessed by the colonizers during Elizabethan times (Dáil, O'Donnell, 12 April 1945: 2021).

Clearly, however, the claim that the Travellers were descended from high-ranking Irish clans did not save the Travellers from negative constructions. The Clann na Talmhan speaker who provided this account stated, 'They [Travellers] have proud traditions, and I would not like to say anything bitter against them, because they come of a grand old stock,' but he went on to add that country people were suffering from the Traveller's 'depredations' and that the Travellers would become 'a race of degenerates' if they were not settled (Dáil, O'Donnell, 12 April 1945: 2023).

In the post-war period other references acknowledged descent as a source of Traveller identity (Dáil, Collins, 11 July 1956: 723), but the suggestion of a genealogical connection to a high status position in pre-colonial Ireland was challenged. In 1955 a Fianna Fáil member expressed 'amazement' that anyone would claim that the Travellers originated from the 'ancient Irish' or 'native "princes"' (Dáil, Moher, 13 July 1955: 745). By this time constructions of pre-colonial origin were being supplanted by claims that the Travellers had a more recent and more humble ethnogenesis as the descendants of dispossessed peasants and/or drop-outs from settled society.

The occasional identification of Travellers as the descendants of the victims of colonial oppression meant that some parliamentarians felt a need to clarify that their calls for action against the Travellers should not be misunderstood as betraying the promise of the post-colonial state by reproducing the domination experienced by Catholic Irish in earlier decades. Making distinctions between 'tinkers' and 'vagrants' was one way that politicians could attempt to reduce any possibility that their anti-Traveller statements might be construed as inappropriate to a post-colonial political sensibility. Some members of parliament, for example, claimed that while the 'tinkers' were linked through descent to 'ancient families' they had to be distinguished from 'newcomer vagrants' who had joined the road more recently. One deputy claimed that it was only the 'newcomer vagrants' who were problematic and that the greatest 'anti-vagrant' sentiment was, in fact, to be found among the more au-thentic 'tinkers': 'Nobody resents the type of vagrant we are getting on the roads now more than the ancient families of tinkers who are good tinsmiths and tradesmen. I think that they would drop with fright if you suggested that these newcomers were tinkers' (Dáil, Linehan, 18 April 1944: 978). In this passage the 'tinkers' were distinguished on the basis of descent and economic legitimacy (defined in terms of current productive occupations) from the 'vagrants' who were implicitly unproductive and who were described as the targets of the call for control.

Another way in which individual politicians attempted to deflect an-ticipated accusations of discrimination against Travellers was through the suggestion that any proposed restrictions should be imposed, not just on the Travellers, but on any citizens who were mobile. Thus, after listing a variety of alleged 'dangers' posed by the 'tinkers' (including trespass, theft, and the spread of disease) a Clann na Talmhan deputy stated that his proposal of imposed licencing did not 'imply any reflection whatever on this class of people' because they would be applied to 'any citizens of this country who wish to camp out, or have no fixed residence – whether they call themselves tourists or tinkers' (Dáil, Cogan, 4 June 1941: 1435; see also Dáil, Cogan, 12 July 1951: 1497; Dáil, Cogan, 18 July 1951: 1831).

Parliamentarians were keen to deny that they were personally prejudiced against Travellers, and they also downplayed or denied the existence of anti-Traveller discrimination among their non-Traveller constituents and the nation as a whole. Thus, one politician claimed that his own constituents were 'kindly disposed' towards the Travellers, but were, as a result, the targets of their abuse: 'In my immediate area in Tipperary we suffer quite a lot from tinkers. The people there are kindly disposed towards them ... Those people play on the kindly feelings of the natives towards them, and they carry on all sorts of depredations' (Dáil, O'Donnell, 12 April 1945: 2020–1).

The same speaker claimed that, while the 'Irish people' were 'very friendly disposed' to both the Travellers and 'poorer people,' none the less 'these beggars [the Travellers] are a nuisance' (Dáil, O'Donnell, 19 April 1944: 1030–1). In these passages the 'kindly' and 'friendly' disposition of politicians, settled communities, and the Irish nation were portrayed as abused and exploited by the Travellers, who were constructed as perpetrators rather than victims of injustice.

Despite their Irishness, then, the Travellers were clearly inferiorized during this period. During the war years one of the central images of Travellers was that they were criminals who threatened the private property of farmers. It was frequently stated by opposition deputies, for example, that the horses or other livestock of the Travellers trespassed on and damaged farmer's fields, crops, and fences, and that Travellers stole such items as milk, poultry, and clothes from house dwellers (e.g., Dáil, Dillon, 16 March 1939: 2108; Dáil, Cogan, 4 June 1941: 1435; Dáil, Linehan, 18 April 1944: 979; Dáil, O'Donnell, 19 April 1944: 1031). Other forms of attributed criminality included cruelty to animals, non-compliance with the School Attendance Act, the spreading of animal and human disease, and creation of danger for motorists (Dáil, Cogan, 4 June 1941: 1434–5; Dáil, Meaney, 4 June 1941: 1444; Dáil, O'Donnell, 19 April 1944: 1032; Dáil, O'Donnell, 12 April 1945: 2022).

Such allegations were accompanied by claims that the Travellers were responsible for creating 'havoc' (Dáil, Linehan, 18 April 1944: 978), 'scenes' (Dáil, O'Donnell, 19 April 1944: 1032), 'pandemonium' (Dáil, Meighan,

19 April 1944: 1100), and posed a collective 'menace to the social order' (Dáil, O'Neill, 19 September 1944: 1528). Animalistic phraseology which described them as 'infesting' remote areas (Dáil, O'Neill, 19 September 1944: 1528) and breeding 'like rabbits' (Dáil, O'Donnell, 19 April 1944: 1031) added a dehumanizing discourse to such allegations. While Travellers were constructed as Irish, such discourses of inferiorization reflected and reproduced the construction of Travellers as an internal threat to the moral community/nation. Such a naturalized inferiorization in turn supported anti-Traveller action.

Constructing Class

As the above discussion has suggested, anti-Traveller racism was closely linked to the concerns of the propertied and their representatives on the political right. Political discourse also included contradictory constructions of Travellers' class position. Many critics of Travellers, for example, argued that Travellers were better off than many other Irish. One politician contrasted the alleged wealth of Travellers with the war-time scarcities being experienced by the urban population, stating: 'It is amazing to me that while unfortunate people in cities and towns are short of necessaries of life these people are apparently able to carry on. They have money' (Dáil, Linehan, 18 April 1944: 978).

Other anti-Traveller deputies of this period, however, noted that Travellers could also be 'regarded as the poorer section of the community' (Dáil, Cogan, 12 July 1951: 1497). The view that the Travellers were uniquely deprived and disadvantaged in fact led some politicians to carefully clarify that their anti-Traveller statements did not imply a lack of sympathy for the poor in general. Thus Dillon from Fine Gael emphasized that 'Nobody likes to be too offhand with persons who are poor or in difficulties ... [but] these people [Travellers] are responsible for more than one very grave abuse' (Dáil, Dillon, 16 March 1939: 2108).

Some members of the Dáil also argued (in ways that were echoed in the Galway press) that Travellers' newer economic activities represented a degeneration from a putatively more productive past when 'they were quite useful citizens – tinsmiths and metal workers' (Dáil, O'Donnell, 19 April 1944: 1030). The productive craftspeople of the past according to this view had been replaced by parasitical traders and/or beggars. Travellers were no longer 'tinkers,' it was claimed, and therefore were of little economic value (Dáil, Cogan, 12 July 1951: 1496).

By the 1950s, however, the Travellers were also being criticized for their alleged economic success. Thus one politician argued that while the government should be sympathetic to 'beggarmen who travel the roads' such sympathy should not be extended to the 'new class of itinerant growing up now, a gipsy-tinker class, with motor cars and hordes of goats, mules and jennets blocking the road' (Dáil, Giles, 11 July 1956: 684). The reference to newly wealthy Travellers was repeated by another contributor who stated that the Travellers were 'no longer a down and out class,' adding that they had 'motor cars and motor vans ... [and] in many cases they have a number of horses the value of which would exceed the stock on a fair-sized farm' (Dáil, Kennedy, 11 July 1956: 681).

In an illuminating passage, a farmer deputy pointed to the Travellers' allegedly lucrative economic activities, and then went on to construct them as 'useless' because they would not work for him:

> There was a time when these travelling men were supposed to be poor people. I do not think they ever were. But now they are in the horse-meat trade and a whole lot of other trades, and there is hardly one of them who is not able to pull out £500 or £600 in ready money. They are going around in their motor vans and station wagons now ... In a very bad year I had to get in some barley. I employed as many local people as I could get, but in the evening I went to the cross-roads. There I saw seven or eight able-bodied men of the itinerant class. I offered twice the usual amount, a good dinner and a couple of bottles of stout but they were not interested. These people are useless. They are no good to themselves or to anyone else. (Dáil, Lynch, 11 July 1956: 666)

In this speech male Travellers were constructed as 'no good to themselves or anyone else' because their apparent success at dealing allowed them to refuse to work as casual labourers for large farmers. As this passage suggests, recognition of a viable Traveller economy, accompanied by suggestions of illegitimacy, allowed even successful Travellers to be described as a 'drag ... on the community' (Dáil, Kennedy, 11 July 1956: 681–2) or as a 'set of hooligans who will not work' (Dáil, Giles, 9 April 1959: 303).

In these constructions the significance of class divisions among both the non-Traveller and Traveller population were downplayed as Travellers were presented as posing a danger to the general populace. By emphasizing that their concern was the 'protection' of the nation as a whole politicians obscured the links between anti-Traveller racism and the more specific class interests of the propertied.

Masculinized Travellers and Terrorized Women

Feminist work has pointed out how racism articulates not only with class but with gender (e.g., Anthias and Yuval-Davis 1992; Yuval-Davis 1997). Here I draw upon the insights of this literature to explore the deeply gendered character of anti-Traveller racism during the early decades of the new state.

Feminist work in Ireland has pointed out how Irish independence was marked not only by the rise to power of the Catholic propertied classes but also by the marginalization of feminist concerns that were originally part of the anti-colonial movement. In the new state it was women's domestic and mothering roles that were emphasized by the male politicians and the Church. Women were increasingly seen as integrally bound to the private rather than public realm of national life and various state and Church initiatives worked against their employment or political involvement (Smythe 1993).

The role of the state in legitimizing the domestication of women was dramatically evident in the 1937 Constitution, where Article 41.2.1 stated that 'the state recognises that by her life within the home, woman gives the State a support without which the common good cannot be achieved,' and Article 41.2.2 proposed that 'the State shall therefore endeavour to ensure that mothers shall not be obliged by economic necessity to engage in labour to the neglect of their duties in the home.'

State-sanctioned domestication for women was a striking feature of anti-Traveller rhetoric, which constructed a masculinized Traveller population as a specific threat to non-Traveller women in their homes. As early as 1926, for example, a medical doctor was quoted in the Galway regional press as claiming that the very social organization of the Travellers was based upon the goal of 'terrifying women': 'Formerly they lived in individual units, but now they go in bands large enough to terrify any isolated woman in a farmhouse, and I believe this is the real cause of their banding' (*CT*, 18 September 1926: 3).

In the national parliamentary debates of the 1940s and 1950s there were a number of references to the alleged threat posed by a masculinized Traveller population to female homemakers. Thus, for example, Travellers were described as 'big, hulking brutes of men' (Dáil, Linehan, 18 April 1944: 978), and it was claimed that while the men of the farming households were working out in the fields, Travellers would 'go into the farm-houses where the wife, the mother, the sister or the daughter is preparing the midday meal ... [and] terrorise the womenfolk' (Dáil,

O'Donnell, 12 April 1945: 2021–2; see also Dáil, O'Donnell, 19 April 1944: 1031). The argument that housewives were in particular danger from 'hulking young men' was also made in the following passage:

> People living in rural areas, particularly housewives who are left in charge of the house while their husbands are out working, find the tinkers a menace. It is not a very pleasant experience for a housewife living in a remote district, perhaps a mile from her nearest neighbour, to see two or three hulking young men appearing at the door or arriving in the middle of the floor, if the door happens to be open. I know that they only ask for alms, but their very appearance is frightening, and it would be a very brave woman who would refuse to help them. (Dáil, Cogan, 12 July 1951: 1496)

The suggestion of more actively threatening Travellers was repeated in 1956: 'In outlying districts they [tinkers] go in and threaten the farmer's wife and daughter, if they happen to be alone when the men are working in the fields' (Dáil, Lynch, 11 July 1956: 665; see also Dáil, Dillon, 9 April 1959: 308–9).

The links between the ideology of female domesticity and anti-Traveller racism are striking. The particular focus upon the need to protect the women of 'remote' 'outlying' rural districts also echoed early twentieth-century discourses of gender and space that identified the 'women of the west' as the symbolic core of the nation (Nash 1993: 44–9). In the 1940s and 1950s women in remote areas were still being used by national politicians as potent symbols of a nation portrayed as vulnerable to assault by a masculinized Traveller population. The gendered anti-Traveller racism drew upon and reinforced a dominant ideology and practice of female domesticity in post-independence Ireland. It also obscured the realities of Traveller women, whose lives were much less domesticated than those of their settled counterparts.

'Saving' Children

Even more striking than the gendered imagery of anti-Traveller discourse was the way in which anti-Traveller discourse was linked in these debates to invocations of children and childhood. One of the recurring themes in the calls for control over the activities of the Travellers, for example, was the claim that intervention was required 'for the protection of the [Traveller and non-Traveller] children.' The parliamentary debates from the 1940s and 1950s reveal that the discourses of 'child-saving' that permeate contemporary discussion of Travellers have a longer history.

In the 1940s critics of the Traveller way of life made links between Traveller children's non-attendance at school and Travellers' alleged criminality. That Travellers were ostensibly ignoring the School Attendance Acts and not being 'brought to justice' was, for example, offered as evidence of a wider Traveller evasion of judicial control (Dáil, Cogan, 4 June 1941: 1435). Traveller children's lack of schooling was also taken as evidence of Traveller deviancy by one deputy who stated: 'these young [Traveller] boys and girls do not go to school and there is no earthly chance of doing anything with them' (Dáil, O'Donnell, 19 April 1944: 1032). Another deputy claimed that 'the children of these people [Travellers] do not attend school and grow up illiterate, learning nothing but the elements of crime to which their conditions make them easy addicts' (Dáil, O' Neill, 19 September 1944: 1528). Descriptions of Traveller children as likely to 'throw stones at the people passing by' (Dáil, Giles, 11 July 1956: 685) and to intimidate house-dwellers into giving them food (Dáil, Kennedy, 11 July 1956: 681) suggested that not only were Traveller children adult criminals-in-the-making, but that some already displayed an 'unchildlike' aggressiveness that threatened settled society.

While Traveller children were constructed as dangerous to the wider community, they were also described more sympathetically as the endangered 'victims' of an adult Traveller lifestyle of mobility and camping. In 1945, for example, government action against camping Travellers was described as necessary for the physical protection of Traveller children who were camping beside major roads. Dillon suggested that his repeated call for government action against camping Travellers was motivated by a concern for their children: 'The poor itinerants have to live like the rest of us but the dangers attendant on their camping beside a road, involving danger to their children who run about the encampment ... are far greater on the trunk road than on the by-road' (Dáil, Dillon, 29 May 1945: 1035).

A few years later he repeated his claim that the prohibition of Traveller camps was necessary and asked the Minister to 'remind the Guards to insist that they [Travellers] should not make encampments on main roads for the protection of their own children' (Dáil, Dillon, 18 July 1951: 1831). The image of parental neglect and resulting vulnerability of (especially younger) children was reiterated once again in 1957: 'My apprehension is that, if tinkers habitually camp on the side of the trunk roads where fast traffic normally passes, the danger to their children is appalling. You have a camp fire set and three or four toddlers rambling around it. Motor cars are passing at high speed. At any moment these babies may toddle out on to the road and be killed' (Dáil, Dillon, 25 April 1957: 419).

In these passages state intervention to evict Travellers from roadside camps was portrayed as appropriate action for a government concerned with the physical well-being of Traveller children. The argument was adopted by the Minister for Justice in 1951 when he stated that he would have the matter of Travellers camping on major roads 'brought to the Guards' [police] attention' because 'the protection of the [Traveller] children is necessary' (Dáil, Boland, 18 July 1951: 1831).

Combined with the suggestion that greater control over Traveller camps was essential to the protection of Traveller children were claims that such action would also protect (with the non-Traveller women previously discussed) non-Traveller children. The suggestion that non-Traveller children were particularly vulnerable to Traveller 'depredations' had a long history in the regional press, where Travellers were blamed for the spread of diseases to non-Traveller children as early as 1923 (CT, 31 March 1923: 2). Likewise, in the parliamentary debates of the 1950s it was stated that non-Traveller children were being frightened (Dáil, Russell, 15 April 1958: 163) and were 'in danger of being trampled under foot' by Traveller horses (Dáil, Larkin, 25 April 1957: 405).

The linking of anti-Traveller discourse to a discourse of child protection was rhetorically effective. The effectiveness was derived from the widespread acceptance that a 'protected' childhood (characterized by, among other things, sedentary residence and full-time schooling) was a necessary foundation for adult Irish citizenship. Childhoods that deviated from this model, including Traveller childhoods, were easily portrayed as both endangered and dangerous. Translating the rhetoric of child protection into policy and practice, however, was limited by a minimalist state and the 1937 Irish Constitution, which emphasized parental rights (Ferguson and Kenny 1995: 20–1).

Although compulsory education for Gypsy/Traveller children took on legislative force with the 1908 Children's Act (which included a section that imposed 'penalties on persons who habitually wander from place to place and thereby prevent children from receiving education') (Commission on Itinerancy 1963: 66) Traveller children do not appear to have experienced any systematic pressure or opportunity to attend school in the Irish Free State.[9]

In 1942 a proposed School Attendance Act included a provision that would have required 'vagrants to register particulars of their families and of the education received by their children' at Local Garda [police] stations' (Commission on Itinerancy 1963: 112), but the act was struck down as unconstitutional on the grounds that it represented state intervention in the constitutionally protected area of parents' rights. In the case of the Travellers, as one deputy remarked, this resulted in the loss of an 'opportunity of dealing with ... the question of vagrancy' (Dáil, Linehan, 18 April 1944: 977).

In addition to the Constitutional obstacles, the political value placed on family life also worked against any plan for Traveller children's schooling that involved separating Traveller children from their parents. In 1959 the Minister for Justice asked rhetorically: 'how can we enforce the School Attendance Acts if we do not actually take the [Traveller] children away from the parents altogether? Will any Deputy advocate that we do that, even if the Constitution would permit it?' (Dáil, Traynor, 21 April 1959: 784).

Such hesitation was paralleled in the courts, where (according to the later Report of the Commission on Itinerancy) many judges were 'reluctant to commit [Traveller] children to industrial schools solely on the grounds that the parents [did] not exercise proper guardianship by reason of failing to send their children to school' (Commission on Itinerancy, 1963: 66). At the same time, local authorities who were lobbying the central government for more powers to deal with the Traveller problem were 'stoutly opposed' to the committal of Traveller children to industrial schools because this would serve to relieve parents of their responsibilities and allow 'the maintenance of children to become a burden on the ratepayers' (ibid.).

As this suggests, anti-Traveller racism and economic concerns were probably more salient than any concern for the parental rights of Travellers. Traveller parents were in fact described as 'no credit to the nation' because 'They [were] rearing illiterate families' (Dáil, Burke, 13 July 1955: 738; see also Dáil, Maguire, 9 June, 1949: 438), and it was suggested that the state might overrule Traveller parents to impose settlement 'for the sake of the children.' As one deputy put it: 'If you cannot make citizens of [the Travellers], put them into homes. It would be better than [having] them going around rearing their children without education and giving them no chances. You may not succeed in one generation but you might succeed with the second generation' (Dáil, Burke, 16 April 1958: 190).

Despite the rhetoric of 'child saving' that permeated anti-Traveller discourse, however, there were no concrete efforts at intervention. The lived experience of Traveller children was instead one of harassment and 'official neglect.' Political rhetoric framed in terms of the needs and interests of Traveller and non-Traveller 'children,' then, only served to reinscribe anti-Traveller racism while simultaneously legitimizing hegemonic constructions of proper childhood and parent–child relations.

Defending Travellers

The rare challenges to the overwhelmingly negative construction of Travellers in the parliamentary debates came from the leftist parties of Labour and Clann na Poblachta and took the form of emphasizing Travellers' putative links to a nationalist history and their economic utility. One deputy, for example, identified the Travellers as victims of the former colonial authorities and their agents ('the crown,' 'the Black and Tans,' and the 'Royal Irish Constabulary'), and established their credentials as active participants in the struggle for independence through their protection of the nationalist rebels of the 'flying columns:'

> Somebody mentioned tinkers and said that they should have no part in Irish life, that they should be ostracised and that regulations should be made to confine camping to certain limits. I believe they are God's own people. During the Black and Tan days, when we were on the flying columns, the second best friends we had, next to those who gave us homes and shelter, were the people of the road. From the time of the old RIC, [Royal Irish Constabulary] these people were bludgeoned with the wrath of the Crown and of the RIC itself. I think they are part of our history and that we need not be ashamed of them. (Dáil, Collins, 11 July 1956: 723)

Others, such as a Labour deputy from Wexford, countered the dominant discourse of economic illegitimacy by insisting that Travellers were in fact economically 'useful' to 'small farmers':

> Those travelling people buy donkeys from small farmers in the district, and in the course of their journeys at the present time they do very useful work making galvanized buckets, when buckets are not to be had in the hardware shops. They are not as dangerous as certain speakers made them out to be. They are human beings and they have to live. (Dáil, O'Leary, 19 April 1944: 1104)

Repeating his argument some years later, the same deputy stated: 'I do not think that the tinkers are a great menace at all. I see them in my own town on a fair day, spending money, buying horses from small farmers and selling other ones. They have their own way of living' (Dáil, O'Leary, 9 June 1949: 458).

In the late 1950s, in the context of intensifying calls for action against Travellers, another member distanced himself from the anti-Traveller comments of other politicians, noting that 'the class of people described as itinerants ... have been condemned without qualification, and I do not think it is really fair' (Dáil, Corish, 15 April 1958: 165). He went on to argue that international tourists 'almost break their necks looking out the windows of cars or trains to see what they describe as attractive no-mads.' The removal of these 'colourful people' from the roads, he argued, would represent a loss to the nation: 'It would be a sad day for this country if what are often called "the real Irish" were banned from the roads of Ireland' (Dáil, Corish, 15 April 1958: 165-6).

This unusually sympathetic portrayal of the Travellers was dismissed by a Dublin deputy who referred to such views as 'sentimental' and restated the dominant position that the Travellers were threatening urban property and needed to be controlled: 'We have sentimental people who will say that these itinerants are the knights of the road. I do not mind if they are the knights of all the roads in Ireland, they have no right to allow horses to roam into a garden and destroy it' (Dáil, Burke, 16 April 1958: 189).

Anti-Traveller Action

Local and national politicians, with the limited exceptions described above, were active in the elaboration and dissemination of anti-Traveller discourse. They were also involved in explicitly condoning extra-legal or illegal actions against Travellers by other citizens. Patrolling of the roads at night by groups of farmers was, for example, described by one deputy as necessary for the defence of property against trespass by Travellers (Dáil, Cogan, 12 July 1951: 1497), while vigilante attacks on Traveller camps by farmers were publicly defended by another (Dáil, Moher, 13 July 1955: 746).

Along with offering support for anti-Traveller actions by others, local and national politicians initiated police harassment of Travellers themselves (Dáil, Burke, 13 July 1955: 738; Dáil, Moher, 13 July 1955: 745; Dáil, Everett, 7 November 1956: 633; Dáil, Dillon, 9 April 1959: 308; Dáil,

Burke, 16 April 1958: 189). In 1940, for example, the Minister for Justice noted that the police 'have [political] instructions already to pay particular attention to people who camp on the roads' (Dáil, Boland, 2 October 1940: 40), and another deputy described how he became involved in directing anti-Traveller action by the police at the local level: 'Time and again people have come to my office and asked me could I get in touch with the local superintendent and get him to authorise the local sergeant to send out four or five guards to shift them [Travellers] out of a particular place' (Dáil, Linehan, 18 April 1944: 978–9).

Politicians' own accounts of their involvement in such actions contradict repeated claims in these same speeches that Travellers were 'immune from the law' (Dáil, Cogan, 3 April 1946: 1200) and enjoyed 'immense privileges over people who live in a fixed place, as they cannot be amenable to prosecution if they break the law' (Dáil, Cogan, 18 July 1951: 1830–1; see also Dáil, Cogan, 4 June 1941: 1436; Dáil, Meaney, 4 June 1941: 1444; Dáil, Linehan, 18 April 1944: 978). On the contrary, it is clear that Travellers were the targets not only of anti-Traveller discourse but of active surveillance, control, and harassment that was supported by politicians during this period.[10]

Local and national sources for the 1922–59 period reveal that Travellers were constructed in élite discourses as inferiorized Others and that this construction was linked to a number of exclusionary actions, including prohibition of camping, the denial of housing, and support for unofficial and official harassment. These findings contest claims that the Traveller 'problem' is a recent phenomenon. Anti-Traveller racism, already evident at the turn of the century, was very much part of the ethos and practice of the post-colonial state.

Chapter 3

The Politics and Practice of Traveller Settlement Policy

Existing accounts of Traveller history often begin with a discussion of origins and then move rapidly to a consideration of the introduction of a national settlement policy in the 1960s.[1] The fundamental significance of the settlement program for subsequent Traveller experience makes this an understandable starting point for contemporary discussion, but as the previous chapters have shown the lack of attention to the decades that preceded the 1960s has obscured a longer history of anti-Traveller racism at both local and national levels. While the formation of the Commisson on Itinerancy in 1960 was clearly responding to increased pressure from local authorities, especially in urban areas, we have seen that tensions between Travellers and non-Travellers were not a 'new' phenomenon.

George Gmelch has argued that the increased official concern with the Traveller 'problem' in the mid to late 1950s, and subsequent formulation of a settlement policy in the 1960s, can be traced to a shifting Irish economy, notably post-war changes in Irish agriculture (e.g., mechanization) that eroded the basis of the Traveller economy, leading to a process of Traveller urbanization. This urbanization, he goes on to suggest, resulted in growing conflict between Travellers and other urban Irish, and these tensions prompted state intervention (G. Gmelch 1977: 41–51).

While I do not disagree with this account, I suggest that these changes need to be located within much broader national and global processes that include Ireland's abandonment of a short-lived policy of economic nationalism in favour of global (especially American) capital on the one hand, and the local politics of class on the other. In this chapter I place the introduction of a comprehensive national Traveller settlement policy in the 1960s within the context of the opening up of the Irish economy to global capitalism and a political project of economic and social 'modernization' associated with the First Program for Economic Expansion. I then examine the implementation of Traveller settlement policy in Galway City, emphasizing the ways in which a localized anti-Traveller racism articulated with a shifting urban geography of class.

The First Program for Economic Expansion and the Commission on Itinerancy

O'Hearn has pointed out how international developments – notably American pressure on Europe to open its economies to foreign investment – resulted in Ireland, in concert with the Organization for European Economic Co-operation, beginning to abandon its policy of protectionism in the post-war period. It was not until the late 1950s, however, that a new strategy of foreign-led industrialization became official policy (facilitated by Ireland joining the IMF and World Bank in 1957) (O'Hearn 1998: 39).

The adoption of an economic policy based on foreign investment and increasing export production was dramatic, occurring as it did under the aegis of a Fianna Fáil government that had earlier advocated protectionist policies. Bew and Patterson (1982) emphasize how the government garnered support for the new policies from the domestic bourgeoisie as well as trade union leaders by emphasizing the need for apolitical and corporatist economic and social planning that would facilitate modernization. A major shift in social policy, from an anti-interventionist position supported by the Church toward increased state involvement in the provision of social welfare, was, they suggest, one of the ways in which the compliance and political support of the working class and trade unions in particular was ensured (Bew and Patterson 1982).

It is within this context that we can place the formation of the Commission on Itinerancy, the content of its 1963 Report, and the subsequent acceptance of its proposed settlement program as government policy in 1964. The 1963 Report of the Commission on Itinerancy, I suggest, can be read as an example of 'official discourse' (Burton and Carlen 1979: 13–14), which served to redefine the 'itinerant problem' in such a way that a new policy of settlement and absorption of Travellers became part of the platform of the government goals of economic and social 'modernization.'

One of the effects of the formation of the Commission on Itinerancy was the categorizing under one term of those that had been referred to by a myriad of labels during the previous decades. The Report of the Commission on Itinerancy was extremely influential in codifying the term 'itinerant' to refer to 'a person who had no fixed place of abode and habitually wandered from place to place,' with 'travelling show-people and travelling entertainers' explicitly excluded from the definition (Commission on Itinerancy [henceforth CI] 1963: 13). In this formulation itinerants were defined as a category of individuals united only by the common characteristics of 'no fixed abode' and mobility, and the suggestion of a Traveller 'community' or 'ethnic' identity was explicitly denied:

> Itinerants (or travellers as they prefer themselves to be called) do not constitute a single homogeneous group, tribe or community within the nation, although the settled population are inclined to regard them as such. Neither do they constitute a separate ethnic group (CI 1963: 37).

The denial of Traveller 'community' and ethnicity was strengthened by the location of Traveller origins within the colonial period (i.e., somewhere between a 'few centuries' and the 'last century') and an emphasis on a forced 'economic' nomadism (CI 1963: 34). The suggestion that the 'itinerants' had become mobile as a result of colonial oppression allowed settlement to be portrayed as part of a national project to '*re*-settle' Irish victims of British domination. Indeed, much of the rhetorical power of the Report came from its successful pairing of post-colonial nationalist discourse with the new modernization project. Traveller settlement, the Commissioners proposed, was crucial to the economic, social, and moral development of the nation.

While the central government had long viewed the itinerants as a problem it had also recognized that the anti-Traveller measures demanded by the propertied classes and right-wing politicians could not be implemented without catching other more privileged and valued nomads, especially tourists, in the same net. This problem had been identified by earlier legislators and was clearly articulated by Charles Haughey, then parliamentary secretary to the Minister for Justice (and later Irish Prime Minister), at the inaugural meeting of the Commission on Itinerancy in 1960:

> The Department of Local Government have had under consideration for several years the question of promoting further legislation regarding temporary dwellings. *As a general principle, of course, our legislation could not*

distinguish itinerants from other users of temporary dwellings so that any type
of compulsory action under the sanitary services law would affect tourists
using trailer caravans, seaside huts and so on. (CI 1963: 113) [my emphasis]

Of course, in practice itinerants were regularly 'moved on' by the
police while tourists were not, but it was recognized that such discriminatory practices could not be supported if challenged in court. The
dilemma facing lawmakers was how to create laws that could be specifically aimed at 'itinerants' without being seen to discriminate against
fellow Irish citizens.

The formation of the Commission on Itinerancy provided an opportunity to construct an elaborated justification of a new settlement policy
aimed at increasing control over the Travellers while maintaining and re-
asserting the government's claim to be a fair and progressive protector of
all its citizens. Charles Haughey at the inaugural meeting of the Commission stated: 'Of paramount importance ... is the simple fact that the
humblest itinerant is entitled to a place in the sun and to a share in the
benefits of our society' (CI 1963: 114).

As part of its work the Commission on Itinerancy conducted two
censuses of Travellers in 1960 and 1961. The results provided an unprecedented amount of data regarding the living conditions of Travellers
during this period, and many of these results are presented in the Report.
What is important to note here, however, is that the policy of settlement
and 'absorption' recommended by the Commission did not arise out of a
careful consideration of the data which it collected, but rather was pre-
determined by the Commission's own terms of reference.

At their first meeting, for example, the Commission members were
told by Haughey that 'there can be no final solution of the problem
created by itinerants until they are absorbed into the general community'
(CI 1963: 111). It was the role of the Commission to elaborate upon this
premise, to specify the precise steps required to accomplish the goal of
'absorption' through settlement, and, importantly, to legitimize the new
'solution' to the itinerant 'problem.'

Significantly, apart from the administration of the census question-
naires, there was little direct consultation with Travellers. On the occasions when Commissioners did make visits to camps their ability to
'consult' in a meaningful way was compromised by the fact that their
visits were often unannounced and made in the company of city officials
and/or police involved in the eviction of Travellers. The Commissioners
did hear from one organized deputation – a group of Dublin Travellers

who protested against state harassment and evictions – but the Report stated that 'the formality of the occasion' worked against the gathering of Travellers' views (CI 1963: 30).

The legitimacy of the Commission, then, rested not on Traveller participation, but on the reputation of the non-Traveller Commissioners who had been selected 'with great care' by the state on the basis of their 'expertise' on the itinerant issue (CI 1963: 30). Within the text itself the findings and recommendations were presented as the result of close examination of the census data and a strong sense of national and Christian duty. Recommendations were authoritatively presented in a single voice (in contrast with the individual and joint 'reservations' that were appended to its successors, the 1983 Report of the Travelling People Review Body and the 1995 Task Force on the Travelling Community).

The intended 'readers' of the 1963 Commission's Report were non-Traveller politicians, government officials, the clergy, and those involved in voluntary organizations. These readers were urged to act as both implementors of the Report's recommendations and educators of the wider non-Traveller public. Clergy and religious, charitable, and welfare organizations, for instance, were asked to assist in Traveller settlement and to 'condition the [settled community's] feelings towards the newcomers' (CI 1963: 105). The 'settled community,' it was hoped, could be persuaded to give up their 'attitude of hostility' and adopt one of 'Christian charity and brotherly love' towards the itinerants in the interests of successful absorption (CI 1963: 105). Community leaders were urged to 'educate [the settled population] to the fact that not only do the dictates of charity and common humanity require that steps should be taken to rescue the itinerant population from its present plight but that the material and social interests of the settled population itself will be advanced by a just solution of the itinerant problem' (CI 1963: 104).

Traveller settlement, then, was identified as part of a larger national project of social and economic modernization that would be threatened by the development of a 'closed and separate' Traveller community (CI 1963: 104). Settlement was presented as good for the nation as a whole, as well as being in the best interests of, and indeed desired by, the 'itinerants' themselves.

Implementation in Galway City

By 1964, the program of Traveller settlement outlined in the Report of the Commission on Itinerancy had been adopted as central government policy. Its implementation, however, was delegated to local authorities, i.e., city and county councils. At the local level the contradiction inherent in placing responsibility for the settlement of a mobile population in the hands of territorially-defined local authorities with a long history of anti-Traveller action was immediately apparent. Local authorities, claiming that an extensive provision would result in an 'influx' of more Travellers into their respective jurisdictions, moved slowly and unevenly in the provision of accommodation and other services to Travelling People.

In Galway City there was from the beginning complaint about the lack of western representation on the Commission on Itinerancy (CT, 25 June 1960: 9), but an early Connacht Tribune editorial applauded the formation of the Commission and adopted the new discourse of social welfarism:

'[The Commission's] main purpose is based upon the Christian virtue of charity. The aim is to help and not to curb. Its terms of reference recognize the dignity of the itinerants as human beings, and the economic, educational, health and social handicaps imposed on them by their way of life.' (CT, 6 August 1960: 6)

The view that some provision would have to be made for the Travellers if greater control was to be achieved had been gaining adherents such as the Galway City Chamber of Commerce, which suggested in 1960 that Travellers' vehicles should be registered and that 'areas in the country with water and sanitation and perhaps schools should be allotted for the use of itinerants' (GBC, 24 March 1960: 474) [my emphasis]. There was no suggestion, however, that such provision might be made by the city itself. Indeed, two years later Galway Corporation supported a resolution from Bray Urban District Council stating 'that camping by Itinerants on Public Roadways in Urban districts be prohibited' (GBC, 19 September 1962: 78).

The formation of the national Commission on Itinerancy in 1960 was in fact accompanied by increased evictions of Traveller camps from Galway city (perhaps in anticipation of the Commission-sponsored censuses) and in the years that followed Travellers continued to be prosecuted for camping as well as for a variety of other activities, such as, begging and keeping 'wandering' horses. City politicians also engaged in advocating more everyday forms of exclusion, for example, by exhorting Galway City publicans to refuse to serve Travellers (CT, 11 March 1961: 9; CT, 6 August 1966: 1). More dramatically, Travellers were victims of vigilante attacks on their camps, which included the shooting of dogs and horses, and the burning of caravans (*CT*, 2 January 1960: 7; *CT*, 20 February 1960: 9; *CT*, 4 November 1961: 4).

As mentioned in chapter 2, by the early 1960s there were concentrations of Traveller families in particular areas of council housing – concentrations which the city implicitly recognized by continuing to house the few Travellers that it appointed as tenants in the same areas (GBC, 19 November 1962: 102). For the most part, however, a negative housing policy continued to be followed (GBC, 20 September 1961: 145; GBC, 19 November 1962: 102), despite efforts by some officials, such as the following, to promote Traveller applications:

> From a public health point of view [the individual's] claim for rehousing is one of the most urgent, but then [the individual] is an itinerant, and their [the itinerants'] record with Corporation houses is not good. But that was the fault of the parents and is in the past ... perhaps for the children's sake the Corporation would review their decision on the application? (Housing files, 1961)

The failure of such arguments was apparent in the backlog of requests for housing from Travellers. By November of 1967, for example, there were thirty-one outstanding applications for houses from 'persons living in tents and caravans' (GBC, 13 November 1967: 1032).

The applications for housing by some Travellers may have reflected the increased harassment of camping Travellers at this time. City officials and the courts, sometimes in collaboration with residents, were forcing camping Travellers outside the city boundaries (*CT*, 23 May 1964: 9; *CT*, 13 June 1964: 12). For camping Travellers, however, there was little relief to be found in the countryside. By 1964 the County Council had also adopted by-laws that allowed for the prosecution of camping Travellers (*CT*, 17 October 1964: 5), and Galway City kept pressure on the county to evict camping Travellers near its boundaries (GBC, 28 June 1965: 572).

There is no doubt that the position of Travellers during this period was worse than it had been previously. The Secretary of the Trades Council expressed the view that the new county council by-laws had effectively 'denied the tinkers the right to park any place' (*CT*, 24 October 1964: 9), and even the city solicitor involved in prosecuting five Traveller families for camping acknowledged that 'the [Travelling] people seemed to be suffering from a social injustice, but the law was the law. People in the locality had to be protected' (*CT*, 16 February 1963: 6).

After the publication of the Commission Report in 1963 Galway Corporation, in response to a suggestion from the local Trades Council, had submitted a motion to the Association for Municipal Authorities of Ireland calling upon the Government 'to give urgent consideration to the report of the Commission on the itinerant problem ' (GBC, 17 June 1964: 380), but when a Galway county-wide committee on itinerancy began a search for possible locations for such serviced camping sites (GBC, 16 December 1964: 455; GBC, 22 September 1965: 616) it did not take long before it was claimed that 'no suitable' sites were to be found in or near the city (CT, 2 October 1965: 1). It was only direct pressure from the Minister for Local Government that led to city politicians agreeing to 'accelerate the provision of a camping site for itinerants' (GBC, 3 October 1966: 826).[2]

The impetus for movement on the Traveller settlement in Galway City can be linked to changes in the local political economy during the late 1960s. The national Programme for Economic Expansion had targeted Galway City as a regional growth centre, and in 1966 the city's first industrial estate was constructed. The new investment had the effect of generating more industrial jobs, as well as growth in the service sector (Ó Cearbhaill and Cawley 1984: 259–60). The economic buoyancy of the urban area relative to the poverty of the surrounding rural region led to a dramatic increase in the urban population and a spatial expansion of the city. One result was a displacement of pre-existing Traveller camps by new industrial and housing estates. At the same time, the remaining camps were considered detrimental for a city intent on attracting and keeping international and especially American investment.

These developments were accompanied by new currents of social welfarism that were also part of the Programme for Economic Expansion and given additional impetus by the reforms of the Second Vatican Council (1962–5). In 1966, for example, the city granted the Legion of Mary permission to set up a temporary school for Travellers, and in 1967 a branch of the voluntary national Itinerant Settlement Council was formed in Galway City as part of a national network of such committees (see Gmelch and Gmelch 1974).

The Galway Itinerant Settlement Council (later Committee) was a voluntary group initially composed of several influential and relatively well-off citizens of Galway. Some of the members of the council were motivated by a concern for the economic development of the city and region, while others were inspired to social activism by Vatican II, and later by the civil rights movement of the North (which led to parallels being drawn between the plight of the Catholic minority in Ulster and

Travellers in the Republic). All shared the view that the project of Traveller settlement represented a necessary, and long overdue, national duty consistent with the goals of a modernizing Catholic city and country. They also assumed that, given sufficient political will, this project could be accomplished in a relatively short time.

The Settlement Council embarked upon a campaign of public education in order to build support for Traveller settlement. This involved a series of newspaper articles outlining the plight of Travellers and the organizing of an Itinerant Settlement Week. In their public statements members of the council promoted settlement through the invocation of religious and nationalist references. For example, the Travellers were compared to the 'holy itinerant family' who had found 'no room at the inn' (CT, 12 May 1967: 3). Detractors were also reminded that the Travellers 'may have been descendants of our own kith and kin who were evicted during the Famine' (CT, 12 January 1968: 10).

That such arguments were becoming part of dominant discourse was apparent in a 1967 *Connacht Tribune* editorial marking Itinerant Settlement Week in Galway City. The editorial echoed the language of the Report of the Commission on Itinerancy and the Galway Itinerant Settlement Council when it called for greater public sympathy and charity towards Travellers, and urged support for the settlement efforts to facilitate the 'ultimate aim of integrating the itinerants into full community life' (CT, 29 September 1967: 10). Within this context of a plea for sympathy, however, the editorial also included a characterization of Traveller life and behaviour in terms that echoed decades of anti-Traveller discourse:

> they are an annoyance in the towns as beggars, and farmers will say they are a greater nuisance in the country because of deliberate trespass in fields and gardens and damage to crops and because of a feeling of unease that household clothes put out to dry on a line may disappear when they are about. It is probable that the sweeping generalizations are true in a great many instances – undoubtedly many roadside camps are sickeningly filthy and undoubtedly the begging habit is widespread and annoying. Understandably people do not want to see them about. (CT, 29 September 1967: 10)

The editorial then went on to argue, however, that sympathy for Travellers would be forthcoming once people realized that 'the itinerants are not people who rejected the normal pattern of community life' but rather 'were born and reared to the wretched life they lead ... they never had a chance to sample the normal pattern of living and to develop to human dignity' (*CT*, 29 September 1967: 10).

In characterizing Travellers as having failed to develop 'human dignity' the editorial provided ideological support for assimilation through settlement, but also provided ample justification for the continuation of discrimination and violence against Travellers. Indeed, the progress of Traveller settlement in the city was marked by ongoing conflict which fed on such racist characterizations of Travellers.

As part of their publicity campaign the voluntary Itinerant Settlement Council criticized the role of the city and county councils' by-laws in perpetuating mobility and poverty among the Travellers. They also acted more directly to increase pressure on politicians to provide an official camping spot for Travellers within the city. This involved hiring legal defence to test the validity of the cases taken against camping Travellers and advancing loans to those Travellers who were being fined (Itinerant Settlement Council, 2 June 1967). As the committee took on a more activist role those who remained involved became the targets of threats and harassment in an increasingly conflicted and politicized arena.

While initially in favour of direct housing the Galway Settlement Council had decided (following its Dublin counterpart) to lobby for the provision of a camping site in the city as a temporary step toward settlement. After fruitless searching for land both the committee and the city returned to a proposed program of direct housing – allocating two out of every ten local authority houses to Travellers. The second allocation under this policy, however, prompted protests from non-Traveller tenants, and nervous politicians returned to the camping site plan, purchasing a two-acre site for that purpose (GBC, 27 November 1967).

As the new plan became known local landowners and private residents in the area of the proposed camping site objected and politicians, concerned by the opposition and by new vigilante attacks on Traveller camps in the region, halted construction. The reversal of the plan to provide the first official camping site in the city attracted national attention to the city's lack of progress on the settlement issue.[3]

Under pressure to implement the settlement policy, politicians returned once again to the housing option, but galvanized by the success of private land owners and residents in reversing the planned camping site, working-class tenants of housing estates in the city organized protests against new allocations to Travellers. In one publicized case there were demonstrations against housing an 'itinerant' who had in fact not been on the city's special 'itinerant housing list' but rather on the general list for many years because she was living in a condemned building in the city (CT, 25 October 1968: 1). Under pressure from the tenants, the allocation was withdrawn.

The national coverage given these events was extensive, and the Mayor of Galway felt compelled to state defensively that 'there is no community in Ireland which feels the responsibility regarding the settlement of itinerants as strongly as do the people of Galway' (CT, 8 November 1968: 11). After some delay the city indicated that it would construct several smaller camping sites – a proposal that again ran into opposition from residents. Two months after the announcement there was a violent attack on several Traveller families camping in the area of one of the proposed sites.

The August 1969 attack in the area of Rahoon once again put the city in the national spotlight and resulted in the direct intervention of the Minister of Local Government and prominent members of the National Council for Itinerant Settlement. After this events moved quickly. Less than a week after the attack, the city council voted unanimously to implement a plan in which a limited number of local 'city-attached' families (selected by the local settlement council) would be moved to temporary serviced sites to be 'dispersed equitably around the city.' Those politicians who were reluctant to go along with the plan were assured that, once such sites had been set up, the city would use the by-laws against all other Travellers (GBC, 29 August 1969: 1344).

Serviced Sites

The establishment of four official sites within the city was accompanied by a public embrace of the cause of itinerant settlement by several city organizations concerned to repair the alleged damage done to Galway's image and its related capacity to attract and retain foreign investment by media coverage of earlier conflicts. The President of the Chamber of Commerce and Industry, for example, complained that the media's use of the term 'Rahoonery' (from the area of Rahoon, the scene of the August 1969 attack) to describe attacks on Travellers elsewhere in Ireland was unjust now that Galway had provided sites (CT, 13 February 1970: 1).

The mood of self-congratulation did not last long. For many city politicians and officials an important motive for establishing sites was to provide for a limited number of Travellers while at the same time preventing others from camping in the city. Additional Travellers continued to camp, however, often just outside the official sites, and these the city continued to prosecute for unauthorized camping. The Itinerant Settlement Committee (previously the Itinerant Settlement Council) had promoted the idea of providing for a limited number of 'Galway City' Travellers, but felt that the city had not yet created adequate spaces for these families. As a result the Committee decided to sue the city in court, and the case (Galway Corporation versus John Warde) remained in the courts for many years, effectively halting further prosecutions.

While the Settlement Committee was acting against the city in court, it co-operated with the city in many other ways, most notably by undertaking the 'rehabilitation' of itinerants. As part of their work members of the Committee also visited the official city sites to ensure their 'cleanliness.' After several months, however, these visitors noted that the sites were showing signs of 'deterioration' and that some Travellers were planning to move out for the summer (ISC, 6 April 1970). In one site which was situated near a private residential area on donated land the landowner complained that, due to inadequate supervision, 'few of the children were going to school and other itinerants were squatting on the roadside leading to the site, and horses were wandering all over the place' (CT, 16 October 1970: 16).[4]

As external criticism of the sites grew, and some Travellers expressed their own dissatisfaction, the Itinerant Settlement Committee reminded the public that the sites were 'only the first step and by no means the most ideal first step [toward settlement]' and that they would 'soon need to be replaced by more permanent accommodation' (ISC, 16 June 1970). Complaints, however, continued to mount as both the city and the Settlement Committee were accused of not maintaining sufficient 'control' over Travellers. Members of the Chamber of Commerce and Industry complained about the begging of itinerants which, they alleged, was 'increasingly annoying, especially to tourists' (CT, 7 May 1971: 18), and accused the Settlement Committee of 'inviting' itinerants to the city through their lobbying work. Politicians were told that while

> those people ... who live in the encampments, have the sympathy of all because of those conditions ... sympathy does not necessarily mean that the public will tolerate the filth of the encampments until such a time as the itinerants are taken from the roadside. In looking after the interests of the itinerants the Borough Council should not be unmindful of the interest of the citizens who want Galway to be preserved as Tidy Town. (CT, 30 April 1971: 6)

As the number of camping families within the city increased, city politicians asked the Minister for Justice for greater police co-operation in keeping additional Travellers out of areas where authorized camps had been provided (GBC, 14 June 1971). The Minister responded, however, that the police could not 'treat itinerants any differently to other citizens and that if itinerants were not breaking the law the gardai [police] would be unable to interfere with them just for the sake of getting them moved on' (ibid.). Prosecutions were impossible while the court case supported by the Settlement Committee remained unresolved, and there was continuing pressure from the national government to proceed with settlement. The city responded by revising the provision of housing to Travellers.

Housing

The renewed push for housing steered those involved with Traveller settlement back onto a collision course with the tenants of local authority housing estates. This became apparent in 1970, when another dwelling was allocated to the 'itinerant' woman who had earlier had her housing allocation withdrawn as a result of protests. This second allocation, like the first, was greeted by protests from existing residents, who stated that this woman should be accommodated elsewhere, either in a caravan or else a newly constructed estate (GBC, 3 September 1970: 1466). Others suggested that some non-Traveller tenants were 'living in worse conditions [than the woman and her children] and were not re-housed' (CT, 4 September 1970: 9). Indeed, an editorial noted that the tenants protesting any further housing of Travellers had a legitimate grievance as the city's chronic housing shortage had resulted in a state of 'emergency' (ibid.).

The response to these working-class protests revealed that an important shift had taken place at the political level as this time, unlike in 1968, the politicians stood firm in their decision to uphold the 'democratic and fundamental rights of the [itinerant] tenant' despite demonstrations outside their meetings and the threat of a rent strike by non-Traveller tenants (CT, 11 September 1970: 1, 6). The politicians were joined by a powerful ally, the Bishop of Galway, who publicly supported the city officials and politicians and reminded his parishioners that it was their civic and Christian duty to settle the Travellers.

The commentary on the working-class protests included assertions about the links between these protests and Irish modernization. The

Bishop, for example, told protestors that 'to refuse shelter to one of our own people is contrary to the noblest traditions of the Irish Catholic people' and that 'it is only by co-operation that the city can develop and meet the needs of the modern age' (CT, 4 September 1970: 9). A similar invoking of modernization (in the form of Europeanization) appeared in an editorial which criticized the protestors as displaying a tendency in the 'Irish character' toward 'prejudice and intolerance,' and went on to suggest that this tendency might be mitigated by 'closer contact with other cultures' initiated by membership in the European Common Market (CT, 11 September 1970: 6). A letter to the editor from this same period also invoked modernization, but as a source of a new materialism that was the cause of (rather than the solution to) resistance to the housing of Travellers in the city:

> We, the Irish[,] know what it is to suffer, we know the despondency of being down-trodden, the despair of being shunned by those who claimed to be our betters – or do we? Have we become in a few years so far removed from that as to deny it, have we ceased to revel in our new-found freedom or are we slaves to another master now – avarice? (CT, 11 September 1970: 16)

These varying statements of support for Traveller housing drew upon the powerful discourses of nationalism and modernization to criticize the actions of the working-class tenants who eventually lost their battle to keep the Traveller family out.

Tigeens

While the case described above marked a new political willingness to house Travellers in local authority estates, politicians remained sensitive to the accusation that the settlement program was being unfairly foisted upon local authority tenants. Some months later city officials introduced a new plan for Traveller settlement in both private and public estates. The plan involved accommodating some Travellers in the new housing estates being constructed on the perimeter of the city, and providing others with 'tigeens' or small 'halfway houses' in private areas (GBC, 19 July 1971).

Despite an earlier recognition by some private residents that 'the afflu-ent area of the city [must] give the example in the settlement project[,] otherwise the problem would not be solved' (CT, 4 December 1970: 9), the proposed tigeen plan ran into difficulties. In the wealthiest area of the city opposition from private residents made it impossible for the city to acquire any land for the project. The degree of resistance was such that when the Bishop intervened to offer some land held by the Church in the area, his offer was not accepted and the plan was quietly dropped by the city (*CT*, 11 February 1972: 1; GBC, 4 March 1974; *CT*, 8 March 1974: 1; GBC, 6 May 1974).

The provision of four tigeens for Travellers nevertheless went ahead on the northeastern side of the city in an area that was slated for industrial use and was some distance from private residences. These tigeens were intended as an interim form of accommodation which would allow the itinerants 'to make the transition from their old way of life to a new one in council houses' (*CT*, 17 March 1972: 1). While there was no organized opposition, one nearby resident wrote to complain that the families had moved into the new site with their horses and carts and caravans and that, rather than 'beginning a new life,' Travellers were going to create another 'slum' (*CT*, 22 September 1972: 18). The Settlement Committee defended the Traveller families by repeating the now familiar argument that Traveller settlement constituted a national duty toward the underprivileged in the context of successful modernization:

> One of the greatest diseases of our modern society is our insistence on our 'rights as rate-payers' and 'rights of property.' Perhaps if for once our 'rights as rate-payers' took second place to our 'responsibilities as rate payers' and to our 'neighbourly' duties to underprivileged citizens the world might be a warmer and more cheerful place for all. (*CT*, 6 October 1972: 6)

Housing in the New Estates

Along with the provision of this tigeen site, city officials asked politicians to agree to further direct housing of Travellers in the public estates that were being constructed in the east, west, and north sections of the city (GBC, 2 October 1972). While the plan went ahead, it evoked a rearguard action from some members of the Borough Council, who challenged the settlement policy and advocated forcible extralegal removal of Travellers from the city (*CT*, 1 December 1972: 20). Such sentiments were also expressed in a newspaper editorial which praised the efforts at Traveller 'rehabilitation,' but asked city politicians and officials not to 'forget their duty to protect those people who have fixed homes and who pay rates' (*CT*, 8 September 1972: 6). The editorial went on to state that if the Travellers did not comply with the requirements of public health 'they should be sent out of the city' (ibid.) and, in apparent support for the earlier 1969 attack, added, 'let there be Rahoonery in the public interest, in the interest of both itinerants and the ratepayers' (ibid.).

Despite the reluctance of some politicians Travellers were allocated houses and flats in the newer estates where the absence of established tenants' associations ensured that there was little resistance. By May of 1974 the city claimed to have housed twenty six Traveller families in either houses or flats under the new program.[5] Tenants' associations, however, often quickly formed in these new estates and these associations began to resist further Traveller housing in their areas.

Class and 'Modernization'

The anti-Travellerism of the inhabitants of both older and newer public housing estates can be located within the context of the uneven distribution of the fruits of foreign investment and 'modernization.' As had been the case earlier, the politics of Traveller settlement were shaped by class-based divisions that were exacerbated in the context of the hollowing out of indigenous industry and the expansion of American transnational corporations (in computers and pharmaceuticals). While Galway City experienced a period of economic growth after the 1960s, many new, better-paid jobs went to well-educated migrants from other areas of Ireland rather than to the urban working class or those leaving agricultural production in the region. In fact, despite the new employment opportunities in the city, the latter groups experienced increased unemployment during the 1970s and 1980s (Grimes 1984: 264).

Throughout the 1970s those living in public housing estates accused politicians of making the poor bear the brunt of the Traveller settlement program. The following excerpt from a letter to the editor expressed the argument:

> Not one Corporation member ever voiced an opinion against the housing of itinerants in large numbers in a certain local authority housing estate. No! because the people of that area are poor and they had to shut their mouths and take what they got and that meant having several itinerant families as neighbours, but now in the case of [a private estate], of course, this cannot be let happen. It is only fair that [the private estate] should have its share of itinerants, since its [sic] the residents of such areas that are usually over enthusiastic about settling itinerants. (CT, 6 April 1973: 8)

As this letter suggests, the settlement project itself was often identified as being a project of the wealthy of the city, and the demand was made that both public and private areas of the city should 'take their share' of Travellers – whether in camps or in houses. One letter to the editor complained of dogs, horses, and the health hazard posed by a Traveller camp, and argued that 'if this was not a mainly working class area the "No Temporary Dwellings" signs would be more prominently displayed and enforced' (*CT*, 9 January 1976: 11).

Resistance to the housing of Travellers in poorer areas of the city often involved challenges to the image of 'itinerants' developed in the Report of the Commission on Itinerancy. In particular, the argument that the Travellers were poorer than other classes and therefore in need of assistance was disputed by those who felt that their own allegedly more legitimate claims on the state (e.g., for employment and housing) were not being met. During the 1970s, when the construction of local authority housing was not keeping pace with the expansion of the city's population, Travellers were often portrayed as 'outsiders' taking houses from local people despite the comment by the City Manager (the chief city official) that those camping in the city were 'mostly offshoots of older families' already in the city (GBC, 4 February 1974).

Some politicians responded to class-based protests by trying to distance themselves from the settlement policy, publicly challenging assignments of tenancies (e.g., one politician criticized the housing of an 'itinerant' in preference to a 'fourth generation Galwegian') (*CT*, 26 July 1974: 1), and by demanding to see housing lists in advance of allocations (*CT*, 6 September 1974: 1). When allocations to two Traveller families resulted in protest marches, petitions, and a night-time vigil by tenants to prevent the 'sneaking' in of more 'itinerants' (*CT*, 14 March 1975: 1), the elected representative for the area lent support to these actions by publically stating that: 'itinerants are not fit to be moved into the estate. You can't cart people off the side of the road and put them into a house' (*CT*, 28 February 1975: 20). The same councillor later spoke against any housing of Travellers in the city: 'I would like to see the itinerants housed in the heart of Connemara, a place where nobody lives. I will not stand by as a member of this Council and watch them being housed ... in any part of the city or its precincts' (CT, 25 April 1975: 1). Several politicians also suggested that the city was housing 'more than its proportional share of itinerant families in the country' and that additional accommodation 'would only encourage an influx of itinerants'

(*CT*, 8 February 1974: 1). One politician claimed that 'every tinker in Ireland is on his way to ... the softies in Galway' (*CT*, 6 April 1973: 8), while another stated:

> The officials of every other county in Ireland are sitting back and laughing at the Galway Corporation officials, as the itinerants swarm out of those counties and into Galway City where they are guaranteed a house ... It's time for a get-tough policy on itinerants in Galway and officials should drive these outsider families back out of the city as soon as they arrive here, other wise [*sic*] we will have every itinerant in Ireland housed here before the summer. (*CT*, 15 February 1974: 1)

By the mid-1970s the continuing resistance from tenants, and the continued presence of camping Travellers in the city, was forcing a reconsideration of settlement plans. Early settlement rhetoric had argued that the itinerants were poor Irish, who, if provided with houses, education, and wage labour, would become members of the 'settled community' within a short period of time. Settlement advocates, however, were beginning to suggest that the itinerant way of life was something more substantial, more deeply ingrained. In the newer arguments the degree of material deprivation of Travellers was downplayed (the claim was often made that the extension of the 'dole' had eliminated Traveller poverty), but social and cultural deprivation were emphasized. The new argument was supported by an academic study (based largely upon six weeks of fieldwork among Travellers just outside Galway City) which introduced the concept of an itinerant 'subculture' arising out of 'inherited poverty' and 'adaptations to deprivation and discrimination' (Walsh 1971: 155).

In Galway City the newer arguments were marshalled in support of the need for more 'interim' forms of accommodation. It was suggested, for instance, that Travellers required greater 're-education' before being housed in regular estates (GBC, 20 January 1975). The discussion downplayed the class-based divisions (within both the non-Traveller and Traveller populations) that had surfaced in the course of settlement policy implementation by emphasizing the allegedly *cultural* division between the Travellers and the non-Traveller 'settled community.'

The Traveller 'Village'

The new argument about the need for 'interim' accommodation for Travellers was articulated in an editorial responding to a threat by a tenant 'action group' to 'burn out' Travellers camping in their area. The editorial condemned the threat of violence, but put forward the view that the 'rights' of settled people were being threatened by the direct housing policy. The editorial argued that what Travellers required was an 'intermediate step between the roadside and full integration into the community.' This would involve the help of 'trained social workers' as an 'essential part of the preparation for the new life' (CT, 9 January 1976: 8).

Consistent with such arguments was a new plan introduced by city officials for the settlement of Travellers. This plan proposed the construction, some distance away from existing residential estates, of a 'village' where only Travellers would be accommodated. The village would consist of twenty houses as well as a pre-school and community hall. A compound for horses and an area for storing scrap would be provided and caretakers and social workers would be hired as supervisors (CT, 5 October 1976: 1). While the plan was not unanimously supported by politicians and attracted protests from residents of the area (GBC, 6 June 1975: 7; CT, 14 May 1976: 1; GBC, 14 June 1976), pressure on the city council to act led to its submission to the Minister for Local Government for approval.

The submission of the plan appeared to be a victory for city tenants – but it was short-lived. Soon after the plan was submitted, a group of businessmen and industrialists working in the region of the proposed village produced a brochure expressing their concerns to the politicians. Their opposition was given tacit support by the Minister for Industry and Commerce who, while visiting the city, referred to a nearby Traveller camp as an 'industrial embarrassment.' The result was that local politicians, concerned about any threat to the industry or commerce of the city, voted to reject the village plan (GBC, 18 October 1976; CT, 22 October 1976: 1, 20).

With the shelving of the village project there remained only two options for Travellers, either camping in unofficial camps or entering houses in public housing estates. In evident frustration at the turn of events, the Assistant City Manager declared that he would now be forced to house twenty-five camping families in public housing estates (CT, 22 October 1976: 1, 20). His comments confirmed the fears of many tenants that the shelving of the village plan meant accelerated housing of Travellers in their neighbourhoods and the Galway branch of the National Association of Tenants Organisations claimed that those living in public housing estates were being unfairly victimized by the settlement (CT, 29 October 1976: 1). The rejection of the village proposal resulted in a mobilization of tenants, as well as many Travellers camping in the city, fifty of whom marched first to the industrial estate and then to the city offices to demand that they be provided with accommodation (*CT*, 5 November 1976: 1; *CT*, 12 November 1976: 16).

Any alliance between Travellers and tenants, however, was weakened by the continuing anti-Traveller actions of tenants. One of the more dramatic incidents occurred when non-Traveller tenants blocked the entrance to a new estate in order to forestall the entry of three Traveller tenants, claiming that their area had housed twenty-five itinerant families since 1934 and that in resisting further allocations to Travellers they were only doing what those living in private housing estates had done before (*CT*, 8 July 1977: 1).

Seven politicians expressed support for the actions of these tenants, as did the local branch of Fianna Fáil. A motion was introduced at the city council stating that no more Travellers should be housed in the area but some city officials spoke against it, pointing out that they had followed the proper procedure for the letting of houses and that it was not 'open to the Council to discriminate ... against any section of the community for whom the Council is responsible' (*CT*, 15 July 1977: 1).

After a month of negotiations, during which time one of the Travellers went to court in order to gain access to his allocated house, representatives of the protesting tenants agreed to accept two of the three allocations in exchange for assurances from the city that no more Travellers would be housed in the area for a period of twenty-five years. Other tenant grievances against the city, such as outstanding repairs, were also to be dealt with as part of the bargain (*CT*, 5 August 1977: 1; *CT*, 12 August 1977: 1). Not long after this, the third Traveller was allocated a house in another estate. Again there were protests, and the family was kept under house siege for six days by picketing non-Travellers. The dispute ended only after the city agreed that no more Travellers would be housed in the estate for five years. It was also agreed that social workers would visit the Traveller home on a regular basis, that wandering animals would be impounded, and that repairs and dampness in the estate would be attended to (*CT*, 4 November 1977: 16).

These incidents represented the height of tenant success in using their resistance to settlement policy to wring concessions from the city. The incidents also led to increased pressure on politicians to reconsider the 'village' plan. By November, 3,000 signatures had been collected by an organization called 'The Group for Action on Housing Itinerants,' which urged 'all Trade Unionists, Tenants and progressive citizens of Galway'

(*CT*, 7 October 1977: 16) to support a petition that called for the implementation of the original 'itinerant village' plan as well as the provision of serviced hardstands and fields for travellers who did not want to stop travelling (*CT*, 26 August 1977: 1).

In May 1978, an internal city report on Traveller settlement outlined what the city had done so far, and made proposals for the future. This report stated that the city had provided accommodation in houses and flats for forty-four Traveller family units since 1967, and that thirty-four of these were still living in such accommodation. Another forty-one family units were subtenants in corporation dwellings, or living in tigeens, or unauthorized camps in the city. The report stated that thirty-one of these forty-one families had to be provided with some form of permanent accommodation because of their 'long association' with the city (*CT*, 26 May 1978: 20). In addition to these, the report pointed out that the city would also be responsible for housing the estimated forty new family units that would be formed through the marriages of young Travellers in the city over the next five years.

The report emphasized that the projected need for seventy-one units of accommodation over the next five years was unlikely to be met through regular allocations. Moreover, the report went on argue that many of the Travellers were 'not ready' for housing and that to house them would 'impose a burden upon the traveller who is unable to cope as well as upon his adjoining neighbour in the Corporation estate' (ibid.). As a result, the report proposed the stepping up of a 'special programme' to augment direct housing.

The 'special programme' was, in fact, a resuscitation of the earlier 'village' plan. It was proposed that there would be a group housing scheme just for Travellers, which would have a pre-school, adult training facilities, recreational facilities, provision for animals, and an area for scrap and vehicle parking. In addition, there would be 'intensive welfare,' involving two social workers who would arrange for instruction in 'personal and domestic hygiene, health, school attendance, [and] housekeeping,' and discourage begging. Travellers would enter this housing estate 'on the understanding that they were agreeable to undergo a process of familiarisation in settled circumstances as a transitional stage to qualify for a Local Authority dwelling in the normal way' (ibid.).

While the councillors deliberated over the proposal (GBC, 19 June 1978), there was a media story on the primitive living conditions of a Traveller mother and her newborn who were living in a tent in the city. A reinvigorated Galway Council for Travelling People (the new name for the earlier Itinerant Settlement Committee) used money donated by the public in response to the story to buy a trailer for the mother. When the trailer was parked, however, the Council for Travelling People was accused of not respecting the rights of the nearby residents, whose property values were allegedly lowered (*CT*, 20 October 1978: 1).

The incident revealed the continuing tension surrounding Traveller camps and increased pressure on politicians to implement the group housing scheme. One newspaper columnist suggested that the Travellers were the victims of 'something bordering on racialism ... the unfortunate travellers just don't happen to be blacks or Pakistanis' (*CT*, 20 October 1978: 8), and the Galway Council of Trade Unions called for implementation of the village plan to 'prevent the unfortunate people from experiencing the rigours of another winter by the roadside' (GBC, 20 November 1978).

By January of 1979, the politicians decided to go ahead with the village plan, a major factor in its favour being that it was located on an area of undeveloped land on the eastern outskirts of the city and would be fully occupied *before* other regular estates were built, thereby eliminating the possibility of neighbourhood opposition (GBC, 5 January 1979). By 1981 the project was ready, and twenty-four Traveller families entered the scheme.

The sudden accommodation of twenty-four families resulted in some positive publicity for the city, but the continued existence of several Traveller camps frustrated those who had seen the group scheme as a means of eliminating unofficial camps without housing Travellers directly into local authority estates. Indeed, many politicians had expected that the provision of the group housing scheme would allow the city to more successfully prosecute Travellers for roadside camping (GBC, 15 January 1979).

One of the places where Travellers were camping was a new location just outside the group housing project, and this camp became the target of complaints from non-Travellers who moved into the area when new estates were built nearby (GBC, 22 March 1982). A public debate ensued about the 'success' of the group housing scheme less than two years after its opening, with city officials defending it (GBC, 4 October 1982) and others claiming that it had been a failure. A member of the police was quoted as stating:

Many of [the Travellers] are not settling in. Some are stealing and begging. In my view there are too many housed in Galway already and there should be no more housing of itinerants in Galway.

If something concrete is not done I can see them taking over the city completely and we will have a similar situation to Dublin.

The only way to tackle the problem is to set up an institution to rehabilitate these children and show them how to settle in houses as well as proper parental control, which is not there now. (*CT*, 11 June 1982: 24)

Fourteen Traveller parents from the scheme denied these allegations in a letter to the editor (*CT*, 18 June ,1982: 1, 24), but tensions were revealed again the following year when relations between Travellers and non-Travellers in the area were described as 'explosive' (*CT*, 15 July 1983: 1).

While the city tried unsuccessfully to prosecute camping Travellers (GBC, 24 October 1983) non-Traveller tenants formed an Itinerant Action Committee with the purpose of forcibly stopping further caravans coming into the area. A spokesperson for these tenants told the city council: 'This was supposed to be a model village to try and rehabilitate ... the itinerants, but it can't work where there's caravans, horses and goats all over the place – to me that's a hardstand' (*CT*, 28 October 1983: 1). Several months later a Traveller living in the group housing scheme also expressed concern about the presence of the camp so close to the village project, suggesting that the only solution to unauthorized camping by Travellers in the city lay in the provision of official serviced sites or hardstands (*Galway Advertiser*, 5 April 1984: 12).

Camping

As the above suggests, despite the extensive housing of Travellers that had occurred by the early 1980s, the focus of attention remained on the Traveller camps.[6] Between the mid-1970s and early 1980s there were at any one time from four to seven different camps within the city. None of these, however, were official hardstands. All of the 'official' serviced sites that had been provided by the city in 1969–70 had been closed down when their original occupants left or were housed.

For some time there were three 'semi-official' camps in the city. Two of these were former tigeen sites. In one case, despite the fact that the original four tigeens had deteriorated and finally been demolished by the city, Travellers continued to camp in trailers on the site, which retained minimal services. A second site, originally situated outside but since incorporated within city boundaries, retained two of its original tigeens but was also used as a camping place for others living in trailers. A third site had been 'opened up' by the city for Travellers evicted from another area of the city, but had then been 'closed up' when most of the inhabitants were relocated to the group housing scheme. The remaining camping places in the city lacked even 'semi-official' status.

For most of this period the largest cluster of tents and trailers was found in a camp that had once been on the outskirts of the city but was, by the 1980s, surrounded by new housing estates. This camp was the subject of protests from tenants and residents, who complained that the lack of running water or toilets made it a health hazard, that wandering horses posed a danger to pedestrians and gardens, and that the Traveller practice of hanging their laundry on the fences of a new American company in the area constituted a civic and national embarassment (CT, 27 November 1981: 3). By 1980 the camp was threatened not only by protests from non-Travellers living in the area but also by plans for a shopping-centre development (CT, 1 February 1980: 3).

A proposal by city officials that the affected Travellers be relocated to a serviced hardstand elsewhere in the city was resisted by politicians, who argued that such provision would only attract Travellers from elsewhere to the city and/or attract local opposition (GBC, 22 March 1982). At the same time, the Travellers themselves resisted any relocation. One was reported as stating:

> We won't move into any serviced site with strange families who might be rowdy. We have been living here for 12 years. We went to local schools and we all made our First Holy Communion and Confirmation in the parish. Local people know us well by now and we haven't caused any trouble. (CT, 4 June 1982: 1)

Subsequently however, several of the camping Travellers moved their trailers a couple of hundred feet in order to allow the completion of the shopping centre. They claimed that they had moved only because they had been assured that they were 'there to stay' and had been promised water and electricity by the city. This claim was later denied by the Town Clerk, who declared that the camp would remain an unserviced site until a suitable hardstand site was found (CT, 15 October 1982: 1, 22). The residents' and tenants' association for the surrounding area meanwhile expressed its opposition to their continuing presence (CT, 8 July 1983: 1), while declaring support for the provision of hardstands for Travellers away from built-up areas. This position, which in effect meant that no hardstands would be provided within the city, was described in an editorial as 'reasonable and realistic' (Galway Advertiser, 29 March 1984: 6) and was supported by several politicians. The result was that no action was taken on the provision of hardstands.

The 1983 Report of the Travelling People Review Body

The struggles in Galway City over the type and location of accommodation for Travellers, while dramatic, were not unique. Elsewhere in Ireland there were also intense conflicts, and progress on implementation of the settlement program was slow. In 1981 a Travelling People Review Body was established by the central government with a mandate to review current policies and services and to recommend ways to 'improve the existing situation' (Review Body [henceforth RB] 1983: 1). The Review Body report published in 1983 was less path-breaking than the 1963 Commission Report, but provided an indication of some shifts in official thinking.

The Review Body, which included two Travellers (one from Galway City), incorporated some of the more culturalist discourse that was identifiable in Galway City by the late 1970s. The Report explicitly rejected the term 'itinerant' in favour of 'traveller' but avoided any statement on the issue of ethnicity, referring instead to Travellers as an 'identifiable group of people ... with their own distinctive life style, traditionally of a nomadic nature' (RB 1983: 6).

The Report also replaced the concept of 'absorption' with that of 'integration,' thereby acknowledging the possible retention of Traveller identity and 'traditions peculiar to the traveller way of life' (RB 1983: 6–7). In its recommendations, however, it prioritized the provision of standard housing and mainstream education and health services. While there was reference to an obligation to provide serviced sites for those Travellers who did not wish to live in houses, those desiring such an alternative were described as being in the minority (RB 1983: 19–20). Despite an ostensible recognition and valuing of a distinctive way of life and identity, the Report in fact supported the thrust of the existing settlement program.

In Galway City the implementation of the settlement program was shaped by anti-Travellerism and its articulation with an urban geography of class. As we have seen, public authority tenants found themselves newly implicated in 'solving' the Traveller 'problem' as they were pitted against wealthier areas in struggles over the location of Traveller accommodation. Local politicians followed a program of accommodating Travellers slowly and in areas where resistance was weakest. In practice this resulted in a pattern of housing Travellers in newer public estates (where there were no established neighbourhoods to oppose Traveller settlement), and eventually in a group housing scheme for Travellers. By the early 1980s, Galway City and County were distinguished from County

Dublin – the other major area of Traveller concentration – by a high percentage of housed Travellers, and by the lack of any serviced camp provision (Rottman, Tussing, and Wiley 1986: 85–6).[7]

The struggles of working-class tenants to resist Traveller housing complicated the dominant discourse of 'itinerants' and the 'settled community' by insisting on the significance of class divisions within the 'settled community' (and to a lesser extent among 'itinerants'). Such efforts contested claims made by the élite that the larger modernization project of which the Traveller settlement project was a part was class neutral in its costs and benefits.

While local class-based conflict complicated the 'itinerant' versus 'settled community' language of the 1963 Report, it did not ultimately challenge this categorization. For many working-class tenants, resisting the housing of Travellers in their respective neighbourhoods was part of an attempt to maintain a claim to superiority based on membership in the 'settled community' – in the context of class-based marginalization. Working-class struggles to resist Traveller settlement, while highlighting class, paradoxically drew upon and strengthened the ethnicized boundary that the settlement program was intended to eliminate.

An increasingly reified Traveller/non-Traveller boundary was, by the end of the 1970s, beginning to be culturalized in ways that 'explained' the apparent failure of the Travellers to be rapidly 'absorbed,' and supported proposals for the provision of segregated and differentiated services. The 1983 Review Body's references to Traveller identity and tradition exemplified this shift while retaining a commitment to Traveller settlement as necessary to Irish modernization.

Chapter 4

Travelling, Racism, and the Politics of Culture

The previous discussion has focused on the relationship between anti-Traveller racism at both national and local levels and tensions and divisions within the 'settled community.'[1] In this and the following chapters I move from the documentation of the history of anti-Traveller racism as articulated and practised by outsiders to an examination of Travellers' own struggles to forge their lives within the unequal structures of power that have produced this history.

Using textual and ethnographic material I explore Travellers' lived experiences of travelling, work, gender, and childhood, locating these within the context of a wider political economy and an oppressive anti-Traveller racism. Drawing on anthropological models that focus on the dynamic production of cultures and identities in the context of wider fields of unequal power relations, I argue that Traveller culture and identity have been and continue to be produced out of sets of unequal social relations that simultaneously link Travellers to the wider political economy and create the more intimate ties of family and community. These social relations are, like anti-Traveller racism, deeply structured by class, gender, and generation, with the result that a dynamic 'politics of culture' is produced and reproduced within externally imposed constraints.

To begin to illustrate these processes I focus on the phenomenon of travelling, which has been described by some commentators, including some Travellers, as the primary source of anti-Traveller racism as well as the central 'core' of Traveller identity. I begin with a discussion of the links between mobility, political economy, and anti-Traveller racism, and then move to a more extensive discussion of Travellers' lived experiences of movement and accommodation, emphasizing the ways in which these

experiences are the outcome of their active engagement with and challenge to exclusion.

'Sedentarism' and Anti-Traveller Racism

Some writers have linked anti-Traveller racism in Ireland to a wider ideology and practice of 'sedentarism,' which, it is argued, reproduces hegemonic capitalist social relations of work and property by denigrating and controlling mobility (McVeigh 1992). This argument is provided with some support by the historical discussion of the previous chapters, which revealed how anti-Traveller racism has been linked to the class interests of a domestic bourgeoisie, and later the ostensible needs of global capital.

The historical material, however, also points to how Traveller mobility has not always been outside of, or even in opposition to, capital. Indeed, Travellers through their mobile family economies facilitated and/or mediated links between less commodified rural households and wider commodified markets, while also supplying cheap, mobile, and short-term labour to larger farmers. Traveller mobility, moreover, was often violently produced by state-sponsored evictions and harassment, exclusion, and neglect. When the state finally initiated a project of settlement, moreover, implementation was still, as we have seen, far from systematic.

As Okely pointed out some time ago with respect to Traveller-Gypsies in England, 'modern capitalism generates nomads, it does not simply inherit them' (1983: 32), a process well demonstrated by the phenomenon of 'new age travellers' in Ireland and Britain. An expanding literature has in fact devoted itself to the documentation of how the globalizing political economy of late capitalism has intensified mobility, creating diverse streams of refugees, migrants, and entrepreneurs of global capital (Ong 1999).

Within Ireland, it is useful to point out that the policy makers of the latter half of the twentieth century were in fact preoccupied with facilitating the 'mobility' of tourists and international capitalists even as they attempted to settle Travellers, whose movement was problematized. This apparent contradiction highlights the importance of locating histories and cultures of travelling within relations of 'class, gender, race, cultural/historical location, and privilege' (Clifford 1992: 105). In the Irish case, Travellers' travelling was identified as dangerous to the nation (with particular threats to 'women and children'), while other forms of mobility deemed central to economic development and modernity were encouraged.

If there is no straightforward link between mobility and the experience of racism, claims regarding the centrality of travelling to Traveller culture and identity are similarly complicated by historical and ethnographic material. As the Galway City case study makes clear, Traveller patterns of mobility and residence have been shaped by a national political economy combined with localized class-based political struggle. Within these constraints, however, Travellers have forged various patterns of mobility and usage of accommodation in accordance with their own goals and available resources. Although some have identified nomadism, or at least a 'nomadic mind-set,' as central to Traveller ethnicity, such an identification, I suggest, obscures the reality of more complex histories and experiences of travelling.[2]

The 1986 Court Case and Attack in Galway City

The relationship between wider forces and Travellers' patterns of travel and accommodation was apparent when I returned to Galway City in 1986 to conduct fieldwork. The relatively large number of housed Travellers at the time of the 1986 count (i.e., two-thirds of the 125 Traveller families living in some form of 'standard accommodation' versus one-third living in trailers in camps) was a product of earlier struggles over accommodation and land use that had resulted in a focus on housing rather than official camping sites.

In 1986 pressure on camping space was increasing as city workers 'closed up' existing and potential parking spots in the city by placing large boulders along roadsides and in other undeveloped areas, and the absence of any hardstands in Galway City or County meant that the minority of camping Travellers were living with insecure access to land for parking and with limited or no basic services.[3]

The scarcity of secure camping spaces was dramatized shortly after my arrival, when the district court granted Galway Corporation an injunction for the removal of sixteen Traveller family units from two camps located on land slated for recreational development. The city had argued that its legal obligation to the affected Travellers had been fulfilled by offers of permanent accommodation in housing; however, the Travellers involved refused these offers and asked instead for an alternative *camping* site. One young Traveller woman explained their position to the local press in the following way: 'We've lived in caravans all our lives and we don't like living in a house. It's just like asking people who live in a house to come and live in a caravan – they wouldn't like it' (*Galway Observer*, 27 August 1986: 1). Although there was an existing 'agreement in principle' on the part of local politicians to provide hardstands in several areas in the city (*CT*, 29 September 1986: 1), the Travellers' request was not granted and they were ordered to leave.

The Traveller claim that they had the right to be offered an alternative *camping* location, rather than a house or flat, was based on an emergent public assertion of ethnic and cultural distinctiveness. Such an assertion, however, was rejected by the court. As one of those present at the case indicated, the judge ruled that the city had to offer 'reasonable accommodation' but that it was not obligated to meet the 'specific needs of every single ethnic group or cultural ghetto.'

The decision of the Galway court was consistent with other similar cases across the country. The precedent-setting 1980 Supreme Court judgment on the MacDonald versus Feely (City and County of Dublin) case had established the right of Travellers to be offered accommodation when threatened with eviction, but had also ruled that housing authorities' obligations to Travellers were fulfilled by the offer of tigeens, flats, or houses, rather than serviced camping space (Supreme Court 1980).[4]

One of the women involved in the Galway case explained how, prior to the case going to court, the city had offered her housing in order to meet the legal requirements necessary for her subsequent eviction. The city's strategy was successful and those Travellers served with injunctions after the ruling were harassed by the police and threatened with imprisonment and the institutionalization of their children. While some of the families responded by trying to 'open up' alternative camps in the city their efforts were blocked by non-Traveller residents.

Under mounting pressure one of the camps disbanded and eventually re-grouped in an existing unofficial camp on the other side of the city. The Travellers of the second camp, however, insisted that they would not leave until they were provided with an alternative camping location in the immediate vicinity. According to these Travellers, the impasse was broken when a city official told them that they could move into a nearby field. They were advised to move in the early hours of the morning in order to avoid any confrontation or obstruction from non-Travellers living in the area.

The Travellers acted on the advice, but shortly after they parked their trailers in the field they were attacked by a group of non-Travellers who dragged their trailers out and onto the roadside. The incident, which I described in the introduction to this book, received a great deal of media coverage and focused national attention on Traveller/non-Traveller relations in Galway. The exposure provided the affected Travellers with the chance to voice their demand for an official campsite, and one of the women living in the camp, Margaret Sweeney, emerged as an articulate spokesperson for the camp residents.

Shortly after the attack Traveller families involved issued a formal request for an official hardstand, stating: 'some Travellers wish to live in houses and some do not. We do not want to live in houses. We want places to park our trailers. We have been asking the Corporation for years for properly supervized and serviced hardstands.' This action was followed by the formation of a larger Galway Traveller Committee, with Margaret Sweeney as the spokesperson.

Travelling, Settlement, and the Commission on Itinerancy

Political mobilization around the provision of hardstands directly challenged an explicit premise of early settlement policy, namely that housing and settlement was the goal of all Travellers. This conclusion was an interpretation of the more ambiguous finding, reported by the 1963 Report of the Commission on Itinerancy, that an overwhelming majority of itinerants had answered positively to a census question about whether they would 'prefer to settle in one place if [a] means of livelihood [was] available' (CI 1963: 143–4).

Other statements in the 1963 Report were similarly ambiguous with respect to Travellers' desires in the area of accommodation and mobility. The Report noted, for example, that the only Travellers who formally approached the Commission (a group living in Dublin) presented a case 'of strong complaint against the policy of continually moving them from camping places without providing any alternative place for them to go (CI 1963: 30) – evidence, it could be argued, of a Traveller concern with accessing secure camping places as much as a desire for housing and settlement. Elsewhere in the Report it was also stated that 'Some itinerants ... said that they were prepared to pay rents for sites if they could get them' (CI 1963: 52) and it was acknowledged that a *minority* of Travellers might retain an itinerant lifestyle, in particular 'those who are not very poor and whose families are already reared' (CI 1963: 106).

The Report, however, emphasized the need for housing and settlement. The argument was advanced in part by describing Travellers' tents as 'completely unfit, unhygienic, and unhealthy for the occupiers,' and therefore in need of outright prohibition as a form of dwelling (CI 1963: 44). The suitability of horse-drawn caravans or wagons as dwellings was also 'questionable' (CI 1963: 41), and applications for houses from itinerants were to be given priority as they were said to be 'living in totally unfit and overcrowded conditions' (CI 1963: 61).

That some Travellers in Galway were interested in housing was clear from the existence of Traveller applications for tenancies, but there were also local reports of Traveller concern that the newly formed Commission would lead to greater restrictions on mobility. The Galway regional press, for example, ran a story about how the formation of the Commission on Itinerancy had been greeted with suspicion by some Travellers in the region because of its emphasis on settlement. One man, described by the press as the 'king of the Tinkers,' was reported to be concerned about the purpose of the census of Travellers taken for the Commission and was quoted as stating that he would lead a movement against [Travellers] being confined to any kind of 'reservation' or 'concentration camp.' (CT, 15 April 1961: 7). Some months later he was reported as declaring his intention to leave Ireland because 'when there is talk of putting the travelling folk into compounds or concentration camps, it's time to go' (CT, 2 September 1961: 4).[5]

In the face of increased prosecution for camping in the Galway region there were also reports of Traveller interest in paying for fixed camping places that would be secure from eviction (e.g., CT, 16 February 1963: 6). Such was the request of a Traveller 'spokesperson' quoted during a local court case in 1964.

> Speaking for eleven itinerant families, fifty-year-old tinsmith ... made a strong plea at Galway Court this week for his people's right to live in their own way ... 'If we leave Galway, the farmers are chasing us and if we stay in Galway, the Corporation is chasing us.'
>
> 'We are human beings like everyone else and all we ask is the right to live in our own way and some place to park. Why aren't we given parking places where we could stay the night and pay.' (CT, 27 June 1964: 9)

By the 1970s Traveller demands for serviced camping sites were, nevertheless, still being ignored or considered illegitimate by policy makers and implementors. Even when there was official acknowledgment that some Travellers in Galway City wished to continue camping the city labelled such Travellers 'transients,' thereby (along with many other local authorities) absolving itself of any responsibility to provide services to them (see GBC, 31 May 1976; Ennis 1984: 15). While the housing program was clearly meeting the needs of some Travellers (and was an important corrective to the earlier negative housing policy), by the 1980s it appeared to be reaching the limit of Traveller demand. The 1982 annual Traveller count revealed that, of forty camping family units in the city at the time, only five had expressed a desire for permanent accommodation (GBC, 22 March 1982). By the fieldwork period it had become increasingly clear that the priority of most camping Travellers was not to enter housing but to gain a place to park without threat of eviction. Combined with ongoing resistance from non-residents to further housing of Travellers, this reality had led the city to a new agreement 'in principle' to provide hardstands. The Traveller Committee lobbied for the translation of this agreement into action.

Camping in Galway City

My return to Galway City in 1986 coincided with the court case described above, and from the beginning my ethnographic research was shaped by the local politics of Traveller mobility and accommodation. When I approached Travellers about the possibility of buying a trailer and entering one of the existing camps I found that my enquiries were greeted positively despite the politically-charged atmosphere. Although a majority of Travellers in the city at the time were living in some form of housing, my explanation that I wanted to enter a camp in order to learn about the Traveller way of life was well received and I was offered invitations to join several different camping clusters – perhaps a reflection of hopes that my presence might increase leverage with the city.

'Camping' was identified by many Travellers as the core of a distinctive 'travelling' way of life even when there was little mobility involved. After many months of living in a trailer I was surprised when one of my camp neighbours described me as 'travelling' despite the fact that I had been stationary for my entire stay; however, as another of my co-residents declared: 'in a trailer you always want to move – you aren't settled.' Travellers associated camping with a *potential* for movement, and this in turn was linked to a distinctive Traveller identity.

Camping and 'travelling' were identified as positive symbols of Traveller identity, but the realities of struggle over access to secure parking land and the lack of basic services such as toilets, electricity, water, and rubbish removal meant that camping was also a source of frustration and shame. Camping Travellers identified the cause of their living conditions as a combination of systematic official neglect and harassment, and understood their continued presence in camps under such conditions as a form of active resistance. As one woman told me in anger, 'they [the city] want us to suffer but we won't leave for them.' There was also agreement that geographical mobility was being reduced due to external pressures. As one of my neighbours commented, 'the days of the travelling are coming to an end, and it's all because the Corporations, and the County Councils, and the residential people, are getting their own way.'

While understanding their circumstances to be politically created, camping Travellers none the less lived daily with the stigma of being 'dirty' in the eyes of non-Travellers and some housed Travellers. The result was that the meanings attached to camping were simultaneously and ambivalently those of cultural pride and stigma.

As described in the introduction, after buying a trailer my husband and I entered into a camp where we stayed for a total of nine months. During this time I was able to observe the movements and accommodation changes of those who spent time in the camp. I was also able to gather family travel and accommodation histories from my neighbours. Such histories were not difficult to collect; indeed, many people enjoyed recounting for me the places they had lived and the different forms of accommodation they had experienced. This material was augmented by an examination of the available annual counts of Travellers and housing files kept by the city.

During the nine months of my residence in the camp a total of fourteen nuclear family units (comprising eighty-one individuals) spent varying periods of time there. The birth and movement of children and the arrival and departure of visitors altered the composition and population of the camp over the course of the fieldwork period, but the most dramatic cause of changed camp membership came from movement of entire family units in or out of the camp.

Seven of the fourteen families that spent time in the camp entered and/or left during my residence. Three of these arrived after they were threatened with eviction from another camping spot in the city, while in the other four cases the moves in and/or out were more 'voluntary' in nature and involved a change in accommodation either from trailer to housing or vice versa.

Two of these latter families had left the city's group housing scheme in order to take up residence in a trailer in the camp, while another two left the camp in order to move into 'standard accommodation' – one to a flat (where they stayed for a few months before leaving for England), and the other to a house in the city. In these cases the movement in and/or out of the camp was occurring within the city itself, although all had spent earlier periods living in other parts of Ireland and in several cases in Britain.

The remaining seven families remained stationary in the camp for the entire nine months of my own residence. Two of these had been living there for many years. An older married couple in their sixties had spent at least fourteen years in the camp, and a younger couple with four children had resided there since their marriage five years earlier (before their marriage both the wife and husband had lived in houses in the city with their parents). While these two families were long-term camp residents, the histories of the other five families that were stationary over the course of the nine months of fieldwork revealed earlier experiences of travel and changes in accommodation usage.

In the case of one family that had 'pulled in' to the camp just prior to my own arrival, the husband and wife had been married for six years and had four children. Before her marriage, the wife had been living in her parents' house in Northern Ireland, while the husband had spent most of his childhood camping in Galway City. After they married they moved into a trailer and camped near the wife's people in Northern Ireland, but after a few months came to camp in Galway City with the husband's people. Shortly after their arrival in Galway they entered the group housing scheme, but less than a year later they had left the scheme to travel back to the North. There they moved into a house, but left it after ten months to camp in a trailer closer to the wife's relatives. They remained camping in the North for another four years before returning to live in the Galway camp.

Another husband and wife who had been married for seven years and had three children had both spent most of their childhood camping, but the wife had lived in a house in another town for a couple of years prior to her marriage. After their marriage the couple camped in a number of towns and cities in Ireland and England, including Galway City, where they had also spent two separate periods of several months living in the group housing scheme. Just prior to moving into the camp they had spent a third period of almost a year in this housing project.

These histories of movement and experiences with both housing and trailer-living revealed that there was no straightforward equation between forms of accommodation and degrees of travelling and settlement. Just as some of those living in trailers in the camp were essentially 'settled' in the sense of having remained stationary in the camp for many years, others had combined mobility with short-term accommodation in housing.

This reality stood in contrast to the dominant 'official discourse' of Traveller settlement, which categorized Travellers according to accommodation and frequently equated housing with settlement and camping with travelling. Camping (and therefore ostensibly 'travelling') family units were sometimes further sub-divided into 'local' versus 'non-local' families in Galway City. Categorizing Travellers in such terms, however, obscured ongoing patterns of both geographical and residential mobility and deflected attention from other alliances and divisions among Travellers.

Mobility, Accommodation, and Kinship

While I have emphasized the role of state provision or lack of provision in determining mobility and accommodation usage, within these constraints Travellers worked to organize their patterns of travel and accommodation in accordance with particular goals. One of these was the maximization of proximity to particular sets of close kin.

Decision-making about geographical and residential mobility was identified as a male prerogative, and while Travellers often stayed close to the wife's parents early in the marriage, thereafter disproportionately more time was usually spent with the husbands 'people,' i.e., his parents and brothers. With the death of elderly parents, sons would tend to cluster alongside brothers and paternal uncles until they themselves became the centre of a cluster of their own married children, and especially sons. The loss of the opportunity for fathers and sons to experience camping 'on the one road' was described as one of the drawbacks of housing. Given the lack of control by Travellers over land and housing, the achievement of such co-residential patterns required various strategies of engagement with structures of power as well as creative forms of co-operation.

While the number of camps in the city shifted during the fieldwork period, each comprised one or more clusters of family units linked to one another by close kinship and/or affinal links usually based on close ties between males. In most cases the kin-based residential clusters had been established in the particular camping location for many years, although the specific composition of the cluster had changed as individual families moved in and out.

Localized kin-based clusters of family units were closely linked through kinship and affinal ties to other such clusters in geographically dispersed locations in Ireland and the British Isles. The oldest married couple in the camp where I was living, for example, had thirteen married children. While five of their married sons lived with them in the camp as part of a clearly identifiable kin-based cluster, they also retained close ties to several married children who were living elsewhere in houses in the city.

Two additional married children were camping in Northern Ireland, while a son was living in Dublin. Many more of their married nephews and nieces were camped or housed in England, Wales, and Scotland.

Two married sons who lived in houses in the city visited the camp almost daily, often bringing some of their children along, while their married daughters also living in Galway visited once or twice a week. Contact was less frequent with those living outside the city, but a son who lived in Northern Ireland visited his parents several times during the fieldwork period and a daughter who also lived in the North arrived with her children and stayed with her parents for an extended period. There were also short visits from some of the more distant relatives who were living in Britain. In lieu of direct contact, communication with close relatives was maintained through phone calls (usually made to and from pubs, training centres, and other pay phones), letters, and messages brought by other Travellers.

Ties to close relatives living in other towns and cities provided family units and wider clusters with potential access to other areas of Ireland and Britain, and relatives coming to the city for visits often urged siblings and cousins to join them. The making, cancelling, and remaking of travel plans by those living in the camp was in fact a major source of excitement throughout the year.

Travel could be motivated by a desire to renew ties with geographically distant kin, but other family-related events could also dictate movement. The need to be close to a hospitalized child, parent, or sibling, for example, often required 'staying around' a particular town or city for an extended period. As has been described by G. Gmelch (1977: 108) and Okely for Traveller-Gypsies in Britain (1983: 194–6), some Travellers also preferred to move away from a place that had become 'too lonesome' after the death of a close relative. Death could also prompt a change in accommodation, with some Travellers burning trailers after the death of a member of the family, while others sold them to a 'stranger.' Deaths could also result in Travellers leaving houses and failure to do so could attract criticism. As one Traveller woman said of a Traveller mother whose child had died: 'If I was her I wouldn't have stayed twenty-four hours in a house with my child dead.'

Those planning moves often mentioned economic opportunities as a reason for travelling to join kin elsewhere, but movement required a careful calculation of economic viability. Some of my neighbours spoke of the challenge of accumulating sufficient savings to tide them over until they were able to generate income in the new location. Those

without access to sufficient resources were as a result sometimes sedentary out of necessity rather than inclination. In the case of one younger
family with few resources a decision to join relatives in Northern Ireland
had to be continually put off due to a lack of income with which to
purchase reliable transportation. The mobility of this family unit was
dependent upon the arrival of a wealthier uncle who agreed to tow their
trailer. The enforced dependence was experienced as a shamefully visible sign of economic failure.

The impact of external constraints and limited resources on mobility
and accommodation 'choices' was well illustrated when the sister of one
of my neighbours explained how she and her husband had decided to
leave the city after her husband was fined for not having sufficient
insurance on his vehicle. Unable to pay the fines, they decided to avoid
his imprisonment by travelling to join some cousins in England and they
sold their trailer in order to finance the trip. On the day that they were
going to leave, however, they got a letter from the city offering them a
flat. The city's offer allowed them to use the money received from the
sale of the caravan to pay off the court fine, and instead of going to
England they took the flat and stayed in the city. This case reveals
something of the multiple factors that shaped Travellers' patterns of
mobility and accommodation usage.

City-Wide Patterns

The complexity of the patterns found among my camp neighbours led
me to look more closely at the material available from the city's annual
counts and housing files. While limited as a source of information, these
sources confirmed that there was no straightforward link between camping and mobility or housing and 'settlement.'[6]

Six of the forty-one households recorded as 'camping' in 1986, for
example, had been parked at the same location two years earlier and in
some cases for much longer periods of time (i.e., up to seventeen years).
The figures for long-term stationary residence in trailers would in fact
have been higher but for the court proceedings against two of the larger
camps in the city, which had resulted in the relocation of thirteen families
in the months prior to the count. Most of these thirteen had been in their
respective camps for at least three years and in many cases considerably
longer.

The records for the group housing scheme meanwhile revealed that
while about half of those who had entered the scheme had remained

'settled' for a fairly long period (including those who had moved on to regular corporation housing), the other half had made more short-term use of the houses.[7] Although a pattern of short-term use was consistent with outsider's views of the group housing scheme as 'transitional' accommodation for Travellers who were preparing for permanent settlement in houses in regular estates, the assumption that those who left the project were simply not 'ready' for settlement meant that a pattern of mobility that entailed the short-term use of housing was not officially acknowledged.

The other form of transitional accommodation provided by the city were the corporation flats which were assigned to both non-Travellers and Traveller tenants alike. In the case of Travellers, city housing officials viewed granting tenancy as a first step toward permanent settlement in regular housing. Again, approximately half of those who entered the flats had remained 'settled' either in the flats themselves or in subsequent corporation housing. For the remainder the flats, like the group housing scheme, appeared to have served as more short-term, sometimes seasonal accommodation. One family in the camp where I was living, for example, had spent the winter before my arrival living in the flats before returning to the camp in the summer, and another left the camp in order to move into the flats, saying that this was only for the winter.[8]

By the early 1970s Travellers who had demonstrated their willingness to 'settle' by a period of residence in a transitional form of accommodation (e.g., tigeens, flats, and later the group housing scheme) were being offered regular corporation tenancies. Many Travellers that I spoke with were positive about these standard houses and were willing to temporarily put up with less desirable accommodation, such as the flats, in order to be later granted a tenancy.

Unlike the flats and group housing, houses in regular corporation estates were seen by outsiders as permanent rather than transitional accommodation for Travellers. There was a similar understanding among many Travellers who described entry into a regular corporation house as evidence of a decision to 'settle down.' The housing files supported this perception, revealing that most of the tenancies were long term.[9]

In several cases, however, 'housed' Travellers pursued short-term trailer travelling outside of the city while retaining their houses. Some also made it clear that their entry into housing was the result of a lack of options. An older woman, for example, described how her entry into a house in the early years of the settlement program had been in response to the repeated jailing of her husband for an inability to pay fines for camping. Similar pressures existed during the fieldwork period. One camping family faced with eviction, for example, agreed under severe pressure from the city to take a house even though, as the mother told me with frustration, they did not want to live in a house and would try to move out again.

Travel and accommodation histories, as well as the city counts and housing files, made it clear that there was no simple equation between 'travelling' and 'settlement' and particular forms of accommodation. Travellers living in various forms of housing were not necessarily 'settled,' while Travellers camping 'on the road' were not necessarily mobile. Travellers had in the past and were continuing to combine residence in housing and/or camping in trailers with diverse patterns of travelling and settlement.

Housing and Traveller Identity

As mentioned earlier, there was a presence of Travellers in houses in Galway City well before the settlement policy of the 1960s, and autobiographical and fieldwork accounts of parents and/or grandparents revealed that the experience of living in a house was not unusual during this earlier period. The status of those who had lived in houses prior to the introduction of the settlement policy, however, was sometimes ambiguous.

Some Travellers encountered during fieldwork, for example, described their own housed ancestors as 'settled' or as having married 'settled' people. One older woman living in a house first described her father and father's father to me as 'settled people,' but then added that 'there was still a little drop of the Traveller in them.' The description was then further augmented by her statement that 'they were still considered Travelling People but they were years settled.' There was a similar ambiguity in the claim by another woman that her own housed mother was not a 'real Traveller.' Despite the fact that 'her mother's father used to sell little ends and odds alright she wasn't the real Travelling People ... not the camping out life.' Some referred to families that had entered and stayed in housing in the city in the 1940s and 1950s as 'a different sort of Traveller,' while others suggested that they were not Travellers at all. Such apparent lack of consistency in identification may have represented attempts to 'fit' more fluid past identities into the present dichotomous categories of 'Traveller' and 'settled' people.

With the introduction of the settlement program the definition of who was and who was not an 'itinerant' became important to local authorities. While those living in houses prior to the adoption of the policy were not consistently labelled as 'tinkers' or 'itinerants,' those who were housed under the new policy were consistently labelled as such in order to demonstrate the city's progress in implementation of the program. The result was that some of those that the city identified as 'itinerants' in the 1970s had parents who, because they had entered housing at an earlier point, were never officially identified in this way. Official labels, however, sometimes contradicted popular understandings of these older individuals. In 1977 some of them were referred to as itinerants when non-Traveller tenants protested the housing of three new Traveller families in their area, claiming that their area had already 'done its share' because it had been housing such families since the 1930s.

The history of housing found among Travellers disrupts one of the premises of early settlement policy – that housing in and of itself would lead to settlement and that settlement, in turn, would lead to the 'absorption' of Travellers into the 'settled community.' By the 1980s a majority of Travellers were living in some form of housing – many for long periods of time – but they had not been 'absorbed.' In local newspaper reports there was increasing use of such terms as 'settled Travellers,' 'housed Travellers,' and even 'former Travellers' to refer to this population, but while the experience of long-term accommodation in housing shaped social relations in new ways, it did not necessarily result in a reduced experience of racism or loss of Traveller identity.

In both the group housing scheme and in the regular corporation estates there were identifiable clusters of closely related Traveller family units. Residential clusters of housed Travellers were partially facilitated by the actions of the city. In contrast to the 1960s, when it was argued that Travellers had to be housed apart from one another in order to encourage assimilation, by the 1980s housing officials sometimes argued that settlement and integration were more likely to be achieved if closely related Travellers were accommodated near one another. In some cases the result was the transfer of residential clusters en masse out of camps and into housing estates.

More commonly, however, residential clusters were created through a series of moves by individual Traveller households. Some Travellers, for example, would tell housing officials that they would only move off the road if they were allocated a house in a particular estate, close to other relatives. In other cases housed Travellers threatened to return to the road if they were not transferred to accommodation closer to family members. In such cases a limited degree of negotiating space was gained within the imposed housing program that allowed Travellers to recreate important co-residential relations with close kin and affines.

Most housed Travellers pursued the same kinds of economic activities as those in camps and from the outside the houses of Travellers in regular housing estates were often identified by the van and/or trailer parked in front. Some who had remained in housing for many years were criticized by others for downplaying their Traveller identity. As one Traveller said of another family in a housing estate, 'They've gone the way they wouldn't tell you they were Travellers. They've got that used to the house.' In other cases, however, it was clear that a Traveller identity was impossible to escape due to externally imposed categorization. Those who conducted the 1986 count of Travellers, for example, noted that four housed respondents who were approached indicated to the census taker that they 'did not wish to be referred to as Travellers.' Despite the recording of this preference the four households were none the less included in the 'Traveller' count.

One young woman suggested in an interview with me that those living in houses in fact had little choice but to be identified as Travellers. She pointed out that while she and her family had remained in a house for well over a decade (and were considered sufficiently integrated to receive little assistance from service workers), they continued to experience discrimination from non-Travellers.

> We're not supposed to be Travellers ... they say ... that we're not Travelling People, but how ... can we not be Travelling People when I just go out to [the local supermarket] ... and I mean I'm discriminated against ... we're still Travellers, we're equal to those on the road ... we're supposed to be different, but we don't feel any different.

The issue of the status of Travellers living in houses articulated with class-based struggles over Traveller accommodation. At a residents' and tenants' meeting held to address the issue of the provision of hardstands in the area, a member repeated the organization's position on hardstands: that it was opposed to the provision of a hardstand in the area because it had already accommodated 'more than its fair share' of Travellers.

A young Traveller woman in attendance objected to the criticism of housed Travellers that was implicit in this argument and challenged the chairperson by asking: 'Do you call me a Travelling person?' The chairperson, clearly unsure of how this young woman wanted to be classified, suggested: 'If you were born [in an estate in the area] we're not classing you as a Traveller.' To this, however, the young woman angrily retorted: '[then] you say we're *not* Travellers?' The chairperson, in confusion, tried to redirect the discussion back to the hardstand issue by telling her that: 'nobody is objecting to people [i.e., Travellers] in houses. We 're objecting to a hardstand. Never has it been stated at any stage or any meeting that there is any objection to people in houses, or that they are not wanted in houses.'

While the chairperson's comments were intended to assuage the feelings of the young housed Traveller woman, the comments led to an interjection by a supporter of the Workers' Party who demanded to know why the Association was now suggesting that, while it was opposed to a hardstand, it was not opposed to further housing of Travellers in the area. The implication was that the Association was only concerned with the interests of those non-Travellers living in private estates near the proposed hardstand, and not with those of non-Traveller tenants who were already housed beside Travellers. This in turn led to other speakers blaming the housed Travellers for problems such as vandalism. One speaker stated: 'I think everyone will agree that they're just not integrating into society because of the amount of them that are located here.'

The problems involved in asserting a distinctive identity as housed Travellers without playing into the hands of those opposed to further provision of services were also apparent at a Traveller Committee meeting. When one of the non-Traveller organizers mentioned that some non-Traveller residents and tenants were opposed to a hardstand because of the number of Travellers already housed in the area, one Traveller man who lived in a trailer (but whose parents lived in a house) responded with frustration:

What annoys me about that, and it really riles me up, is ... that how many thousand settled people live over there in those houses? Now, any Travellers that are in those houses, are paying their rent, their electricity ... They're getting nothing free, they're paying and they are keeping themselves in them [the houses]. Now, they should be put down [referred to] as settled people when they are in the houses. [Non-Traveller settled people] should not be saying, well, we have so many itinerants in such a house and such a house [as a reason not to provide hardstands].

The suggestion by this Traveller that those who lived in houses should be 'put down [i.e., identified] as settled people,' however, was immediately opposed by a housed Traveller present at the meeting.

> Housed Traveller: I don't think that's a very good idea because I'm in a house, but I'm a Traveller.

> First Traveller: OK you're a Traveller, but you're still in the house there. The man next door to you, we'll say he's a country man [a settled person] ... aren't you paying the same rent as him for the house? Why should the settled people come along and say: 'Oh he's an itinerant, there's another Traveller.

> Housed Traveller: But if you were living in a house tomorrow morning, which would you rather be known as? A settled person, or a Traveller that went into a house?

> First Traveller: I'd like to be known as a Traveller ... but do you see? When you're in a house, they shouldn't be coming along saying they already have so many when you want a site. What they want to do is discriminate.

The particular position of housed Travellers in the local politics of provision for Travellers was obscured by the focus in the late 1980s on camping families and the pressing need for hardstands. As the participation of some housed Travellers in the Traveller committee suggested, however, the issues facing those in camps were not easily separated from the issues facing those in houses due to the movement in and out of houses and the shared experience of anti-Traveller racism by those in both camps and housing estates.

Mobility, Accommodation, and the Domestic Cycle

One of the reasons for the interest and involvement of some housed Travellers in the mobilization around the provision of hardstands was a pattern linking housing and camping to different phases of the domestic cycle. The 1986 Traveller count revealed that twenty-one of the forty-one camping households at the time were headed by young adults in their twenties, with an additional eleven headed by adults in their thirties. A majority of the households 'on the road,' then, were younger, while older Travellers were more likely to be in some form of housing. The pattern was clear in the camp where I lived. Of the fourteen family units that spent time in the camp during my research period twelve were headed by couples in their twenties or thirties.[10]

Many of the younger couples living in camps had spent part or all of their childhood in houses where their parents had been 'settled,' but had left to camp at marriage. The movement of young people out of housing upon marriage had attracted concern as early as 1978, when city officials had noted that Traveller newlyweds were moving into camps and a report stated that young couples 'should be housed as early as possible in their married lives so as to avoid risk of their acquiring anti-social patterns of behaviour' [i.e., camping] (CT, 26 May 1978: 20).

While the scheme of renting priorities in the city was amended in order to give young Traveller couples high priority, the 1986 count revealed that, of eleven newlywed Traveller couples in the city, eight were camping in trailers. The relatively inexpensive life on the road was a major factor that led young couples to camping. A trailer which could be bought and resold was viewed as a better investment than paying rent for a flat or a house. When married couples had come from families in different parts of the country, the decision to live in a trailer was also linked to an expectation and/or experience of movement between the wives' and husbands' people.

While most younger couples were not very interested in permanent housing, some used housing on a short-term basis. Such usage, however, ran the risk of alienating local service providers, who tended to be most sympathetic toward those who indicated their desire to settle by staying in housing. In order to avoid jeopardizing future chances for housing or other services, many younger couples preferred to remain in trailers in camps rather than enter housing temporarily. As this consideration suggests, young people who had entered trailers at marriage had not rejected housing as an option. On the contrary, most emphasized that, while they did not want houses now, they would later on when their families had expanded and the oldest children were teenagers.

The reasons offered for moving into a house at a later stage of the domestic cycle were various. Older Travellers often explained to me that they had done so because of their 'crowd of kids.' Traveller women pointed to the importance of such basic services as running water, toilets, and electricity to a large family, and it was also suggested that living in a house made it easier to ensure that children went to school. Some adults also raised particular concerns about adolescents in camps. One comment was that teen-aged girls and boys should have separate sleeping quarters and that because this necessitated at least two trailers (an expensive proposition and one requiring adequate camping space) the housing option became more attractive.

There were, however, disadvantages to abandoning trailer living. One was the procedure whereby Travellers had to spend time in either the flats or the group housing scheme before gaining a tenancy in a regular corporation estate. The flats were particularly unpopular, being described as too 'close' – i.e., allegedly overheated – a feature which was said to cause illness (see also G. Gmelch 1977: 148; Okely 1983: 96). They were also considered to be too small for larger families. The units of the group housing scheme were also considered to be cramped, and, like some of the camps, the 'village' was viewed as being dominated by particular Traveller families, making it less attractive to those who were 'strangers.' Many of my neighbours, for example, suggested that they would be too 'lonely' in this scheme without close relatives.

Along with the specific limitations of these forms of interim accommodation, the rent payments in both cases made them more expensive than trailer-living. One mother of nine children told me that she wanted to move into a house soon because it was becoming more difficult to look after the children in the camp. She described how such a move would require her to budget well in order to keep up with the weekly rent payments in either the group housing scheme or the flats. Having demonstrated her ability to make the payments, she hoped she would then be offered a house in a regular corporation estate – which was her real goal. Once she had this house, she suggested, then she would 'settle down.'

While camping was most attractive for younger families and housing was more characteristic of middle-aged adults with teen-aged children, this operated in conjunction with various other factors which meant that there were exceptions to the general pattern. In the case of some middle-aged couples with teenagers who were living in camps a crucial consideration appeared to be the ability to gain access to space for two or more caravans.

One older Traveller man who was camped beside the group housing project, for example, was reported as describing how he had left his small house in the 'village' because it was not big enough for his large family. By camping he could have two caravans which, he pointed out, provided more space (*Connacht Sentinel*, 7 January 1986). In the camp where I lived a middle-aged couple also had two large trailers, which provided gender-segregated sleeping room for their teen-aged children as well as an increased communal area for visiting, watching television, cooking, and eating.

The few elderly Travellers who continued to camp in the city did so among married children. One older woman who was part of a cluster of closely related families that had been housed together in an estate described to me how they had tried to 'keep themselves in it' and had in fact stayed eight months in total – 'not like some Travellers who are in and out' – but the entire cluster eventually returned to camping because she claimed the houses were too 'close' and threatened her physical health.

An older couple in the camp where I lived were the centre of an ever-changing residential cluster of married sons, daughters, nephews, nieces, and grandchildren. The desire of older Travellers to be among their married children (who were more likely to be camping) appeared to have been the cause of some movement out of houses by elderly Travellers. In four cases recorded by the 1986 count older Traveller couples had recently left their houses after many years of 'settlement' to join married children living elsewhere.

The Traveller Committee, Hardstands, and the Politics of Culture

The movement out of housing, especially in the case of younger married couples, explained why many Travellers living in houses were interested in and supportive of the efforts of the Traveller Committee to lobby for hardstands. As one member of the committee pointed out to me:

> You've got to, when you get married, pack up, buy a caravan and then move into it ... when your children get grown up, well, you might say, well, I'll settle now. But the way it is now with the young couple, they've no choice but to go back out into a caravan and there's no place for them to go. I mean do they expect the fathers and mothers to keep these couples in the houses with them? And then they're coming along and saying, well, you've got lodgers ... They're not making any accommodation for them, there's no sites.

One Traveller man living in another camp also told me, 'I think even the housed Travellers are beginning to realize that even their own families sooner or later have to come back on to the road,' and suggested that this explained why some of the older housed Travellers were involved in the Committee. That such involvement was risky, however, was suggested by one man who expressed concern that if the city knew of his participation in the committee it might take away his house.

The impetus for the formation of the Traveller Committee was the attack on a particular camp in the area of Rahoon, but it was the larger issue of hardstand provision across the city that was addressed. At the time there was no formal representation of Travellers in the local decision-making structures of the city, and the formation of the committee represented a significant attempt to create space for a Traveller 'voice' in the debate over the provision of Traveller accommodation. The majority of the Committee members were Travellers from three different camps within the city, although as mentioned there were some from houses.

The 'spokesperson' for the Committee was Margaret Sweeney, a Traveller woman who claimed to represent twenty-seven to thirty 'long-term city families' who were camping in trailers and who did not want to move into permanent accommodation. Non-Travellers included members of the Galway Civil Rights Group as well as service providers, who provided some of the initial impetus and organizational expertise for the Committee.

The formation of a committee with a city-wide focus was unprecedented and contrasted with the independent and separate strategies pursued only a few weeks before, when the residents of the two camps facing eviction had in fact distanced themselves from one another in public. For example, one Traveller had commented: 'We're a different crowd to the Travellers there, that had horses and everything else. We cannot speak for them people. We are a group on our own – non-drinkers.'

The primary goal of the Traveller Committee was to pressure local politicians into implementing the existing agreement in principle to build several hardstands within the city and a 'transient' site on the outskirts. Toward this end, the Committee attempted to mobilize public opinion in favour of hardstands, and to win over those politicians who were delaying action. Several high-profile events were organized, including pickets of the city council building, marches, the distribution of flyers, and public speeches. A number of months after the committee had been formed additional publicity was generated when Margaret Sweeney decided to run as an independent candidate in the national election of February 1987, becoming the second Traveller in the country to stand for public office.[11]

The archival record reveals earlier attempts at organization among Travellers in the area, including what was described as a 'votes for itinerants' campaign in the 1960s (CT, 26 March 1966: 6), liaison with the Itinerant Settlement Committee of the 1960s, marches to support the 'village' plan in the 1970s, and representation from Galway on the 1983 Travelling People Review Body.[12] One older Traveller woman who had been involved in earlier struggles over sites and housing in the 1970s recalled, however, that Travellers had little voice and that she had repeatedly challenged non-Traveller 'spokespersons' to let Travellers speak for themselves. The emergence of the Traveller Committee represented an attempt by Travellers to enter the public debate over Traveller issues in the city.

The formation of the Traveller Committee was path-breaking, but its entry into local politics was marked by a largely pragmatic strategy. Those involved felt that, given the pressing need for secure camping sites and the relative powerlessness of Travellers vis-à-vis other constituencies in the city, the focus of the Committee should be on lobbying for the implementation of the existing city plan for hardstand provision rather than the proposal of any modifications or alternatives. The decision not to challenge the specifics of the existing hardstand plan, while perhaps a realistic assessment of the capacity of the committee to affect political decision-making, caused some Travellers to have reservations about the Committee's efforts.

One of the striking aspects of the Traveller Committee was its acceptance of the dominant discourse of settlement. Members of the committee were convinced that the key to hardstand provision in the city was to persuade the public and city council members that Travellers would remain stationary in the proposed sites. Thus, while many Travellers viewed hardstands as necessary for the maintenance of geographic mobility, the Traveller Committee emphasized that the provision of hardstands was consistent with a policy of Traveller settlement.

One member of the Committee, for example, stated that while a Dublin Travellers' Committee of the time was called Mincéir Misli or 'Traveller Go,' the Galway City Travellers wanted the opposite, i.e., 'Traveller Stay.' This statement had a great deal of local resonance given the history of harassment and evictions of camping Travellers but did not reflect the realities of Traveller mobility, and some wider Traveller support was alienated by the strategy.[13]

The Traveller Committee also promoted the notion, originally proposed by the city, that hardstands would only be provided for a limited number of identifiable 'long-term city families.' Because one of the most frequent arguments against the provision of services to Travellers was the claim that this would encourage an 'influx' of other Travelling People into the area, the committee felt that non-Travellers needed to be reassured on this point. Margaret Sweeney told members of the Traveller Committee that:

> the [settled] people have nothing at all against the [Travelling] people who are within the city for so many years. What they're totally against is the Travellers who come and go. They come and go, they raise trouble, they do things wrong and then we are left there to be blamed. The first thing the people say is: 'well look, you let them in there,' and they assume then they're your relations. [But] you don't know who they were or what they were, they came, and they went. You minded your business and you didn't question them, but the people understand that you did. They think that you're all the one. (Traveller Committee meeting, 29 October 1986)

The committee attempted to counteract non-Traveller fears of an 'influx' by emphasizing that hardstands would only be provided for a limited number of 'long-term city families' and by publicly advocating the provision of barriers on the sites to make the entry of 'strangers' impossible. In addition, it promoted the city plan to provide a 'pull-on/pull-off site' outside the city for 'transient' Travellers. Thus, part of its strategy involved an acceptance of outsiders' categories based on geographic jurisdictions (e.g., 'Galwegian Travellers' versus 'strangers') and geographic mobility (e.g., 'settled Travellers' versus 'transients'). 'Long-term city families,' it was argued, had the right to be provided with hardstands by virtue of the length of their trailer residence in the area.

This argument appealed to those Travellers who already had parking spaces in the city and were anxious about pressure from other Travellers. In the camp where I was living, for example, there was constant concern over the possible arrival of 'strangers' from outside or inside the city. As one woman put it, when you are camping 'you don't know who is going to come in on top of you.' This concern had led some of those living in the camp to ask city officials to erect a barrier to restrict entry to the camp, and shortly before my arrival the city had responded by placing large boulders along the road, thereby reducing the area for parking trailers. The city also, however, later facilitated the move into the camp of three families that it had evicted from another camp. The action of the city in unilaterally imposing these three families dramatized the lack of control over land by those already in the camp.

While my neighbours were anxious to ensure their security of tenure and saw hardstands as one way to do this, there was concern about eligibility for hardstands being based on 'long-term' residence in the city.

Within the camp, for example, the proposed plan for hardstands created tensions as families assessed the relative strength of their claim based on this criterion.

As discussed earlier, many Travellers had moved in and out of the city at various times, and more had close relatives at present living elsewhere who planned to return at a later date. As a result, there was anxiety about definitions and calculations of 'city-families.' At one Traveller Committee meeting a man mentioned that his brother was coming back to the city after an absence and should be considered within the category of 'Galway City Travellers' who would be eligible for hardstands if and when they were provided. Another Traveller replied testily that because this individual was not currently in the city, he would not be eligible for a spot. The first man then retorted that if his brother was not entitled to a parking space, then he probably was not either, because over the course of fifteen years of camping in the city, he had often gone away for a couple of months to his in-laws, just as his brother had done.

The view expressed by another Traveller man was that the Committee should not say anything about other Travellers coming into the city because 'the Travellers coming in are entitled to a place like anybody else.' This statement drew on the experience of mobility familiar to many Travellers, but also on a strong Traveller cultural ideology that 'the road was free' and 'anyone could pull in anywhere.' Discussion of restrictions and claims based on temporal and geographical exclusiveness challenged this deeply held value.

The Committee was dominated, however, by those who argued that hardstands would only be provided if the politicians and the public were convinced that these would be used by 'long-term city families' and that there would be no 'influx' of Travellers into the city. As one supporter of this position put it: 'If we are thinking of the Travellers who are coming and going to Galway that is no good. We've got to think of ourselves.' The decision to limit the work of the Committee to the interests of those presently defined as 'city families' not only weakened support for the Committee within the city, but it worked against the development of political networks with Travellers elsewhere in the country.

Emphasizing its role as advocating exclusively for 'long-term city families,' the Committee also argued that hardstands should only be provided for those *presently* living in camps rather than for those who might wish to leave houses or flats in the future. Although the Committee was aware that some housed Travellers were interested in moving to hardstands if these were provided, Committee members considered that such a movement out of housing would be viewed as a backward step by politicians and the general public, and would, as a result, undermine support for the hardstand plan. Thus the Committee reiterated that the priority was to provide for *currently* camping households. Again, the strategy weakened possible support among the majority of housed Travellers in the city – although, as mentioned previously, some Travellers living in houses were involved in committee activities.

Political pressure to 'spread [the Travellers] evenly throughout the city' had resulted in a city plan which called for four or five hardstands, each of which would accommodate six or seven households, and which would be located within different city wards. Again the Traveller Committee's decision not to contest this particular arrangement created some tension as such specifications bore little relationship to Travellers' own existing residential clusters of related families.

As already indicated, kinship-based groupings were apparent in both housing and camps. At the broadest level particular families were associated with one of two distinct 'sides' of the city, and within these 'sides' there were more localized kin-based clusters in both housing estates and camps. In the case of camps, while Travellers emphasized that no single household or group of households 'owned' or had exclusionary control over the parking areas, the existing configuration of clusters was the result of some kin-based clusters successfully holding on to particular areas through time. As one elderly man explained, he would not leave a particular camp until he died because his continued presence ensured that his married children (many of whom were living elsewhere) had ongoing access to the space when they needed it.

In the context of increasingly limited and insecure access to camping land in the city it was the more powerful families that had managed to ensure sufficient access to land to establish kin-based clusters, and Travellers without close ties to those already living in these areas were unlikely to enter over the objections of the established residents.

In an effort to have some control over the process of allocating hardstand spaces to Travellers within the imposed spatial and numerical constraints of the city's hardstand plan, Margaret Sweeney had offered to assist the city in determining which families should be together. The Traveller Committee's proposed involvement in the re-organization of residential clusters, however, threatened existing relations. The prospect of city control (assisted by the Traveller Committee) in determining priority of access to particular hardstands directly threatened those who had established long-term claims to particular parking spots, and Margaret Sweeney's admission that conforming with the existing city plan would require larger clusters of related families to be divided and smaller clusters amalgamated increased the degree of concern.

The result of the Traveller Committee's adoption of a pragmatic strategy of publicly accepting, rather than contesting, the general concept as well as the specifics of the existing city plan for hardstands was a loss of manœuvring room and some wider Traveller support. Where the Committee did achieve a degree of successful challenge to dominant discourse, however, was in the development and promotion of a positive Traveller identity and culture. Unlike settlement advocates who presented the Traveller way of life as something problematic to be eliminated in the course of 'integration,' the Traveller Committee presented Traveller identity and culture as worthy of defence and celebration.

In speeches and interviews the Committee spokesperson argued that Travellers were entitled to hardstands on the basis of a particular history and tradition. The argument was extended further in the claim that this tradition was that of the 'true Ireland.' Travellers, according to Margaret Sweeney, were entitled to live in caravans on serviced sites because their distinctive way of life, culture, and tradition represented the essence of Irishness.

> I think that the Travelling people are the true Irish people of Ireland and no Travelling person should be ashamed of what we are. We should be proud of it because we came from real Irish people. Our ancestors fought for this country and they had to leave their homes just the same as I'm sure some of yours had to years ago ... Now is the time for the politicians to stand up and realise that we are Irish people. We have a right to be in this country. We have a right to say where we want to live. We have a right to live the way we want to live and it's not up to anybody else to plan how we should live. (Margaret Sweeney, University College Galway, 14 October 1986)

Some months later, at a meeting of tenants and residents for the area where she was camped, Margaret Sweeney in her capacity as spokesperson also stated:

> We are the real Irish. We're as Irish as they come. I've no need to be ashamed because I am a Traveller and I'm not going to let you or anyone else in this town take over and try to tell me how to live. I'm living right and natural

and if I want a hardstand then I'm going to go out there and fight for them. (Combined Tenants' and Residents' Association, West Ward, 10 February 1987)

The argument represented a crucial challenge to dominant discourse in its embrace of a positive Traveller cultural identity. Consistent with the arguments of the Traveller Committee, this Traveller identity was linked to a form of accommodation usage, i.e., 'trailer living,' rather than mobility, i.e., 'travelling.' At one university meeting, Margaret Sweeney was asked to elaborate on this position:

Q: You say you've lived in that site ... for the last 15 years and you don't want to leave it. Why would you still call yourself a Traveller?
A: Well I was born a Traveller and I want to remain as a Traveller. Let's put it this way, if I never travelled I was born a Traveller. My father and mother, my grandparents, all them were Travellers, and I want to bring my children up under the name of a Traveller ... I'm not one bit ashamed of being a Traveller. I'm as proud as any Irish person in Ireland, and I don't think I have anything to be ashamed of by being a Traveller ... I wish to be known as a Traveller for the length I live ... I've no wish to travel, all I'm asking for is a proper serviced site in which we can live our lives in the way we want to live. (University College Galway, 14 October 1986)

Later in a television interview the host asked a similar question, and in her response Margaret Sweeney linked Traveller identity to a rejection of houses:

I feel ... a lot of people are under the opinion in this country, that the only way for Travelling People to live is in a house, and I think this is wrong. I think that Travelling People – that's the culture behind them ... were brought up where a lot of Travelling people travelled all over the country. Then Travelling people settled into cities, their children were going to school, but they still didn't wish to live in houses. In fact, I know Travelling people who are in houses for the past 15–20 years, and they have said to me recently, only for my family, I wouldn't be in it. So they never really settled, it was because of the reasons of the family that they settled into it. (*Hanly's People*, 12 January 1987)

While the above response downplayed a direct relationship between trailer living and 'travelling,' a more ambiguous relationship was suggested elsewhere in the interview when Margaret Sweeney stated:

> Travelling is your life, if you're born a Traveller ... it's in your blood. You
> love to travel. Even if you live in a house, [you're] always [thinking] 'when I
> was in the caravan, I did such and such a thing – I was happy in it,' no
> matter how many years you live in a house. (*Hanly's People*, 12 January
> 1987)

Even in this case, however, it was trailer-living that was being highlighted as the essence of a Traveller identity, while 'travelling' was more
tenuously invoked. The focus on trailer-living as a basis of Traveller
cultural identity was one that resonated widely with other Travellers
despite the reality that a majority of the Travellers living in Galway City
were living in houses and flats.

Travellers in the camp where I lived followed the activities of the
Traveller Committee with interest, but most remained uninvolved in any
of the political activities. Some who were concerned about the city's
hardstand plan found justifications for their fears in some of the statements of Traveller Committee members, while others expressed pessi-
mism about the ability of the Committee to influence the actions of the
city.

Several people suggested to me that the members of the Traveller
Committee were, in fact, only 'in it for themselves' – attempting to derive
benefits for their respective households by developing ties with powerful non-Travellers. Similar criticism was made of other Travellers across
Ireland who had emerged at various points as spokespersons for Travellers. The characteristically 'individualist' logic was expressed by one
successful Traveller man who refused to make a financial donation to the
Committee, and said: 'What's that got to do with me? I got a house years
ago through my own efforts.'

The Committee spokesperson in turn voiced frustration with the lack
of support from Travellers, commenting to me that Travellers 'aren't
loyal and won't come together.' The reality of division among Travellers
contrasted with the dangerous pan-Traveller political capacity imagined
by some non-Travellers, including one housewife who anxiously informed me that Margaret Sweeney would do well in the elections because 'they'll [Travellers] all come in to register and vote for her and the
town will be full of tinkers.'

Much of the Committee's energy in the end did not go into organizing
Travellers, but rather into trying to develop support among non-Travel-

lers. Along with approaches to city politicians and officials, the Labour party and the Trades Council were addressed by Committee members. Invitations to attend Traveller Committee meetings were also issued to tenants' and residents' associations in the city. Such efforts, however, had little success. One attempt at joint action between the Traveller Committee and a tenants' and residents' association dissolved when tensions between those living in the estate and Travellers in a nearby camp erupted into threats and confrontation between the two groups (*City Tribune*, 28 April 1987: 1).

The actions of the Traveller Committee revealed the constraints on political agency in the context of oppression. In their attempt to reproduce a distinctive identity and way of life, especially trailer living and travelling, Travellers were limited by their powerlessness. The struggle for hardstands was as a result conducted largely within the constraints of an imposed dominant discourse and practice of settlement that did not respond to the complexities of Traveller mobility and accommodation patterns. Just as the struggles over Traveller settlement revealed the 'settled community' to be internally divided by class, so, too, the attempt to organize a Traveller Committee often made existing divisions among Travellers more salient. The Committee, however, revealed that some Travellers were actively engaged in trying to secure and improve the position of camping Travellers and challenging anti-Traveller racism by redefining Traveller identity and culture in positive ways.

Although the Traveller Committee did not achieve its goal of hardstands immediately, a limited number of sites were constructed a few years later. The provision of the official camping sites was a response to many pressures, including the lobbying efforts of the Traveller Committee. While inadequate to demand, the provision of hardstands represented a partial shift toward official recognition of a cultural alternative in the area of accommodation.

Chapter 5

Work, Class, and the Politics of Culture

Some accounts of Traveller history have pointed to an alleged occupational obsolescence brought on by changes in the wider Irish political economy as the source of anti-Traveller racism. Past anti-Travellerism, however, as we have seen, sometimes took the form of allegations that Travellers' were enjoying an illegitimate degree of economic success. Such apparently competing accounts are also present in Travellers' own understandings of the relationship between the past and present Traveller economy and experiences of racism.

After presenting some of my research to a largely Traveller audience in Dublin discussion turned to these issues. Some Travellers made reference to a past of Traveller economic utility and positive relations with non-Travellers and contrasted this with the experience of a loss of economic niche and intensified racism of the present. Others, however, reversed this scenario by emphasizing the vitality of the contemporary Traveller economy and improving relations with the 'settled community,' which they juxtaposed with the poverty and persecution of the past.

In this chapter I work toward a reconciliation of these apparently contradictory accounts through an examination of the past and present Traveller economy. The discussion requires drawing upon feminist and other scholarship that broadens the understanding of 'work' to include not only formal paid employment but also various forms of informal and domestic work (Pahl 1984; Leonard 1995) – a literature that by emphasizing the significance of the activities pursued by Traveller men, women, and children illuminates more clearly how a distinctive Traveller economy has persisted in the context of a changing Irish political economy.

While emphasizing the resilience of a Traveller economy I also draw attention to the ways in which Travellers' social relations of work and exchange produce and reproduce social inequalities of class, gender, and generation. Reserving a more detailed discussion of gender and generation for subsequent chapters, I focus here on the processes through which class-based divisions among Travellers are created and simultaneously obscured and legitimated by constructions of Traveller cultural identity that emphasize economic self-sufficiency. Archival and ethnographic material is then used to illuminate the dynamics of both resiliency and stratification.

Tinsmithing and Multioccupationality

Discussions of the Traveller economy have frequently focused on an occupational history of tinsmithing, which included the creation and repair of many domestic and agricultural items. The belief that the Travellers were previously tinsmiths has often been 'proven' by etymologies that collapse the two meanings of 'tinker' as (1) Traveller, and (2) the occupational category of tinsmith. Thus, for example, it has been argued that the term 'tinker' was derived from the sound of hammering on metal (i.e., 'tink') and that therefore 'tinkers' were formerly tinsmiths (G. Gmelch 1977: 8).

This folk etymology has served to perpetuate a particular view of Travellers' occupational history but Traveller's own etymologies of the word 'tinker,' recorded in the 1960s and 1970s, did not emphasize tinsmithing as much as occupational flexibility and diversity. A Traveller was quoted by Court, an American folklorist, as saying: 'Well, a Tinker is a man who does every class of job, and he's tinking on every job, tinking on every job. It comes along that that's how we got the title [sic]' (Court 1985: 88). In this etymology (dependent upon the fact that 'think' and 'tink' are often homophones in Irish English), Travellers' cleverness as 'thinkers' is emphasized rather than the occupational specialization of the tinsmith. A similar Traveller account was recorded by S. Gmelch in the 1970s: 'A tinker was a man years ago who thought of a hundred ways of surviving ... This was the real tinker, not just the tinsmith. He was a better survivor than the rest' (S. Gmelch 1975: 28). In these accounts from male Travellers, the economic ingenuity and self-reliance of Travellers was emphasized rather than a particular occupational identity.

A focus on tinsmithing has nevertheless been central to outsiders' claims of a disappearing Traveller economy for over a century. For example, the 1896 entry in the Oxford English Dictionary referred derisively to tinkering as only the 'ostensible trade' of the tinkers and implied that they in fact survived through theft, while at the turn of the last century Lady Gregory was told by country people in County Galway that 'some of [the tinkers] that do smiths work are middling decent ... but the most of them have no trade but to be going to fairs and doing tricks' (1974: 94). In 1925 it was also suggested in the local press of Galway City that the days of the 'travelling tinsmith' were over:

> These nomads ... are in many cases tinsmiths, more popularly known as 'tinkers,' who make a 'tinny' sound as they mend pots, kettles, and pans. But massed manufacture and the cheap standardised article have in great measure restricted the possibilities of employment for the travelling tin-smith, so that many of these wandering bands live by a combination of peddling and begging. (*CT*, 28 March 1925: 5)

A declining demand for tinsmithing was central to outsiders' claims of Travellers' occupational obsolescence. A 1959 editorial in the Galway press provides an example of the argument that this decline had trans-formed the formerly legitimate tinker 'craftsman' into an illegitimate and parasitical 'nuisance.'

> The Irish Census returns show an increase in the number of tinsmiths and sheet metal workers in this country but it is obvious to everyone that the itinerant tinsmith is almost no more. The craftsman who mended pots, kettles, and pans has virtually disappeared from the roads. On the other hand there has been no fall in the number of tinkers of the type usually in mind when that word is used. They are on every road and a nuisance in every town. (*CT*, 29 August 1959: 8)

The demand for and decline of tinsmithing, however, varied through time and across regions. The editorial of 1925 cited above, as well as an account of tinkers in Wexford, for example, suggested that enamel buck-ets and basins had eliminated the rural demand for tinware before the Second World War (Anon 1937: 4), but Patrick Stokes (in Court 1985: 109), who travelled mainly in the west of Ireland, described how war-time demand had to be met by making buckets out of scrap metal due to a lack of tinplate supply. Bridget Murphy (in Court 1985: 76) also described continuing high demand for tinware in post-war Wicklow, and respond-ents for the Irish Folklore Commission in the early 1950s referred to Traveller men making and repairing tinware that was cheaper than that available in the shops (IFC 1952: 1256:18, 31). Traveller men in my own fieldwork area described being employed on a piece-work basis by shops that provided the materials and orders for tinware during the 1950s and 1960s.

Regardless of the timing of its decline, what is more significant is that the historical record clearly reveals that the male trade of tinsmithing was never the sole source of support for Traveller families. As early as the end of the nineteenth century, for example, Sampson had noted that the tinkers were involved in tinsmithing, but were also dealing in calves and asses, counterfeit coining, fortune-telling, and 'thieving' (Sampson 1890). Subsequent descriptions also emphasized the different occupations pursued by Travellers as a collectivity.

By the 1930s the folklorist MacGréine was suggesting that the 'tinkers' or 'travellers' could be subdivided into three classes according to occupational specialization – tinsmiths, hawkers, and dealers in asses and horses (1931: 171). In the 1950s McGrath was offering a similar tripartite division of Traveller families into those who were 'horse blockers [dealers],' tinsmiths, and 'ordinary travelling folk' (including chimney sweeps). These descriptions, however, also made it clear that individuals and family units were multioccupational and that women (and children) were active participants in a Traveller family work strategy. McGrath, for instance, described both the range of activities pursued by men and the additional peddling activities of women:

Most of the men-folk follow the art of 'tangling' (buying and selling horses before the fair) [and] many of them are Tinsmiths and umbrella men in their own right. The women sell anything from paper flowers, to little statues, and of course mothballs and studs, fancy pieces of lace, and approaching the season of Christmas 'Moore's almanac.' (McGrath 1955: 23)

A non-Traveller account collected by the Irish Folklore Commission in the early 1950s also described how 'the women travel the locality selling tin cans, saucepans, etc., which are made by the men. They also sell or barter small articles, collar studs, pins, combs, picture frames, wire files, etc. – also asking for a charity (telling of all the prayers they will say for their benefactors), milk, "mate" [meat], flour, tea, sugar being the most requested' (IFC 1952: 1256:44). Autobiographical accounts also document women's importance in generating income as well as providing the bulk of the subsistence needs, making it clear that their work was not just an adjunct to adult male activities, but was often the mainstay of the Traveller family economy (Gmelch 1986: 52–3; Maher 1972: 11, 57).

In the early part of the century many of the goods peddled by Travellers were made by Travellers out of natural resources. Along with tinware George Gmelch lists such items as paper and wooden flowers, reed baskets, straw brooms, horsehair brushes, wooden clothes pegs, and feather fishing lures (G. Gmelch 1977: 18). By the post-war period, however, the majority of the items hawked by Travellers were being bought from wholesalers. The shift from peddling items of their own manufacture to items purchased from wholesalers (known as 'swag') represented greater commoditization of the Irish and Traveller economy, but non-commodified exchanges such as barter and begging remained important.

It was the capacity for barter that made exchanges with Travellers possible for more subsistence-based and poorer farming households in the west. Traveller Nan Donohoe's description of peddling in Connemara reveals that the rural folk were accustomed to exchanging food and turf for the store-bought wares of the tinkers (Gmelch 1986: 124–5). Likewise, a Traveller woman told me during fieldwork how 'the women in those days [the 1950s] had the job of selling the wares that the men would make. They'd sell them for a few shillings or they would exchange them for food. If the house didn't have the money, they would swop the can or the bucket or whatever it may be, in exchange for some type of food.'

These descriptions suggest that exchanges with Travellers were one way in which poorer non-Traveller households attempted to ensure their own economic survival, and the importance of such opportunities underscores the need to recognize the existence of class-differentiated attitudes toward Travellers. While the propertied complained about trespassing on their land, less well-off households were more likely to welcome the arrival of Travellers as providers of geographically and economically accessible goods and services – as some of the Travellers' defenders in the Dáil suggested.

In the post-war period Travellers met many of their own subsistence needs through barter and begging, but as their wares shifted from handmade crafts to storebought 'swag' they needed cash to reinvest in goods for peddling. One way in which cash was earned was through the collection of 'refuse' items (e.g., rags, feathers, horsehair, scrap metal, bottles, etc.) from householders and the resale of these items to urban-based dealers. Sometimes Travellers delivered their items to these dealers directly; in other cases, the dealer would drive a large lorry around to the camps in order to buy the materials.[1]

In Galway City, Travellers were described as selling rags as early as 1926 (*CT*, 4 December 1926: 7), and a later reference indicates that bottles and feathers, as well as rags, were being collected and resold to a 'general dealer' in the city (*CT*, 8 June 1940: 5). By the 1940s this dealer was reportedly also buying scrap metal and horsehair (*CT*, 9 March 1946: 5). The importance of dealing in recyclable goods appears to have increased during World War II, when many items were not available or were rationed, and continued to grow thereafter. The increased reliance on dealing in refuse items is supported by accounts from non-Travellers in the fieldwork region.

> While camping in any district the men tinkers make cans, tin jugs, etc., and their women go through the villages selling the cans and begging ... the men tinkers also travel through the villages mending pots, pans, cans, buckets, lamps, umbrellas ... they ask for some hay for their ass or horses, *horse hair, old iron, broken pots, ovens*. (IFC 1952: 1256:56) [my emphasis]

An observer from County Mayo noted in the early 1950s that 'more and more [Travellers] today are making a living as buyers of feathers and other junk ... as dealers in horses and asses, [and as] collectors of bottles and scrap' (IFC 1952: 1256:66).

Travellers also provided for some of their subsistence needs directly through self-provisioning – i.e., through rabbit-hunting with dogs, raising goats for milk, fishing, gathering firewood and turf for cooking and heating, and collecting grass and hay for horses (see Court 1985: 95–6; Joyce and Farmar 1985: 11; Sandford 1975). Sometimes this self-provisioning work was combined with work for exchange; rabbit skins, for example, were sold to dealers and, as already mentioned, natural resources were gathered and transformed into commodities such as brooms and fish lures which could be sold.

While the economic activities described so far were organized by the family unit, Travellers were not strangers to casual wage labour. Both men and women worked as agricultural labourers in England and Scotland during the early part of the century, and there was a substantial migration to England to work as labourers on construction sites by the late 1950s (Gmelch and Gmelch 1985: 289). Travellers also worked as agricultural labourers in Ireland itself (Court 1985: 98–100). A western respondent to the Irish Folklore Commission commented: 'Of recent years groups of tinkers take occasional farm jobs (as piece-work) such as pulling an acre of beet or picking potatoes but will not work a full day' (IFC 1952: 256: 1256:44).

An article in the local press a number of years later referred more positively to Travellers providing much needed labour in the region:

> Tinkers, the 'menace' as they have so often been called by farmers, ap-
> peared in a new role in many parts of Roscommon last week when they
> were to be seen picking potatoes in many districts. A family would camp in
> one area until all the farmers there had the work done, then they would
> move on to the next area and their help was greatly welcomed (*CT*,
> 8 November 1958: 16).

As these references suggest Travellers worked as members of family
units on a short-term piece-work or contract basis. Other examples of
past casual wage or contract work mentioned by older Travellers during
fieldwork included working as labourers on the Corrib drainage project
and fixing roofs or cleaning toilets in schools and convents. Like agricultural labour, such activities were integrated within a broader multi-
occupational family work strategy.

While Travellers worked hard to negotiate favourable exchanges with
house-dwellers through flexible arrangements that could include barter,
their room for manœuvre was none the less constrained by relations of
exchange at either end of the work process – notably relations with
wholesalers on the one hand and recycling merchants on the other. Such
exchanges, which appear to have become more significant in the post-
war period, linked Travellers more closely to markets whose prices they
could not control. When prices were low survival depended on an intensification of unpaid family labour. Travellers were thus deeply implicated in a market economy even while the organization of work remained
family-based.

Settlement Policy and Work

Traveller mobility, multioccupationality, and reliance on unpaid family
labour allowed them to continue to provide competitive goods, services,
and labour to the wider population through the economic crises of the
post-war period. Despite this, the suggestion that they were suffering
from occupational obsolescence, with the male trade of tinsmithing as
exemplar, was a central premise of the settlement policy outlined in the
1963 Report of the Commission on Itinerancy (CI 1963: 72).

This influential Report laid out a pessimistic assessment of the Traveller economy, a stance facilitated by the exclusion of 'travelling show-
people and travelling entertainers' from its definition of 'itinerant'

(CI 1963: 13). This omission can be questioned in light of Traveller Michael McDonagh's claim in the 1990s that these groups are 'very much part of Traveller culture now' (M. McDonagh 1993: 13). More importantly, however, the Report also downplayed the significance of its own evidence of Traveller multioccupationality and the significance of women and children's work. Instead, it emphasized how allegedly declining male activities, especially tinsmithing, necessitated settlement and preparation for formal employment.

In contrast to the conclusions of the Report, the evidence collected by the Commission revealed the importance of newer activities. Dealing in refuse, not tinsmithing, was, for example, acknowledged to be widespread. The report stated: 'Almost all itinerants avail of any opportunity that presents itself to obtain scrap or waste material of any description that has a saleable value. Metal of all descriptions, clothes, rags, feathers, horse hair, bottles, jars, and a number of other articles ... provide many itinerants with a livelihood *of sorts*' (CI 1963: 73) [my emphasis]. Along with dealing in recyclable items, there were references to dealing in 'horses and asses' (CI 1963: 71) and working in family groups on a contract basis as seasonal agricultural workers.

As mentioned, the activities of women and children were downplayed or denied. Peddling, which was described by one of my camp neighbours as a 'women's trade,' was not mentioned at all in the Report. Instead there was a discussion of 'begging,' which was placed in a section dealing with 'social and ethical behaviour' rather than in the section on 'economics.' The often inseparable link between peddling and begging was therefore denied as 'begging' was described as being 'practised habitually by almost every itinerant woman and child' (CI 1963: 92) and to provide 'a vitally necessary part of the real income of the majority of itinerant families ... without which most itinerant families would be reduced to starvation level' (CI 1963: 90). Without any reference to peddling it was easy for the Commissioners to identify 'begging' as evidence of the lack of a viable economy and to suggest that the practice, along with trespassing, was 'probably the greatest single cause of hostility on the part of the settled population' (CI 1963: 90). The elimination of begging through stiffer fines and the extension of government payments was advocated and the general population was exhorted to be 'less indiscriminate in their almsgiving' (CI 1963: 92).

The overall thrust of the Commission report equated itinerancy with poverty, but it did refer to a minority of wealthier families who were highly mobile and who lived in motor trailers (rather than horse-drawn caravans or tents). These families were described as having good living conditions and income (CI 1963: 78–83), but the significance of a well-off strata of Travellers for the overall equation of 'itinerancy' with poverty was not pursued. Recognition of a viable way of life would have challenged a central premise of the policy – i.e., that settlement was the only means through which a higher standard of living could be obtained. Official settlement rhetoric thus downplayed both the breadth of Travellers' economic activities and the significance of class disparities within the Traveller population.

Premised on an assumption of occupational obsolescence and poverty, the Report advocated a re-organization of the Traveller family economy. While it recommended support for the collection of scrap as a form of self-employment (CI 1963: 74) and sought to increase the existing casual wage work of Traveller women (CI 1963: 74), most Traveller economic activities were to be replaced as settlement and 'absorption' would require that the itinerants 'adapt themselves to the employment patterns of the ordinary population' (CI 1963: 73). Settlement workers were asked to seek out opportunities for unskilled employment in order to facilitate 'integration "on the job" as well as in the residential sphere' (CI 1963: 75).

The Commissioners also called for increasing Traveller access to government payments. At the time of the Report some Travellers were receiving children's allowance and widow's, orphan's, and old age pensions which could be collected at any post office, but most were not receiving social insurance (which required attendance at regular intervals at a specific centre).[2]

The Commission suggested that obstacles in the way of Travellers 'signing on' for social insurance be removed as the income obtained from this source would reduce begging and would provide a 'means of inducing [itinerants] to settle' (CI 1963: 75). Along with a removal of barriers, it was suggested that Travellers might be required to 'sign on' more frequently than the rest of the population in order to constrain mobility (CI 1963: 76). At the same time it recommended that forms of state and local authority assistance, including children's allowances, be partially paid in voucher (rather than monetary) form to those Travellers who resisted settlement (CI 1963: 77). The explicit discussion of how such payments might be tailored to facilitate the settlement project implicitly acknowledged an existing economy that would have to be replaced if settlement were to be attractive and/or viable for Travellers.

At the local level in Galway City, the voluntary Galway Settlement

Council saw as part of its mandate the need to address the economic aspects of settlement. The Council, which was most involved with the poorer Traveller families of the region, put some effort into finding jobs for Traveller men (CT, 25 October 1968: 11). Members of the Chamber of Commerce and Industry, for example, were told by the Council that 'a lot of these [itinerant] men are fine men. If they get work they will become members of society' (CT, 10 March 1972: 18). These attempts, however, were largely unsuccessful. In a discriminatory labour market few male Travellers were offered jobs, and when they were the wages were too low to provide adequate support for the household or to compensate for the loss of the dole and/or earnings from self-employment. One early settlement worker recalled for me that a Traveller man camped in the city told her that he could earn more money by selling fish and collecting the dole than he could working at a labourer's wage (see also Walsh 1971: 17).

Along with attempts to find employers for Travellers, Settlement Council members supported a short-term project that encouraged the production of tinware and aprons by Traveller men and women. The enterprise provided materials to Travellers and marketed their products (ISC, 2 April 1969). Some of those living in the camp had been involved in this project and suggested to me that it was popular among Travellers. Such an arrangement fit existing social relations of work in that it allowed for a considerable degree of domestic control over the labour process if not relations of exchange.

In 1977, as part of a larger national effort to provide job-related training for Travellers and the unemployed more generally, a training centre for young female Travellers opened in the city's market area with a great deal of positive publicity. Run by a Galway nun trained as a social worker, the centre taught 'domestic skills' such as cooking and sewing and paid an allowance to the trainees (GBC, 22 November 1976; CT, 10 June 1977: 1). This centre was followed in later years by two more, one for boys and another that was co-ed.

Researching Work

Although entry by Travellers into wage labour was a goal of various voluntary and state initiatives, there was little evidence at the time of fieldwork that Travellers were entering formal employment beyond the short-term casual employment that had characterized earlier periods. In the context of 1986–7 when I was conducting fieldwork, Southern Ireland was experiencing recession and high rates of unemployment that had been deepening through the decade (O'Hearn 1998: 49). Anti-Traveller racism combined with economic contraction mitigated against opportunities for Travellers in the formal sector.

There was at the same time an identifiable Traveller economy characterized by a combination of short-term employment and a more economically significant range of income-generating activities in the informal sector. As others have commented, forms of informal work in Ireland have not disappeared but rather increased in the context of globalization. Greater mobility, flexibility, and casualization of labour in fact would appear to be integral rather than antithetical to advanced capitalism (O'Hearn 1998: 103). Travellers had a long history of involvement in the informal economy but, unlike that of other Irish, this involvement was structured by a historical trajectory of anti-Traveller racism and, by the 1960s, a state settlement policy.

The latter had included as part of its program the extension of social welfare payments, or the 'dole,' as a means of facilitating settlement, and in Galway City most Traveller families were receiving social welfare payments by the late 1960s. Travellers encountered during fieldwork in the 1980s denied that signing on for the dole was linked to an erosion of other sources of income; rather, they presented such payments as a resource which was immediately utilized once it became available to Travellers – one man in fact suggested that Travellers had been cheated because they had not been told about this entitlement earlier.

Social welfare payments were viewed by Travellers as a resource which they would be 'fools' not to exploit, but they were also associated with a greater degree of oppressive state intervention in their lives. It was suggested, for instance, that part of the reason city officials wanted them to become tenants of houses was that the government wanted to get back in rent some of the dole money that it had paid out.

Within the camp welfare payments were a major source of income for most families and the week revolved around the Thursday 'dole' day. As for many other Irish, however, such payments were insufficient for the support of Traveller families and were combined with income from other sources.[3] Other forms of work, however, were by definition illegitimate in the context of dole payments based on the premise of unemployment and lack of other income. In order to maintain their access to welfare payments, Travellers then found themselves having to collude with a dominant discourse which portrayed their economy as a thing of the past. Work which had previously been carried out in the open became part of a 'shadow' economy as the taking up of social welfare resulted in a 'delegitimation' of Travellers' economic activities. Occurring as it did as part of a larger state-initiated settlement policy, this process was collectively experienced as creating a shared sense of dependence and vulnerability among Travellers vis-à-vis the state.

Concern about having their payments cut led many Travellers to be cautious about sharing economic information with me. Details of work activities and income were rarely volunteered in the first months of fieldwork and when I asked direct questions I was occasionally challenged to explain why I was being so 'very curious.' I heard later that my arrival in the camp had coincided with an announcement by the Minister for Social Welfare that there would be new measures against social welfare fraud. Given this context it is not surprising that my questions were resisted, usually through indirect methods, but occasionally through more overtly expressed concerns that I might be working as a spy for the dole office. The few who talked to me initially did so in very general terms and emphasized how they needed to 'feed the children.'

Travellers were also concerned about the possibility of having other Travellers 'report' on them. Rumours about Travellers informing on their enemies were rife. One camp resident was allegedly afraid to return to England because some of his relatives there believed that after he had been arrested for dole fraud, he had won his freedom by implicating them.

In fact, however, the state in its local manifestations did not appear to be actively investigating Travellers' economic activities, although Travellers mentioned that their bank accounts were vulnerable to inspection. Some forms of work such as scrap metal collection were readily apparent and well known to service workers, but Travellers, by definition, were labelled unemployed and poor and therefore eligible for payments regardless of such activities. As one service provider remarked, 'It is a recognized fact that Travellers don't have gainful employment ... there are Travellers who deal a lot in scrap but that whole area is much more difficult to prove. Even so, the assumption is always that [they're] unemployed.' The fact that it was their Traveller identity, rather than employment status, that ensured eligibility was significant in that it guaranteed their public assertion of this identity vis-à-vis the social welfare bureaucracy.

Travellers in the city and nation-wide in 1986–7 not only received social welfare payments by virtue of an officially defined identity, but also collected these payments in a discriminatory way. Throughout the country, all Travellers had to 'sign on' at a labour exchange within a single half hour on a particular day each week, a regulation that did not exist for any other group of people and has since been changed. When the requirement was condemned by a Senator as 'racism Irish style' the Department of Social Welfare defended the practice by stating that the procedure 'protected the dignity of Travellers, by ensuring that they were not open to allegations of fraud' (*Sunday Press*, 21 December 1986: 2). As this ostensible defence suggested, the procedure was instituted in the belief that Travellers were defrauding the state by collecting dole payments at more than one exchange, a practice which was also mentioned by Travellers that I encountered.

In Galway City all the Travellers gathered at the same time to collect their payments, a weekly event that intensified social relations among Travellers from different camps and housing estates. Information and gossip were exchanged at the same time as practices such as money-lending and extortion were facilitated. Transfer payments were intended to promote assimilation, but, paradoxically, the externally imposed procedure of dole collection had the result of both increasing interaction among Travellers and dramatizing in a concrete fashion their common relationship vis-à-vis a discriminatory state.

The structure of dole payments at the time (made to family units, but actually paid out to male 'heads of households') also reinforced pre-existing patterns of male dominance. By assuming that the male head was the primary provider and that he would redistribute the funds to the other members of the nuclear family unit, dole payments among Travellers, as for other Irish, served to 'reinforce the power and authority of husbands [as the] controllers and arbiters of resources allocated by society to the family' (Evanson 1987: 196). The smaller monthly child benefit payments were made to mothers, but the children's allowance books of poorer families were often held by money-lenders. During the fieldwork period, however, some Traveller women described how they had 'banded together' in an effort to gain independent access to part of the family income by drawing out their own and their children's portion of the dole payment separately.

As I was trying to learn about Travellers' economic activities, my neighbours were also trying to work out the economic status of myself and my partner. Early on, for example, our lack of apparent income-generation resulted in the offer of a loan as well as the suggestion that my husband sign on for the dole. The limitations of our scooter for any work activity were also pointed out and offers to find us a more 'productive' cheap car were made. When none of these suggestions were taken up the initial perception of us as 'down and out' altered and after some months one young girl surprised me by declaring that my partner and I were 'millionaires' because we had money even when it was not dole day. The perception led to a few requests for small loans, but others clearly still considered our lifestyle to indicate a lack of wealth. When we were selling our trailer in preparation for leaving the field, we were encouraged to keep the price high because, according to one commentator, potential buyers knew that we weren't well off.

While economic information was initially difficult to obtain, the public nature of much of camp life and my presence at evening gatherings allowed me to glean a fair bit of information through careful listening and observation. Later in the fieldwork period I found that many individuals, especially men, became more interested in volunteering aspects of their work activities, emphasizing how hard and creatively they were working to make a living. While it is important to emphasize that the families that I met during fieldwork in the late 1980s did not reflect the entire diversity or degree of stratification found among Travellers as a collectivity, a description of their work activities can illuminate something of the complexity of Traveller social relations of work and exchange.

The variety of forms of work pursued by Travellers included both income-generating activities and various forms of 'reproductive' work, including self-provisioning, budgeting, accessing the state and social services, begging, domestic labour, and child care. I reserve much of the discussion of this 'reproductive' work for the later chapters because it was often the province of women and children.

Relations of Work and Exchange

None of the Travellers living in the camp were involved in formal wage labour although several men described work that they had pursued before marriage, for example, working as a general helper in a hotel and as a construction labourer. Some of the married women who lived in or visited the camp had also worked before marriage as hospital cleaners, babysitters, waitresses, and launderers. Such work was low paid, often part-time, and short-term in nature.

The lack of more extensive involvement in the formal work force was partially the result of a discriminatory labour market. One adult man who was unusually well educated described to me how he went to the labour exchange three times a week looking for jobs but claimed that once employers learned that he lived in a Traveller camp they were not interested in him. It was also clear that the workplace was one of many sites where Travellers experienced overt racism. A Traveller woman living in a house described how anti-Traveller slurs from fellow workers had been a major factor in her decision to leave a hotel job (see also G. Gmelch 1977: 82).

In the context of a racist and, in the 1980s, contracting formal labour market, Traveller families continued to focus on a variety of informal economic activities that offered a high degree of autonomy and control over the work process and at least the potential, if not for many the realization, of economic success. The most significant income-generating activities were forms of petty commodity production and/or trading which, in the case of several camp residents, took the form of gathering recyclable and other saleable items for resale.

Collecting and dealing in recyclable goods had been a source of income for Travellers for several decades in Galway. With the industrial and commercial development of the city, the opportunities for such work increased, although the nature of the work changed. In the past most of the refuse materials were collected by Travellers directly from householders (something which some Travellers also described doing in England), but those that I knew during fieldwork were more likely to scavenge from industrial and commercial refuse bins and from the city dump. The primary material collected was scrap metal, which was then resold to a merchant. Less lucrative was the retrieval of glass bottles, which were also sold for recycling. Other miscellaneous items (e.g., household goods and clothing) were also collected for resale or domestic consumption.

This work was actively pursued by adult members of three family units in the camp. Two of these made daily trips to the city dump, while the third concentrated on driving around to industrial bins in the city. Another five families had adult members who were occasionally involved in these activities and the children of several families also collected items from nearby commercial refuse bins.

Travellers were extremely reluctant to answer questions about the organization of this work or to discuss its economic value. My early questions about the process of cleaning the scrap, for example, elicited evasive or defensive responses. One woman who was telling a story about working at the city dump to a group of people became flustered when she noticed my presence and another woman whispered to her, 'now she will know where you go every day.'

After four months of residence in the camp no opportunity to participate in this activity had presented itself and so one morning, after a married couple had left for the dump in their van, I declared my intention to follow them. I was encouraged in my resolve by the reaction of one of my neighbours who laughed and told me to bring her back 'something nice.'

I rode on my scooter to the dump, which was a few miles outside the city, and entered it, passing a sign declaring 'Trespassers will be prosecuted.' Inside the dump were a number of Traveller adults, standing and chatting in separate groups of men and women. They were mostly married couples who were related to one another in various ways. The wife that I had followed from the camp was talking with three of her sisters-in-law (all of whom lived in houses). I approached this group of women and, after she introduced me, we began to chat. One of the women told me that I would probably get a disease from working in the dump.

Each woman had already collected a small pile of materials – quiz books, magazines, samples of shampoo, pieces of linoleum, some packages of food, and pieces of wire. The men also had individual piles of larger pieces of metal and firewood. After about twenty minutes a garbage truck drove into the dump and all of the men and women gathered around it. One Traveller man joked to the driver, who had noticed my presence, 'We've a Yank here with us today – she won't be long getting into the business.' As the garbage was mechanically pushed out of the back of the truck everyone pushed forward, jostling each other, trying to grab and pull out anything that looked like metal before someone else could reach it.

After this, a second truck pulled in and the same procedure was followed. Once the trucks pulled away, some of the women continued to pick up other items, including a package of flour, a box of custard powder, pieces of firewood, and bottles from the ground. This more leisurely activity ended when a third man driving a bulldozer began spreading the piles of pressed garbage. Unlike the first two truck drivers, this man seemed determined to ignore the presence of the Traveller women as they dove in and out of his path grabbing items as they were uncovered. None of the men engaged in this dangerous activity.

When the spreading was finished, the women wandered around searching through the garbage with little success and then gathered again to talk. At this point, my acquaintance spotted a man at the entrance of the dump and shouted 'we're done' to the others and then whispered to me that he was the boss of the place and might 'run us out.' This, however, did not happen. Shortly afterwards, she declared that she was going off for a walk and I decided to leave and return to the camp. I had spent about two hours at the dump.

A couple of days after my visit, the camp neighbour that I had met there let me know that the other Travellers had been angry with her for 'bringing' me out to the dump, as they suspected that I was working as a spy for the dole office. I asserted my innocence of this charge, but decided not to go again. The renewed apprehension about my true motives after four months of residence in the camp revealed the degree of tension surrounding this and other forms of income-generating work.

My experience at the dump was a stark reminder of the harsh and precarious means by which some Travellers earned income and met some of their domestic needs. This form of work was, however, pursued by those who were already somewhat better off. In order to make money at this work, family units had to already have the use of suitable transportation (trucks, vans, cars) with which to move materials from the dump or industrial bins to the camp and then to the scrap yard. Those who could afford it invested in large vans, which were insured and kept in good repair. Those with smaller forms of transportation such as a car could also be fairly successful. One man, for example, used a car to tow a cart on which he transported the less bulky but still valuable copper wire for resale. For those without access to a fairly new van or car, however, scavenging for recyclable items was difficult. The couple that I had followed from our camp, for example, could only afford older vehicles which they could not insure properly. Their presence at the dump depended on whether their vehicle was working, and even when it was, they risked prosecution for lack of proper insurance.

Others had even more limited means of transportation. For a short period, for example, one father living in the camp had only a bicycle, which he used to get to nearby bins. His ability to collect scrap or other items for the family was limited to what he could transport on his back. Another one of our camp neighbours also had periods when he had no vehicle. During one of these times he was reduced to buying, from his brother, a small amount of scrap, which he then cleaned and sold to the scrap merchant for a somewhat higher amount. Other variations of this kind of relationship involved those without reliable vehicles selling what little material they could collect to relatives with vans, who then transported it to the scrap merchant for a profit.

Successful scavengers needed access to transportation but also access to labour. In the case of two family units parked in the camp, both husband and wife were involved in this activity. My visit to the dump suggested that women and men worked separately, and that they concentrated on the collection of different items. The women seemed to collect smaller recyclable items such as bottles and items for domestic use, while men specialized in the collection of scrap metal, the major item sold for money.

The two wives who worked at the dump could do so because their families were still small and because they had access to child care, usually provided in the home of a mother, mother-in-law, or sister-in-law who was home with her own children. In families with larger numbers of children wives were less likely to work outside the camp or house and fathers were more likely to work alone or with the assistance of older sons. One such father living in the camp relied on his ten-year-old son to assist with the cleaning and loading of scrap.

Many who did not work at the dump suggested that this was because it was already 'packed' with Travellers. Gaining and keeping a regular position at the dump depended on having close kinship or affinal ties to those already established. The couple that I had followed from the camp, for example, were joining a larger group that included the husband's sisters and their husbands. As a larger group they were able to defend their position at the dump against other Travellers.

Successful scavenging also required the creation and maintenance of some kind of relationship with the non-Traveller truck drivers and other dump workers. The tolerance of these city employees was necessary because the activity of scavenging was strictly illegal. Although I did not hear of any cases of prosecutions for working in the dump, some men in the camp had been threatened with prosecution by the police for scavenging from industrial bins.

Along with access to the waste material itself, the work required space in which to sort, clean (by burning off the non-metallic parts), and store the scrap before either transporting it or having it picked up by the scrap metal merchant. Those living in the camp had access to this kind of space but those in houses and flats had little or none. Attempts by Travellers in regular housing estates to use their yards for cleaning and storing scrap frequently led to conflict with non-Traveller neighbours; in one case, a housed Traveller was publicly criticized for having 'scrap in the front garden' by the residents' and tenants' association chairman, who commented, 'This is a new estate and we are anxious to make it a pleasant place to live in. But this kind of thing just destroys the entire image of the place' (*Galway Observer*, 16 April 1986). The Traveller family left the house soon afterwards.

Some Travellers tried to avoid such conflicts by using their ties to close relatives living in the camp in order to gain access to more storage space. Before one man moved into the camp, for example, he was living in a house in the city but he sometimes stored his scrap in the camp. Within the camp, scrap was piled up in shacks or stacked behind trailers. While there was concern about detection by outsiders, some also suggested that scrap had to be carefully guarded against other Travellers who might steal and resell it. One man was sufficiently concerned about this to pay a young nephew to guard it for him when he was not there.

Finally, those involved in scrap metal collection were dependent upon exchanges with merchants. The Travellers that I knew sold their material to one of two scrap metal merchants in the region and Travellers emphasized that the prices they received for scrap had been falling. Travellers were in a vulnerable position in this exchange as the prices for scrap were set by larger forces of demand and supply and bore no relationship to the amount of labour involved. There were few ways for Travellers to alter the terms of trade to their advantage. Most, for instance, had little withholding power as they lacked sufficient space on which to stockpile scrap in anticipation of higher prices. While some spoke of transporting scrap to merchants in other urban centres, this was not pursued. This particular form of 'self-employment,' then, was dependent upon unequal exchanges over which Travellers had little independent control. Those involved in this work could only attempt to partially mitigate their dependence through the combination of this activity with other forms of work.

One of these other forms of work was the intermittent collection and sale of winkles (edible marine snails), cockles, and mussels. Periodically several Traveller families from the camp, with as many members from each unit as possible, would go on picking expeditions to gather these shellfish. Information about the best locations for working were shared between closely related families. Although the winkles could be consumed by the domestic group, the work was clearly geared toward sale rather than direct consumption. This activity was unrestricted by state regulations and was also one of the few forms of income-generating work which could simultaneously involve the entire family unit. Because children could be very productive in this form of work, they were sometimes kept home from school in order to participate. Once gathered the commodity had to be quickly transported to the buyer who, because of its perishability and lack of other buyers, was able to dictate the terms of exchange.

Various forms of petty commodity trading were also part of the economic repertoire. One married man purchased wholesale quantities of dry goods such as blankets, sheets, pillows, and lino, and then travelled in his van reselling these goods outside the city. Another bought fresh fish from fishermen, which he sold to non-Traveller householders. Other housed Travellers described selling carpets, furniture, and televisions within a forty to fifty mile radius of the city. One older Traveller woman who described selling 'bits and pieces' to settled people enjoyed telling me how sometimes Travellers from outside the city appeared at her home offering to sell similar items. She regaled me with an account of how she would string them along by pretending to be interested, and then would show them the trailer in the back garden and reveal her Traveller identity!

Unlike in the past, when peddlers had engaged in both barter and begging, the trading engaged in by these Travellers appeared to be completely commoditized. It also seemed to be dominated by men although in some cases women and older girls did some of the selling. Several women living in the camp, for example, described how before marriage they had been driven by their fathers, who dropped them off to peddle goods from door to door.

Other Traveller men within the camp and in houses were involved in intermittent trading both with non-Travellers and with other Travellers. At Christmastime, two married brothers and their father pooled their money in order to buy a large number of trees from a farmer. They then transported these to the city and sold them on the streets. While this particular endeavour was successful, one of the brothers noted that 'many fellows go broke over the trees.' Success at this kind of work depended on sufficient capital and transportation, space for storage, and a licensed place on the street for selling (the lack of which could lead to fines). A less capital intensive but also less lucrative item was holly, which was picked in the country at no cost, made into bunches, and sold on the street.

At the time of fieldwork at least one cluster of closely related families was deeply involved in horse dealing and attended the horse fairs and 'marts' in the region. Others who were involved on a smaller scale described keeping one or two horses as a 'hobby' to 'pass the time.' One man living in the camp used the land surrounding the camp to graze a couple of horses, including one belonging to his father, who lived in a housing estate. While access to grazing land was easier for those in camps than those in houses, pursuing this activity was difficult because the city had a long history of responding to non-Traveller complaints about 'wandering horses' with 'round-ups' that placed the animals in the pound, from which they could be released only after the payment of large fines.

The spokesperson for the Traveller Committee emphasized the significance of horses to Travellers, stating that 'horses are a part of the travelling people's culture and ... many travelling people would never give them up ... for travellers who own horses, the care of the animals is almost as important as the care of the families; they are after all the families' way of life' (*Galway Advertiser*, 19 March 1987: 33). Another Traveller woman told a television reporter that 'horses [have] been in our life since [the] beginning. We had no vans or cars, we had a horse. So we are going to stand by the horse, as good as the horse stood by us' (*News RTE*, 26 April 1987). Although some insisted that there was 'no money in horses' others described their horses as a 'bank' where capital could be invested.

Another major activity of men was trading or 'swopping' with other Travellers. Used trailers, vans, cars, and car parts as well as smaller items like televisions, video recorders, and pieces of furniture were constantly circulating as they were bought and resold. For some men trading in these items was an important source of income. One man described to me how he bought and sold at least ten caravans a week – responding to the changing cash and/or accommodation needs of Traveller families in the city. Women, who were excluded from the formal 'swopping' process, were none the less quick to offer praise or condemnation of male negotiations.

Swopping could involve straight cash, but more often it involved combinations of goods and cash or outright barter. The latter was common among the poorer families with little capital. In the camp the men of the least well-off units were active in 'swopping' as they continually attempted to gain access to reliable transportation. Invariably, however, the vehicles that they were able to afford broke down and had to be swopped again. At times the trading became so frequent that it was difficult to keep track of which vehicle was owned by whom within the camp. Ambiguity in the area of ownership of property was sometimes a way in which support could be offered to poorer families by wealthier relatives – for example, through long-term 'loans' of needed vehicles.

There were also, however, cases of tension over the outcome of deals and precise rights of ownership.

Successful trading or swopping required access to capital, transportation, some mechanical skills, and knowledge of the supply and demand for particular items – in other words, a wide social network. Those who were most successful in dealing in larger items such as trailers were also those with access to plenty of storage and work space. People living in flats had no such space and those in houses were limited – for example, they could only park one trailer at a time in a driveway. As with scrap metal storage, some of those with close kin in camps tried to use these to advantage. For example, two families that left the camp for a house and a flat both stored their respective trailers in the camp while they were waiting to find buyers for them.

Dealing in scrap, horses, and/or trailers required access to land that was more difficult to obtain for those living in houses, and some Travellers saw hardstands as potentially providing both security from eviction and more flexible land use. A letter to the editor written by a group of young Travellers employed at one of the training centres called for hardstands in part because Travellers in houses found that 'they could no longer collect scrap, which as it is, cannot be accepted in a housing estate' (*Galway Advertiser*, 29 June 1986: 21). Other Travellers, however, were concerned that hardstands might become 'reservations' where their economic activities would be under increased surveillance and restriction and were reluctant to support the plan for this reason.

I have mentioned how in the past Travellers met some of their needs through self-provisioning activities such as hunting and fishing. During fieldwork some of the shellfish gathered by families were consumed by the domestic unit, and a number of men caught fish and were involved in hunting hares with dogs. Much more significant forms of self-provisioning, however, involved the retrieval of items such as clothes, wood for fuel, furniture, and other household items from the dump and bins along with the items that could be recycled for money. Items for direct use were gathered by individuals and either consumed directly or redistributed to relatives in other families. One married son, for example, gave furniture and a television found in the dump to his parents, who lived in the camp.

Those without access to transportation suffered economically not only because they were unable to earn cash through petty commodity production, but also because they could not reduce cash expenditure through self-provisioning – for example, two families had to purchase turf and coal in order to heat their trailers because the men were unable to scavenge for firewood or 'boards' in the dump. In these cases they also suffered from their inability to build up social credit through redistribution.

As these exchanges suggest, a striking aspect of camp life was the exchange of goods and services between closely related families. There were three distinct kinship-based clusters of families in the camp, and within each of these goods and services were constantly circulating and being redistributed. The closely related men of each cluster shared information about potential deals, borrowed tools and transport from one another, and occasionally exchanged labour necessary for their work. Women also, as we shall see, shared information as well as tools, clothes, food, and child care.

The kinship-based residential cluster, however, did not constitute a corporate unit, and each request for assistance between members of different nuclear families had to be independently negotiated. One of the younger married men, for example, had to publicly request each of his married brothers to give him half an hour of their time to help him move a car that he was dismantling. Attempts at cluster-wide co-operation could also collapse under the competing demands for autonomy. For example, an attempt to rotate payment of an electricity bill between the closely related families of one of the camp clusters bogged down in bitter disagreements over which unit had used how much power. When one family unit defaulted on payment the bill accumulated until, under the threat of having the power cut off, one of the wealthier families in the cluster paid it off. In such a case the wealthier family was subsidizing poorer relatives but such actions were a source of tension and resentment, and frequently contributed to the reproduction rather than amelioration of inequality.

Middlemen, Money-Lending, and Inequality

So far I have emphasized the variety of forms of work engaged in by Travellers encountered during fieldwork. Many of these activities can be described as 'self-employment'; however, such terminology has tended to highlight the income-generating activities of men and downplay the extent to which family survival was dependent upon the unpaid work of women and children (a topic explored in more depth in chapters 6 and 7). The terminology of 'self-employment' also obscured the dependence on both co-operative and exploitative relations of exchange with non-Travellers and among Travellers themselves. Here I focus on the significance of such exchanges for the creation and reproduction of economic inequality.

Internal stratification among Travellers was described by early observers such as MacGréine and McGrath and was acknowledged, as I have already discussed, in the 1963 Report of the Commission on Itinerancy. At the local level the early reports of the Settlement Council in Galway contrasted the plight of the poorer tent-dwelling families with the position of other better-off Travellers living in wagons in the 1960s, and at the time of fieldwork in the late 1980s there continued to be dramatic disparities between families. Among the families encountered in the camp there were also significant economic differences. A couple of families, for example, had substantial bank savings, while several others consistently ran out of money each week before dole day.

Relative wealth was indicated in part by the type of accommodation used, with better-off families distinguished by newer trailers and mobiles full of decorative knick-knacks and 'delph.' Admiring comments were made about much wealthier Travellers camping elsewhere in the city, whose new trailers sported ornate chrome decoration on the outside and cut-glass windows. The most revealing indicator of wealth, however, was the form of transportation. As previously discussed, cars, vans, and trucks were the crucial means of production for many income-generating and self-provisioning activities as well as residential mobility, and these were the primary site of familial investment. In the camp, two brothers had sufficient income to invest in brand-new vans on hire-purchase from non-Traveller dealers, and another two men owned large pre-owned vans worth thousands of pounds. Most, however, did not have the necessary income for vans and instead bought second-hand minivans or smaller run-down cars (in the case of the latter for as little as fifteen pounds).

Those with good transportation were able to engage in a variety of income-generating and self-provisioning activities, but those without were excluded from these activities. The three poorest families in the camp had insufficient income to invest in any reliable form of transportation and were constantly involved in swopping and borrowing money from other Travellers in order to improve their transportation prospects. Even when they managed to invest in a vehicle some could not afford to pay (or may, as a result of anti-Traveller racism, have been denied the opportunity to purchase) the insurance and taxes on their vehicles. Some of the cheaper vehicles were also not insurable in the first place. These families had to continually weigh the risks of driving, as being caught for these infractions would lead to fines which they could not afford.

I have discussed how some individuals with access to reliable transportation sometimes assisted poorer relatives by acting as middlemen who would buy up scrap material or other recyclable items and transport them to the merchants (see also G. Gmelch 1977: 65). The middleman role was also visible in the harvesting of winkles. One of the families in the camp, for example, was without any transportation, but the husband's brother, who owned a large van, agreed to transport the entire family to and from the beach to pick winkles. The brother who had provided the transport bought the harvested shellfish and took them to the buyer himself – presumably making a profit on the exchange.

The middleman role was also often closely entwined with another role taken on by wealthier individuals – that of money-lender. Relations of debt between closely related Traveller men, such as older and younger brothers or uncles and nephews, were common. An anticipated visit from England of a wealthy uncle was greeted with apprehension by some of his nephews because they owed him money. While money-lenders may have felt familial pressure to offer loans to close kin in need, such loans were relatively risk-free as it was difficult for a family unit to escape its immediate kinship network.

Inequities between closely related families in the camp and beyond were created and reproduced through both middleman and money-lending relationships. The way in which exchanges produced relations of dependence and exploitation were, however, masked by a tendency to blame poorer individuals and families for their own condition. Poorer families were described as being 'lazy' and sometimes as unwilling to work precisely because of their ability to get loans from wealthier relations. Poorer families who might express resentment of wealthier relatives in private also saw them as providing necessary security in an otherwise precarious existence. They were unlikely to publicly contest the claims of the well off to be redistributing wealth to the extended family in an uncalculating (rather than exploitative) way.

One woman, for example, described how when her brother had died a wealthy uncle had paid for the headstone that her parents had been unable to afford. As she told the story she emphasized that the money involved 'wasn't even a loan,' but clearly it had created a sense of obligation. As this example demonstrated, the distinction between loans and gifts, assistance and exploitation, was easy to blur in close kin exchanges where the obvious disparities of wealth were downplayed or denied through an ideology of familialism.

In cases where the resources of kin were not available or needed to be augmented, poorer Traveller families turned to other non-related Traveller middlemen and/or money-lenders (such a system was also found among the non-Traveller population in the city). In the absence of a close kinship relationship the exploitative nature of these exchanges was much more apparent and easily identified. One small-scale money-lender who lived in the camp told a story which revealed the mechanics of these kinds of loans. He spoke of a fellow who owed him £20. At a chance meeting with the debtor, he asked for the £20 back, but the debtor said he only had £10. The lender took this £10 and told the man that he was treating the missing £10 as another loan, and as a result, the man still owed him £20 because the interest was 100 per cent.

The risk involved in money-lending to non-relatives was often reduced for the lenders by their insisting on holding the family allowance books or coupons as security and/or accompanying their debtors to the dole office. One woman in the camp said that her indebted father had often left the labour exchange with only five pence in his pocket because the rest of the transfer payment had gone immediately to a money-lender. Money-lenders used close kin to assist in real or threatened violence that accompanied enforcement of debt payment and some of the poorer families in the city were described by one service worker as being in the 'death grip' of these lenders.[4]

Loans were usually negotiated independently by men, with the result that wives were sometimes unaware of the extent of their indebtedness. Women expressed frustration over the loss of control of income represented by their husbands' relationships with money-lenders, and occasionally tried to intervene directly in an attempt to establish better terms of repayment or even debt forgiveness. This was particularly likely if the wife had a closer kinship relationship with the lender than her husband. Attempts to protect family income from money-lenders were also a reason for women to draw their own and their children's portion of the dole separately. Women claimed that male money-lenders were less likely to come after women and, moreover, that women were more likely to 'stand up to them' if they did.

Money-lending was linked to the middleman role but also to trading more generally. Some Travellers who dealt in trailers and vans, for example, offered hire-purchase arrangements which tied families to them through debt. Huge profits were sometimes made when debtors suddenly needed money and raised it by selling back their purchases to the dealers at a loss. In one case, for example, a man was fined for having no car insurance, and in order to pay it was forced to sell his trailer. He had already paid over £1200 for it on a hire-purchase arrangement but got only £350 when he sold it back to the dealer.

While there were economic disparities between those in the camp none of them were well off in non-Traveller terms. In this sense they reflected the majority of Travellers. There were some Travellers in the city, however, that were agreed by all to be much more wealthy. Some of these individuals, who were labelled by other Travellers as 'millionaires,' were older men who were large-scale traders and/or money-lenders, and their route to wealth was portrayed as one of entrepreneurship and ingenuity combined with physical and political strength. Some of these individuals were described as having houses which they rented out, and in some cases were said to have non-Traveller men described as 'dossers' or 'servants' working for them in exchange for a place to live, food, cigarettes, and drink (see also Okely 1983: 61–2).

Another route to wealth that was repeatedly mentioned was, however, very different: large out-of-court settlements stemming from accidents. The frequency of serious accidents among Travellers was a direct and stark result of the lack of provision of adequate living conditions. The financial settlements that sometimes resulted occasionally led to tension and conflict within and between kinship groups. One young women, for example, was physically attacked by a group of young women from another family group in retaliation for the fact that one of their relatives had been, in their view, unfairly excluded from a court settlement reached by members of her family. Stories were also told of some individuals who had received money from court cases but had had it 'taken off them' by close relatives through exploitative exchanges.

Along with these sources of wealth there was also speculation that families who had 'come up fast,' i.e., suddenly improved their economic standing, had done so by somehow benefiting disproportionately from programs and funds earmarked for Travellers. Such speculation was spurred by a pervasive sense among Travellers that such funds were not reaching those for whom they were intended. As one women asked me angrily, 'Where does all the money go that is spent on Travellers?'

Other Travellers deemed 'millionaires' by those in the camp included families that spent only a short time in the city and were described as 'traders' by the press and official discourse. Ennis (1984) suggested some time ago that the label of 'trader,' which was first introduced into official discourse in the late 1970s, served to exclude more mobile and prosperous (as evidenced by their new vans and ornate caravans as well as by the value of the goods they traded) families from the definition of Traveller, thereby allowing the latter to continue to be equated in dominant discourse with poverty and a need for settlement.[5]

There was a similar downplaying of Traveller economic success in the

1983 Report of the Travelling People Review Body which, like the 1963 report, acknowledged the existence of wealthy Traveller families (and, significantly, a link between greater mobility and greater wealth), but argued that such families still experienced 'handicaps of illiteracy, social deprivation, and isolation' (Review Body 1983: 46–7). Despite ongoing denial of the possibility of an economically successful Traveller way of life in outsiders' constructions, the obvious wealth of such families was not lost on other Travellers, who strove for similar success. The presence of a minority of wealthy Travellers in the city (both relatively settled and highly mobile) supports an argument made with respect to Traveller-Gypsies in England but also applicable to Ireland, namely that outsiders' assumptions that 'Travellers will spontaneously accept wage-labour and that no Travellers achieve affluence within their own society, on their own terms, are thoroughly ethnocentric' (1983: 54).

Work and Traveller Identity

Travellers portrayed wealth as the outcome of individual hard work and/or ingenuity and poverty as the result of laziness and lack of initiative. This construction of course echoed broader capitalist ideology, and the strength of the construction was rooted in largely male relations of work that supported a high degree of control over the work process. Those men who were most economically successful owned the necessary mode of transportation and the tools for multiple forms of work, and had access to work space. These factors provided the basis for a strong sense of autonomy even within the context of an oppressive state and unequal relations with merchants.

A strong sense of agency was celebrated in story-telling that emphasized individual male initiative and economic success. Men in the camp spoke proudly of their trading activities – vehemently denying that they ever lost out in deals. Male Travellers particularly enjoyed telling stories about exchanges with non-Travellers which demonstrated their skills of persuasiveness, cleverness, and/or trickery in making a profit.

One housed male Traveller, for example, described to me how he outwitted a non-Traveller who had bargained him down to a low price by measuring out linoleum in such a way that the person paid for a larger piece than he actually received. Another man told of how, after puncturing a car's tires, he would approach the non-Traveller owner to buy the car for a low price, then fix the tires and resell it at its real value. Such stories of outwitting settled people, or 'conning the buffer,' were often repeated and offered as evidence that house-dwellers were 'soft' or 'fools.' One such story concerned a non-Traveller man who was offering Travellers drinks in exchange for words in Traveller cant. He was predictably offered many fictitous words – as the teller of the story pointed out he was 'easy to fool.'

While many stories emphasized the independent actions of individuals, some pointed to the virtue of co-operation especially among kin. For instance, one older woman told of how when a merchant refused to accept a bucket of winkles from one of her sons because they were too small, her son then went to one of his brothers who mixed the winkles in with his own and then successfully sold them. The punchline of the story was the buyer's comment to the second brother as he paid for the shellfish: 'You always bring me good winkles.' The story emphasized how the potential vulnerability of Travellers to the vagaries of the non-Traveller buyer could sometimes be minimized through Traveller cleverness and, in this case, co-operation between brothers, which allowed them to deceive the non-Traveller buyer to their mutual economic benefit.

Occupational flexibility and ingenuity in extracting surplus from non-Travellers in even in the most adverse circumstances were described as evidence of a collective superiority of Travellers over non-Travellers. An expression of this can be found in a published Traveller account of the relative fortunes of Travellers and settled people during the vicissitudes of Irish history:

> People were burned out during the Cromwell evictions or they were made homeless during the Famine. The travellers were used to coping with cold and hardship and hunger, they could survive anywhere because they had their own way of working and their own culture. But the settled people weren't used to managing on their own, they slept in old sheds and barns and did a sort of slave work on the farms. (Joyce and Farmar 1985: 2)

A Galway newspaper account also included a quotation from a Traveller woman who said: 'We [the Travellers] are years ahead of most people. We are clever and quick to learn. We are never stuck when we want something and can find some way of getting it'; and another woman added: 'I have taught them [her children] about business and when they want money they can make it ... we were able to turn our hand to anything' (CT, 10 December 1971: 21).

The assertion of Traveller economic agency and denigration of non-

Travellers in such stories must be understood as attempts to counter dominant discourses and practices of stigma and exclusion in a context of relative powerlessness. As one man explained to me, he was keen to share these kinds of stories with me because 'people say Travellers are uneducated and stupid but they aren't.'

The celebratory theme of course downplayed the reality of a racist exclusion from the formal economy, dependence on unequal relations of exchange with non-Travellers, and the sometimes exploitative relations among Travellers themselves. What was emphasized, moreover, were largely male activities rather than the equally significant activities of women and children. The position of the relatively well off was likewise legitimated, while poorer families were negatively implicated in an ideology that linked their poverty to their own laziness or lack of intelligence in the entrepreneurial sphere. The ideology of self-reliance and individualism, while an expression of the reality of Traveller economic resilience and social relations of work outside of wage labour, also masked and legitimated gendered, generational, and class-based inequalities.

As I have demonstrated, however, such inequities were produced and reproduced within a broader context, which required Travellers to publicly collude with an official discourse of economic marginalization unless they were willing to risk reduction or elimination of the dole. In practice this meant that the elaborated ideology and practice of self-sufficiency and economic agency remained largely an internal means of challenging racism through the valorizing of male work as central to an ethnicized Traveller identity. The economic vulnerability of many Travellers meant that it could not become part of a public challenge to a stigmatizing dominant discourse.

Chapter 6

Gender, Racism, and the Politics of Culture

Feminist work on ethnicity and nationalism has drawn attention to the ways in which 'gender relations are at the heart of cultural constructions of social identities and collectivities as well as ... most cultural conflicts and contestations' (Yuval-Davis 1997: 39).[1] Women, it has also been argued, often carry a disproportionate 'burden of representation' as 'symbolic bearers of the collectivity's identity and honour' (ibid., 45).

In earlier chapters I pointed to the ways in which a gendered anti-Traveller racism linked settled women in this way to the Irish nation. Here I use archival, autobiographical, and especially ethnographic material to shift attention toward the ways in which Traveller women in the context of a gendered anti-Traveller racism are positioned from within as embodiments of an ethnicized Traveller identity and boundary vis-à-vis non-Travellers.

I approach a discussion of Traveller women and gender through an examination of the complexities of Traveller women's social relations. My discussion and analysis is prompted by feminist-inspired ethnography that has focused on the relationship between gendered social relations and inequality through the examination of women's lived relations of work, residence, kinship, marriage, and sexuality (Bell, Caplan, and Karim 1993; Moore 1988; Wolf 1996).

Along with attention to the gendered quality of social life, feminist analyses have paid particular attention to various forms of women's agency. In the case of Travellers, recognition of Traveller women's active engagement with often oppressive relations challenges dominant constructions that portray them as victims of Traveller men and/or Traveller culture. Crickley has warned against the importation of such constructions into feminist analyses of Traveller women's lives, noting that 'Settled feminists working for the liberation of Traveller women, may ... be unwittingly contributing to their cultural annihilation, through linking gender oppression primarily to Traveller culture and the nomadic way of life' (1992: 105). This chapter aims toward a more productive conversation between feminist and anti-racist work.

Pre-Settlement Constructions of Traveller Women

Turn of the century Gypsiology and literary images clearly indicate that the Traveller/non-Traveller boundary was gendered and sexualized as outsiders' constructions of Travellers focused on a usually masculinized threat to the reproduction of rural class and gender relations. Likewise, as we have seen, the anti-Traveller racism of the parliamentary debates of the 1940s and 1950s invoked a masculinized Traveller population from which properly domesticated non-Traveller women required 'protection.'

While the available historical sources reveal a largely masculinized population, the smaller number of references to women reveal a diverse set of constructions. In a limited number of cases Traveller women are described in romanticized and sexualized ways. A press report of a horse fair in the western region, for example, included a description of a female Traveller as a 'dusky girl' who sported a 'scarlet and white bandanna round her titian hair, while pendulous ear-rings scintillated and sparkled with every movement of her head' (CT, 28 September 1946: 6). In a later account of the same fair a romanticized description of an 'Irish gipsy' described her as black-eyed and 'raven-haired,' adding that:

> her face is deeply tanned from sun, wind, and wood smoke from the camp fire. Her shoulders are enveloped in a shawl and she never wears stockings. In summer she goes barefoot and in winter wears flimsy sandals. She speaks with a rich accent because so much of her childhood was spent in the counties of Cork and Kerry. (CT, 3 September 1955: 4)

These accounts hint at a non-Traveller male exoticism of Traveller women that fits with Okely's description of Traveller-Gypsy women in England as the 'objects of the dominant society's exotic and erotic projections and disorders' (Okely 1983: 202). A more explicit example of Okely's argument can be found in Liam O'Flaherty's short story *The Tent*, where a male tinker is described as having two wives, one of whom is portrayed as an unattainable object of settled male desire (O'Flaherty 1937).[2]

Along with such imagery, however, were other depictions which masculinized Traveller women, describing their active participation in 'rows,' 'brawls,' or 'tribal feuds,' and portraying them as 'intimidating housewives, shopkeepers, and visitors' (*CT*, 16 May 1959: 3). In 1963 it was claimed, for example, that '[Traveller] women-folk and children ... will no longer take no for an answer and become quite abusive as well as persistent, if their demands are not met every time they "do the rounds"' (*CT*, 2 November 1963: 7).

Constructions of Traveller women as aggressive and 'abusive beggars,' however, coexisted with yet a third set of images that portrayed Traveller women as victims of Traveller men. This construction involved an imposition of gendered ideologies that assumed male dominance in the economic sphere and interpreted the 'begging' of Traveller women as evidence of the failure of Traveller men to measure up to the male breadwinner ideal. According to this view Traveller women involved in peddling and/or begging were suffering from male improvidence.[3] Traveller women themselves drew upon these latter understandings in their appeals to householders to provide them with sustenance for the sake of their children and in (often unsuccessful) attempts to avoid prison terms for begging (see *CT*, 15 October 1960: 12; *CT*, 14 October 1961: 12).

Despite their occasional collusion with a dominant discourse of economic dependence, it is apparent that Traveller women's work was in fact central to the family work strategy during the first half of the twentieth century. In the absence of male controlled property it also seems probable that they experienced a degree of economic control and autonomy vis-à-vis men that was being reduced for other Irish women at this time. It is also likely, however, that as Traveller work activities became more commodified in the post-war period, Traveller women's control over the products of their labour declined as newer income-generating forms of work, i.e., the collection of recyclable items, became concentrated in the hands of men. Women who were disproportionately performing forms of reproductive labour which were essential to family survival but which provided no direct access to income may have found their position within the domestic economy weakened.

Beyond the organization of work, Traveller women, along with many other Irish women, faced gender-based inequities and constraints in the areas of family life, including restrictions on sexuality, arranged marriages at a young age (described in the early 1930s by MacGréine, 1931: 175), and a tendency toward residence with the husband's people that may have weakened kinship ties between women while strengthening those between men (G. Gmelch, 1975: 259).

Within such constraints, however, there is evidence of Traveller women working to protect and promote their interests – sometimes, paradoxically, through engagement with an oppressive state. One poignant example of such action on the part of Traveller women can be seen in the practice of breaking windows.

The regional press reports of the pre-settlement period contain a number of cases of women being charged with the crime of breaking windows of settled businesses, homes, or passing vehicles. The reporting on these cases suggests that the damage was the outcome of a strategy consciously employed by some Traveller wives to engage the attention of outside authorities in the context of marital disputes. In one case, for example, a husband reported that his wife followed him to a public house and, after they had 'a few words,' broke the public house window (CT, 17 March 1956: 12). Another wife threw a bottle that broke a window because her husband, who was drunk, was being obstinate and 'in order to bring him to his senses he had to be given a shock' (CT, 16 April 1960: 3). In a third incident a wife who threw a bottle at her husband but missed and struck another 'girl' was reported to have stated that 'she was only married two months and she did not like to see her husband spending his time in a public house and she threw the bottle at him to try and get him out' (CT, 14 January 1961: 10). The judge commented that it seemed to be a 'common practice with this type of people to throw glasses or bottles around or through public house windows to focus attention on their grievances' (ibid.).

In some of these cases Traveller wives may have been relying on the intervention of outside authorities to punish husbands by forcing them to pay compensation or fines out of the income that they increasingly controlled, but in other cases women were clearly trying to provoke the incarceration of themselves or their husbands. In 1938 a wife charged with damaging a plate glass window by throwing a baby's bottle claimed that:

> The reason I did it was because my husband vexated me. When I didn't beg more money from people around the town for him he vexed me ... and I lost my temper with him. The reason why I did it was to learn my husband and make him do something for the children. I have four children; the youngest is only six months and the eldest is seven years ... I had to do something. I'd like to get not gaol, just to cool him and let him look after his children or go to gaol himself. (CT, 7 May 1938: 10)

In 1940 the same woman broke another window and then turned herself into the police barracks claiming that her husband and others had accused her of 'going with other men' and had threatened to kill her. Arguing that: 'I had no place to go with my two-months-old baby. I'm giving myself up here now. You'll have to keep me in now; I'm not going out again tonight as I have no place to go. They would attack me again' (*CT*, 8 June 1940: 7).

The case of yet another woman suggested that economic desperation could also lead to attempts at self-incarceration. This woman reportedly wanted to go to jail because: 'she had nine children and had to scour the country for food for them as her husband would not go with her. Her husband often left her for months and last year had been imprisoned for failing to maintain her' (*CT*, 21 September 1946: 7). In such cases, Traveller women appeared to be engaging the structures of an oppressive state in an effort to mitigate more intimate inequities.

Such attempts were, however, limited by the pervasive anti-Traveller racism and sexism of the state. Although one judge commented that 'it was starange [*sic*] that it was always the females of the tribes who broke windows' (*CT*, 27 February 1960: 7), there is no evidence of state concern with the position of Traveller women at this time. Indeed, in one case a charge against a Traveller man for assaulting his wife with a knife was dismissed after the wife refused to give evidence against him and the couple promised to leave the jurisdiction (*CT*, 11 July 1953: 7). In this case there was more concern with moving the Travellers out of the region than pursuing the issue of domestic violence involving Traveller women.

Women and Settlement

State interest in Traveller women, however, increased in the context of the formulation and implementation of a settlement policy. The 1963 Report of the Commission on Itinerancy in fact identified women and girls as being the 'greatest hope' for the settlement policy that it was advocating:

A number of itinerants, particularly women and girls, have expressed to members of the Commission a desire for a better way of life, and it is the view of the Commission that the greatest hope for a movement to settle lies in the desire of the young married women and the girls to improve their lot. As the women are more in contact with the homes of the settled population they see what is enjoyed by others. (CI 1963: 87)

While the reference to the 'desire' of 'women and girls' inaccurately suggests extensive consultation with female Travellers it is possible that some Traveller women and girls were willing to express unhappiness with their lives to outsiders. The assumption that 'a better way of life' was exemplified by the lives of the settled housewives with whom Traveller women came into contact while peddling and/or begging, however, revealed the culture, class, and gender-bound character of the Commission Report. Only a few years later a re-emerging Irish women's movement (Mahon 1995) would begin to challenge the ideology of domestication that was the basis for recommendations regarding Traveller women.

As discussed earlier, the Commission Report's construction of the itinerant way of life as one that was 'harsh' and 'primitive' relied heavily on the contention that male Travellers could no longer support their households due to reduced demand for their traditional activities, especially tinsmithing. The Report advocated reorganizing the Traveller economy in such a way that it would be brought into closer conformity with a middle-class model of female homemakers and male breadwinners.

Thus, in a discussion of the need for adult education for Travellers, skills such as carpentry, welding, plumbing, elementary repair, and servicing of machinery (described as those that might assist 'in earning a living') were recommended by implication for males, while it was proposed that 'tuition in housekeeping, cooking, washing, child hygiene, and other domestic knowledge might be made available for the women folk, if necessary, in their dwellings' (CI 1963: 70). As this suggests, the emphasis on domestication was most apparent in the discussion of married women whose mothering and homemaking was to become a full-time occupation (under the guidance of settlement workers).

The Commissioners advocated a reorganized Traveller domestic economy, but expressed approval of other aspects of Traveller gender relations, notably the existence of male family heads who were 'always held in respect by the other members' (CI 1963: 37), the 'strict watch' kept on Traveller 'daughters and women' and the fact that 'girls are always very modest in dress and demeanor' (CI 1963: 90). The Commissioners even articulated their concern that the 'high standards' of sexual morality among Travellers might 'be imperilled' through exposure to 'the less desirable incidents of life in the settled community' (ibid.). These positive comments regarding gender relations and sexuality among Travellers contrasted dramatically with the otherwise assimilationist thrust of the Report – betraying a gendered conservatism on the part of the Commissioners.

Women and Settlement in Galway City

At the local level in Galway City, early work with Travellers had been initiated by female religious orders, and the settlement movement of the 1960s was spearheaded by a largely middle-class and female leadership within the Galway Settlement committee. Organizations such as the Irish Countrywomen's Association and the Galway Young Wives also got involved in early settlement efforts. Settlement advocates often made their case for the provision of permanent accommodation to Travellers in maternalist terms – i.e., by pointing to the living conditions of young Traveller mothers and children. Explicit links were made, for example, between the plight of mothers and infants and the 'holy family' that could find 'no room in the inn' (see *CT*, 11 April 1964: 3), and a letter to the editor in Galway chastised 'lady' politicians in particular for voting against the provision of housing for Travellers, asking: 'Where is their concern for mothers and children shivering in wet and cold?' (*CT*, 10 December 1976: 10).

While there continued to be press reports that featured Traveller women as aggressive beggars, protagonists in assaults, and window-breakers, these efforts led to a new focus on the plight of young Traveller mothers. At the height of conflicts over the housing of Travellers, it was images and sometimes the voices of Traveller mothers that were featured in press reporting on the provision of accommodation – for example, 'Itinerant Mother of 12 Makes Case For House' (*CT*, 19 June 1970: 4).

At the same time as the physical circumstances of Traveller mothers were featured in support of settlement, gendered imagery was also central in the discourse of those resisting settlement plans. As in the past, opponents of initiatives such as the provision of housing and hardstands during the 1970s and 1980s countered claims regarding the putative needs of Traveller mothers with references to the need to protect 'terrified' non-Traveller 'women shoppers,' 'wives,' and 'daughters' from Travellers (see CT, 22 August 1986: 1, 3; *CT*, 18 November 1983: 1, 24). A letter to the editor in the 1970s argued: 'Who can deny the justice of the residents' fears for themselves and their children ... the menace of [Travellers'] hungry dogs and wandering horses is very frightening for nervous [non-Traveller] mothers and young children' (*CT*, 9 January 1976: 11). In the 1980s Travellers' 'wild and savage dogs' were said to 'attack women and children,' and it was claimed that 'residents' wives have to be escorted everywhere as they are terrified of the itinerants' (*Connacht*

Sentinel, 18 December 1984: 1; *Galway Advertiser*, 12 December 1984: 1; see also *CT*, 12 May 1989: 12).

These examples reveal how ethnicized boundaries between Travellers and non-Travellers were partially constructed and reproduced through an essentially gendered racism that problematized and demonized Traveller men while shoring up constructions of (settled and Traveller) women as being in need of 'protection.' That such claims were being made at a time when changes in women's roles and a growing Irish women's movement were challenging such paternalistic ideologies suggests a link between anti-Traveller racism and wider struggles over gender relations in Ireland.

Researching Gendered Relations

In order to better understand how dominant constructions of Traveller women and gender relations articulated with Travellers' own lived experience I turn now to the ethnographic material gathered during the fieldwork period. First, however, it is important to note the degree to which the ethnographic project was shaped by my own gendered status and interactions (see Bell, Caplan, and Karim 1993; Wolf 1996). Models of breadwinner husbands and dependent wives, for instance, ensured that some Travellers (like other Irish) assumed that my husband was the one actually conducting the research project and that I was his assistant. One Traveller woman, having provided me with a detailed genealogy, asked me the following day whether my husband had been pleased with it, and at a Traveller wedding he fielded questions about 'his' research while I was completely free from such inquiries. Given the uneasiness that my researcher status sometimes provoked, the diminution of this role on the basis of my gender and marital status, while frustrating on a personal level, had the side-benefit of removing some of this tension from my interpersonal relations.

Relations between Traveller men and women were quite segregated, and women took care never to be alone with men who were not husbands, fathers, brothers, or sons. Married women also spent more time with each other than with unmarried young women. These gendered and generationed patterns of interaction influenced my own social relations in the camp and elsewhere. Throughout the research period my primary access was to other married women and access to men was limited. When I visited married couples in their trailers, for example, men usually left the trailer to visit elsewhere, leaving me alone with their wives. On the rare occasions when they stayed, however, men always dominated the conversation, allowing me an opportunity to learn something of their activities and concerns. I also tried to maximize my time with men by staying in my own trailer when men arrived to visit my husband there, despite the fact that such behaviour was unusual. Most of my interactions, however, were with women and children, with the result that I learned much more about their lives and perspectives.

Women's Work

In the previous chapter I described how official constructions of Traveller work often highlighted the activities of men, while the value and significance of women's work was often downplayed, problematized, or completely ignored. A similar obscuring of women's work was found in stories that celebrated Traveller skills of ingenuity and self-sufficiency through reference to male work activities.

Fieldwork among Travellers in Dublin by Sharon and George Gmelch in the early 1970s suggested that changes in the Irish economy and the urbanization of the Travellers had resulted in a decline of male trades and an increase in the importance of the Traveller women's income-generating activities, particularly begging (see especially S. Gmelch 1977; Gmelch and Gmelch 1978). Not only were Traveller women seen as economically active, but it was argued that what had been a strongly patriarchal family organization was changing as Traveller women gained power and authority commensurate with their increasing contribution to the family economy. I was intrigued by this analysis and paid attention to women's work and its significance in my own research. My conclusion, however, was closer to that of Okely, who described a reversed situation of a decrease in married women's involvement in income-generation among Traveller-Gypsies in England in the 1970s (1983: 204).

I found that while some women reported having worked in casual jobs in laundries, supermarkets, and hotels this was usually before marriage. Some wives that I encountered spent time working at the dump and/or calling at houses, but the overall involvement of married women in income-generating activities appeared to be minimal in comparison with their non-income generating work of domestic labour, budgeting, accessing goods and services from various sources, and child care.

As previously mentioned, begging by Traveller women had long attracted adverse comment from city council and business interests in

Galway, and the implementation of the settlement policy had included efforts to eliminate this activity in conformity with the recommendations of the Commission on Itinerancy. The Chamber of Commerce, which viewed begging as detrimental to the city's tourist trade, had urged the city council to 'crack down,' and the Settlement Council had announced that with the provision of social welfare it was no longer necessary for the public to provide alms to Travellers. The Council also directly discouraged Traveller women and children from begging, especially in the areas where they had been housed (Itinerant Settlement Council, 6 October 1967). Although prosecutions trailed off in the 1970s, I found that the non-Traveller staff of training centres, school teachers, and the Church (in the course of marriage preparations) all continued to actively discourage Traveller begging.

Given the efforts on the part of outsiders to eliminate the practice it was not surprising that Travellers in the camp were extremely reluctant to discuss this activity with me. Over the course of the research period, however, I learned of a number of Traveller women and children living inside and outside the camp who gathered cash, clothing, and food by going door to door and/or engaged in street begging.

While street begging was stigmatized by some in the camp, who suggested that it was a result of alcoholism, destitution, or simply 'greediness,' there was a more ambivalent response to the practice of door-to-door calling. I was first made aware that one of my close neighbours was involved in this activity when I was told of her visits by a non-Traveller living in a nearby housing estate. When I asked my neighbour about her work she emphasized the personal nature of her interactions; that is, she received things from women who 'knew her' as a result of a long-term relationship (see also S. Gmelch 1977; Gmelch and Gmelch 1978). Other women of the camp admired this individual for her success and were often pleased to receive as gifts some of the items that she had collected, but there was also criticism that her redistribution did not go far enough and that her behaviour was 'shameful' because it involved going out of the camp on her own. In fact, several married women indicated that, while they had begged as children, they would be too 'ashamed' to do so now. Some of these none the less received clothes gathered by their children and/or other relatives through door-to-door collecting.

Domestic Labour

Most married women that I lived among spent much of the day working within their respective trailers and mobiles. Women were ultimately responsible (with the assistance of older children and especially girls), for daily tasks such as cleaning the trailer, washing dishes and clothes, food preparation, and cleaning, dressing, feeding, and supervising children. The work of cleaning was constant as women tried to keep children as well as trailer interiors free of the muck that was constantly tracked in from outside. Meals were usually eaten twice during the day with little formality; breakfast might consist of tea, fried eggs, and bread, and dinner might include cabbage, bacon, and spuds, or tinned spaghetti. All day and into the evening, cups of tea were continually being offered to members of the family and visitors.

The gendered division of labour and lack of male recognition of the value of women's work was sometimes the focus of critical commentary. An older woman in her sixties observed that the men often returned home claiming that they had been working all day 'at the scrap' while their wives had been doing nothing. They wanted their wives to 'treat them like kings,' she said, and often insisted on being served their food first. By the time women got a chance to eat, she observed, they were often too tired to do so. A younger woman responded to this assessment by commenting that it would be great if husbands and wives could 'swop' for a few days – a suggestion that was greeted with gales of laughter by the larger group of women who overheard the exchange.

Ironically, by the 1980s the domestication that was advocated for married women as part of a modernizing settlement project in the 1960s was increasingly viewed by service professionals as evidence of a problematized 'traditional' gendered conservatism among Travellers and was targeted for change. As a result Traveller women were by the 1980s beginning to be singled out for 'liberation' through training for wage employment in an economy that was favouring female over male workers in the expanding low-paid part-time casual labour market (O'Hearn 1998: 99).

It is likely, however, that the domestication of Traveller women was not so much 'traditional' as exacerbated by aspects of the settlement project, including efforts to eliminate begging. Another part of the settlement project that contributed to this was the change in the organization of social life that accompanied the shift in accommodation from smaller tents to trailers and/or various forms of housing. The latter had resulted in activities such as cooking, eating, and visiting, which in the past were often conducted outside in fine weather, being brought inside Traveller dwellings. As a consequence domestic space and women's domestic labour were increasingly privatized and expanded.

The intensity of women's domestic labour within the camp was also directly affected by official neglect – notably by the lack of easily accessible running water, electricity, and toilets. Women made it clear that the existence of such services in flats and houses was a major advantage of 'settlement.' Just as some Travellers living in houses made use of the camp to store scrap or trailers, some Travellers living in the camp used their links to close relatives or affines in houses in order to gain access to clean water and washing machines.

Trailer-living involved particular challenges for women as domestic workers, but it also allowed for a degree of communalism that was more difficult to achieve in houses. Within the camp, for example, tools for domestic work such as mops, buckets, and brooms were constantly circulated among the women of the same closely related cluster of families. There was also some provision of domestic labour across nuclear family boundaries. One grandmother in the camp, for example, spent a great deal of time preparing and serving meals and tea to her married sons, some of their wives, and many of her grandchildren. This work had the effect of freeing some of her daughters-in-law from continual food preparation. They in turn partially compensated her by intermittently stocking her supply of food. Another important form of shared labour across closely related camp neighbours was child-care – a topic that I discuss in the following chapter.

The domestic labour of women was essential to the maintenance of the family unit, but it was also imbued with cultural significance. As Okely (1983) has described, for Traveller-Gypsies in Britain there was a set of ritual practices surrounding domestic work, including the use of 'clean' bowls for the washing of dishes and utensils, and 'dirty' bowls for the washing of clothes, the floor, and the body. Using the wrong bowl for the wrong purpose would lead to impurity for family members. Similar practices occurred in houses or flats, where I was told the kitchen sink was considered 'clean' while the bath was 'dirty.' Once a clean bowl became 'dirty' it could not regain its purity and could only be subsequently used for the washing of the 'dirty' items. Okely (1983) has linked such practices to British Traveller-Gypsy beliefs in the purity of the inner versus outer body – beliefs that produce particular concern about the 'cleanliness' of items (utensils, food) that enter the body.

Travellers differentiated between the 'cleanliness' or 'dirtiness' of families and sometimes kinship groupings according to women's alleged adherence to such practices. Women and men would make critical comments regarding the state of other trailers and commented that in some cases they would not accept a mug of tea made by a woman who appeared to be 'careless,' i.e., insufficiently mindful of purity practices. Other women in contrast were praised for their ability to keep their trailers and children 'clean.' The weight of maintaining the ritual status of the family (and wider kinship grouping) vis-à-vis others thus rested disproportionately on the shoulders of women as domestic labourers. Evaluations of relative cleanliness, however, did not necessarily bear a direct relationship to women's work; rather, they corresponded closely to distinctions of wealth among families. Gendered concepts of purity, then, not only reproduced gendered inequalities, but were also a discourse through which economic disparities were acknowledged and legitimated through evaluations of women.

Along with marking divisions of gender and class, attributions of cleanliness and dirt also served to mark ethnicized boundaries between Travellers and non-Travellers (see also Okely 1975; 1983). I was frequently told that non-Travellers were dirty because they did not follow the domestic cleanliness rules used by Travellers. The most common example I was given of this was that non-Travellers washed their babies' nappies and/or their hair in the kitchen sink, the same place where eating utensils were washed. Such an inability to keep pure and impure separate was always described in tones of disgust, and I was frequently told that Travellers were much cleaner than settled people.

While I followed Traveller practice in my use of separate bowls, my less stringent adherence to these practices may have been a source of concern. Although some of my neighbours accepted tea in my trailer, others turned down offers, claiming they had just had a cup, or would return to their own trailer to retrieve a mug, which I would then fill.

Through their work as domestic labourers, then, Traveller women maintained (or threatened) the ritual purity not only of their families and wider clusters but also of Travellers as whole. The linking of women's everyday practices of domestic work to the maintenance of an ethnicized boundary revealed the gendered processes through which women became signified as 'bearers of the collective' (Yuval-Davis 1997).

Budgeting, Sharing, and Redistribution

Travellers' dependence upon a cash income for daily necessities appeared to be greater than it had been in the past, when, as one older woman claimed, only tea and alcohol were purchased and 'no one ever went hungry.' The ability of camp families to earn enough cash for their needs varied greatly, but in all cases it was primarily the responsibility of married women to meet the basic domestic requirements of their units from week to week.

In the camp, the importance of married women's budgeting work was acknowledged by the men as essential to domestic management. Most families in the camp had to buy food, bottled gas for their cookers, heating fuel such as turf, coal, wood, or gas, and some form of power (from a truck or car battery or generator, or from an electricity outlet). Other basic items requiring at least some cash outlay included clothing, vehicles (which also required insurance, tax, and fuel), and trailers. Entertainment costs (for such items as drink, movies, cigarettes, card games, lottery tickets, the purchase and repair of televisions, and birthday and Christmas presents) could be substantial. Those who could manage it tried to save small amounts of money each week, which they then used to pay for these and other modest luxuries such as decorative items for the trailer and jewellery for women and girls.

For several families, however, the week-to-week budgeting was extremely difficult and unexpected crises or celebrations would necessitate going into debt. The precariousness of some units was revealed by the relief expressed by one of my neighbours when her gas bottle ran out on the day before the weekly dole payment. The timing ensured that there would be enough cash to get another one, whereas if it had happened later in the week, she told me, the money would have already been spent, leaving her without cooking fuel for several days.

Women were generally thought to have more 'sense' with money than men and were admired for their efforts to stretch limited income as far as it would go. One woman in the camp was praised for her ability to keep her husband from drinking or borrowing money, thereby ensuring that high-cost items such as vehicle insurance could be met. The financial success of one of the wealthiest Travellers in the city was also partially attributed to his wife, who 'counted the pennies.'

Despite their work of budgeting, however, women usually lacked ultimate control over family finances. The latter tended to be controlled by men, who dominated the income-generating activities and retained control over the buying and selling of family assets. In an effort to ensure that sufficient funds for the immediate needs of the unit were provided, women often pressured their husbands into going straight from the labour exchange to shop for the week's groceries, fuel, and petrol before the dole money ran out. Income expenditures were a source of tension and occasionally overt conflict between some married couples.

While budgeting occurred at the nuclear family unit level, through sharing and redistribution the women of closely linked families actively and creatively attempted to minimize their dependence on the wider market. Closely (often affinally) linked women continually shared information about such things as the prices for basic grocery items in different city stores, special sales on clothing or household furnishings, and opportunities to buy items second hand. News of short-term promotional deals within the city circulated quickly.

Within these networks there was also continual redistribution of items among women. On a small scale this was demonstrated when women would respond to praise of an item of their jewellery or clothing by immediately offering the item to the woman making the compliment. Before a wedding attended by many in the camp, women completed their outfits through the location and exchange of matching accessories within their female networks. Requests to share or borrow more mundane items such as firelighter, candles, brooms, and mops were also frequent within the co-residential clusters of the camp. Initial approaches for such items were often made through children, and those who claimed that they lacked a requested item (overt refusals were rare) risked being cursed for being 'mean bitches.'

Despite important forms of co-operation, redistribution, and exchange among women, the greater commodification of the Traveller economy and the increased concentration of income in the hands of men ensured that women's task of ensuring the maintenance of the family unit was often challenging. Part of the challenge of ensuring subsistence was met through successful interactions with more powerful bureaucracies of state and voluntary agencies.

Women, the State, and Voluntary Agencies

Married women spent a considerable amount of time negotiating on behalf of their families with those clergy, social workers, volunteer workers, doctors, teachers, lawyers, local government officials, and, of course, the resident anthropologist, involved in Traveller-related work (see also G. Gmelch 1977: 115). Through these negotiations they attempted to ensure their family's access to such things as secure camping sites, housing, part-time jobs, schooling, places in training centres, religious classes, rent subsidies, loans, and health care, as well as goods such as Christmas hampers and second-hand clothes.

While each woman acted on behalf of her own family unit, as with the case of domestic labour and budgeting there was considerable sharing of information among the women of closely linked families. One dramatic example of the dynamics of women's advocacy for their families as well as co-operation with others from closely linked units was provided by the introduction of a European Community food giveaway of stockpiled agricultural products – butter, milk, and meat – during the fieldwork period.

The news of the food giveaway travelled quickly and Traveller women actively sought out ways in which to make the most of the opportunity provided to reduce expenditures on food. Overwhelmed with individual requests, one of the social service agencies involved in the food distribution attempted to impose a system of allocation. The first step of the agency was to ask a 'camp representative' to provide them with a list of the names of those living in the camp and to assist in the distribution. Despite this attempt at systemization, other women from the camp continued to approach the agency claiming that they had not received their share from the assigned 'representative.' In response to this perceived problem, an agency worker came out to the camp itself to distribute some of the food directly.

Arriving after darkness had fallen, the worker was confronted with a group of women, some of whom did not live in the camp but had heard about the planned visit from relatives in the camp. The worker's attempt to use his existing list as a basis for distribution was abandoned under the pressure of direct requests from the women. The worker adapted to the situation by asking each woman how many children she had and then trying to assign portions of meat according to family size. This led to a predictable inflation of family sizes by the women present.

After each woman had exhausted her own claim, there was a second round of attempts to claim meat for others who were not present, such as absent sisters and mothers, etc. As consideration widened beyond those who had already received the food, one woman pointed out that I had not yet received my share (I had been hovering in the background). When the distributor asked how many children I had, I lied and declared that I had two and was immediately rewarded with a large piece of meat. While I could plausibly claim maternal status, an older women whose obvious age made it more difficult angrily challenged the premise of the distribution by declaring (accurately but unsuccessfully) to the agency worker that while she had no children of her own living with her, she was none the less constantly feeding her sons and grandchildren and therefore should receive more.

The incident revealed how women worked within severe constraints to increase resources for their own families but also co-operated with others who were closely related by informing them of the visit and by not contesting each other's fraudulent claims. The co-operation did not, however, extend beyond those closely linked by kinship and marriage. Indeed, other families who lived in the camp but were part of another residential cluster were not informed of the impending visit by the camp 'representative.'

While women worked hard to maximize this particular resource they were also critical of the vagaries of charity that it represented. The quality of the meat was questioned and some complained that, as it had been delivered on the same day that most had already done their shopping, it had not necessarily saved them money because they had already bought perishables which (like the meat) had to be eaten within a limited time. One poorer woman told me that she could have saved one pound off her food bill (an amount that she considered quite significant) if she had known for certain that the meat was coming.

Traveller women's work to minimize cash expenditure and maximize access to goods and services was ongoing and essential to the survival of their families, but this work did not necessarily translate into increased power within the family or wider community. While the skills of women in dealing with non-Travellers who controlled important resources and services were acknowledged by men, this work did not provide independent access to income. In their encounters with non-Travellers, Traveller women also experienced various forms of racism, stigma, and humiliation. Many were refused service outright or were served in unseemly haste by shopkeepers anxious to have them leave. When I went shopping with Traveller women in a larger supermarket we were often under conspicuous surveillance by security guards.

The ability of women to represent the interests of their families effectively to service providers also often depended on collusion with stigmatizing constructions of Traveller gender relations. As mentioned, the dominant assumption that men should be primary providers meant that Traveller men, much more than Traveller women, were held responsible for the poor economic position of many Traveller families. A number of service workers described Traveller men as lazy for not working, or for abusing the system of social welfare if they did. Traveller women, in contrast, were often regarded more positively. One service provider, for example, commented: 'the women move much faster than the men ... They have more ability. They're more downtrodden, they're a bit more accepting ... and they're more intelligent.' Traveller women who found themselves in a position of relative powerlessness vis-à-vis service providers sometimes acquiesced in dominant constructions of Traveller male irresponsibility by, for example, attributing failure to stay in a house or in a job to the demands of their husbands, a strategy which sometimes repaired strained relationships with outsiders to the benefit of the family unit (see also G. Gmelch 1977: 74).

While women's access to income has declined, the previous discussion emphasizes the ongoing importance of Traveller women's forms of work to the survival of their families and wider clusters. Such activities, I have emphasized, involved women in skilled negotiations within often unequal relations. Despite the significance of this work, however, it was rarely valorized as evidence of Traveller self-sufficiency, autonomy, and cleverness. Such evaluations remained disproportionately attached to the income-generating activities of men.

Gender, Residence, and Kinship

Traveller women's work occurred within the context of social relations of residence that were in turn based on close kinship and affinal ties. As mentioned, these social relations were, like work activities, deeply gendered. A tendency toward close residence between closely related men observed in the past continued to be evident among Travellers in both camps and housing estates. In the camp where I was living twelve of the fourteen families that spent time there were living among the husband's 'people' – his parents, brothers, cousins, uncles, and/or grandparents.

The presence of the two 'exceptions' to virilocal residence, however, revealed that the pattern of residence with the husband's people was far from absolute. Traveller women in fact vigorously resisted any suggestion of a residence 'rule' and often spoke of their hope that in the future they would spend more time living close to their own natal families. Available 'snapshots' of earlier camp composition provided by the city records in fact revealed many cases of residence with women's kin. One year, for example, an elderly couple were recorded as living in the camp with two of their married daughters as well as two of their married sons, while in another year an older couple were camped alongside three of their married daughters with no married sons present at all. Residence with the wife's people, then, was not unusual, but it was less common and often associated with the early years of marriage (as was the case for the two families in the camp).

Over the course of the fieldwork period there were three distinct clusters of families linked to one another through close kin and affinal ties. Each cluster of families was spatially marked by the positioning of the trailers in the camp and by more intense social interaction among its members. While there were some links of kinship, marriage, and friendship between individuals of different clusters, these tended to be of less social significance.

The major residential cluster of the camp included an older married couple, several of their married sons and their families, a married grandson and his family, and a married granddaughter and her family. A second cluster consisted of two married brothers and their wives and children, and the third cluster, which moved in during the fieldwork period, was made up of a middle-aged married couple and their family and the trailers of their recently married son and daughter and their respective spouses.

Although less often co-residential, close kinship ties among women were actively maintained across geographical distances. Women worked to preserve links to their 'own people' through visits, letters, and phone calls, and evening conversations were filled with fascinating news and speculation about Traveller engagements, weddings, illnesses, and deaths in other towns and cities. My greater access to women provided me with a vivid sense of the networks that linked them to others across Ireland and the British Isles. Precisely because they were less likely to be residentially based, ties among women were an important part of the openness and breadth of Traveller social networks.

Travellers referred to their parents, children, siblings, and grandparents or grandchildren as 'my people,' 'those belonging to me,' or 'my own.' Such phrases could also, in some contexts, refer to uncles, aunts, nephews, nieces, and first cousins. While Travellers could easily recite the names of relatives on both their mother's and father's side out to the range of first cousin, the latter relatives were more often referred to as 'close friends' or 'friends' (my own description of some visitors to the camp as my 'friends' led to the incorrect assumption that they were my relatives).

Kinship reckoning was bilateral, with both mother's and father's 'people' recognized as relatives, but ties through women were given less cultural weight than ties through men. This was apparent when, after a dispute with her spouse, one women told me that her marital troubles stemmed primarily from the fact that she had no one 'belonging' to her living in the camp. I presumed from this comment that she had no close kin living in the camp, but when I repeated her comment to another woman I was told that the wife was 'denying her own,' because in fact her husbands' paternal grandfather who lived in the camp was simultaneously her own maternal uncle. In this case a link between a maternal uncle and niece, while recognized, was given less cultural weight than the patrilineal link between grandfather and grandson.

Patterns of virilocality meant that there was usually greater personal knowledge of those on the father's side. Travellers' knowledge of more distant relatives, such as second and third cousins, great aunts and uncles, great nephews and nieces, were skewed toward the patrilateral kin, who were variously referred to as 'friends,' 'far out friends' or 'strangers,' depending on a combination of genealogical and social distance. The term 'friend,' for example, could refer to first and second cousins, 'far out friend' could include second and third cousins, but both second and third cousins could also be referred to as 'strangers.'

When I asked people to specify the genealogical link indicated by terms such as 'far out friends' or 'strangers' the precise kinship link was not always immediately evident, although people were usually able to work it out for my benefit. One of my neighbours described herself as being a 'stranger' to her husband, but when I pressed on the precise relationship, she worked out a series of kinship ties which revealed that she and her husband were in fact third cousins. In such cases, however, the genealogical link clearly had little significance in the absence of other factors. This point was underscored for me by the comment, frequently made in response to my requests for genealogical information, that 'all Travellers are related if you look into it.'

Outsiders and Travellers occasionally used terms such as 'tribe' and 'clan,' which suggested the existence of exclusive kin groups beyond the immediate family unit. Because these were identified by patronyms the significance of ties among women was again obscured. One service worker, for example, described to me how the city's group housing scheme was dominated by the A ____ 'clan.' What she was referring to was the fact that for some years a major residential cluster found within the scheme consisted of the household of an older man with the surname A ____ and the households of several of his married sons *and daughters*. The, latter, however did not share the same surname and their importance was hidden by the use of the patronym to identify the residential cluster.[4]

Within the context of residential arrangements that favoured ties among men, co-residential women who were less likely to be closely related to one another none the less forged important ties. It was this group of women who socialized together each evening in the camp and, as I have indicated, exchanged goods and services readily with one another. Sometimes such ties would be given ideological strength through the use of fictive kin terms. Two unrelated women who were neighbours married to two brothers, for example, told me that they were 'like sisters' to one another. Through such relationships with other women, Traveller women established important forms of emotional, social, and economic support within the context of residential arrangements that favoured and strengthened ties among males.

Gender and Marriage

When non-Travellers expressed concern about the oppressive aspects of Traveller culture for Traveller women, their concerns frequently centred on practices associated with Traveller marriage and especially the practice of arranging marriages or 'matchmaking.' This practice was viewed as particularly problematic for young women and many service workers made conscious efforts to discourage the practice. Consistent with the view that Travellers were the descendants of dispossessed peasants, many outsiders believed that matchmaking among Travellers was the legacy of an outdated peasant tradition. Sharon Gmelch implies a similar view in her comment that 'common to all travellers is a form of arranged marriage known as the "match". Until this century it was the accepted practice in most of rural Ireland as well' (1975: 66).

Matchmaking among Travellers, however, differed from the 'classic' Irish matchmaking of the post-famine small farmer, which was bound up with the inheritance of land and dowry payments and was associated with a relatively late age of marriage and a high rate of non-marriage. Traveller marriages, in contrast, involved little property transfer, marriage at a young age, and a very low rate of non-marriage. To view Traveller marriage practices as peasant survivals obscures the significance of arranged marriage for Traveller life in the past and at present.

The most common reason offered by Travellers for arranged marriages was the avoidance of marriages with non-Travellers. Such marriages, I was told, were extremely risky because there was no way of knowing whether your partner would be suitable until it was too late. Cases of desertion or marriage breakdown were offered as proof of the dangers of such relationships, and a repeated theme was that such marriages often dissolved when the settled partner 'discovered' that their spouse was a Traveller. One woman, in telling me of her cousin who was separated from her English non-Traveller husband, commented: 'I don't know why. It might be that he found out that she was an itinerant because you wouldn't know she was to look at her.' Another night she told a story about how an engagement between a Traveller boy and non-Traveller girl was broken off when the young man's mother came to his engagement party and his girlfriend realized that he was a Traveller.

These stories of discovery of hidden ethnic identity presumed a stigmatized rejection by non-Travellers, but Travellers were themselves active in discouraging such relationships. The parents and siblings of one young Traveller man responded to the discovery that he had a non-Traveller girlfriend by trying to break up the relationship by repeatedly threatening the young woman with violence and by telling her (incorrectly) that her boyfriend was already married and had a child. I was told that the actions of the boy's family were motivated by the fear that if they got married the settled woman would eventually leave him.[5]

Marriage was a favourite topic at the evening gatherings of women. By participating in these gatherings I became aware of several matches that were made, broken off, and sometimes remade among Travellers living in the city and elsewhere. As described to me the dynamics of matchmaking were deeply gendered and generationed. An engagement, I was told, was formalized only after first the boy and then the girl were asked, in the presence of their parents and a designated 'matchmaker,' whether they were 'satisfied' to marry one another.

Typically the initiative came from the boy's 'side' and he had the first right of refusal. Only after the negotiations had been made among the adults of the two families, and the boy had formally agreed, was the girl approached for her consent. Women describing these dynamics made it clear that girls did not 'choose' but were 'chosen,' and that there was often pressure to agree to a match that one's close relatives had already negotiated. While girls could refuse a match (and the option of elopement remained ever-present), women suggested that a girl who refused a match might find it 'hard to find another.' In cases where the matchmaking process had begun and then was called off there was also potential for the girl to get a 'bad name' and/or for 'trouble' between the two family groups involved. These dynamics supported male and adult privilege (see similar descriptions of this sequence and the particular pressure on girls in M. McDonagh 1993: 16 and W. McDonagh 1993: 21).

In all of the cases described to me the designated 'matchmaker' was male and was closely connected through kinship and/or affinal links to the prospective couple. During the fieldwork period an uncle used a visit to the city to act as matchmaker for the children of his siblings. In one case he 'rematched' his sister's son and brother's daughter, who had quarrelled, and at the same time he 'drew down' a second match between a brother's daughter and yet another brother's son. In this case the matchmaker was an uncle to all of the young people involved.

In other examples described to me matchmakers were uncles or older brothers to one of the young people involved, and often married to the sister or aunt of the other young person. In such a situation, the matchmaker was working to perpetuate the affinal link represented by his own marriage, and his wife, being related to the other set of parents, could be active in the negotiations as well. In such cases the wife might in fact be the most familiar with the personal qualities of the proposed partner and therefore well positioned to encourage or discourage the match. One young woman living in the camp told me how her aunt had influenced her decision to accept a proposed match in just such circumstances by telling her that the young man in question was 'good, quiet, and lovely.'

As this suggests, older women, while not formally identified as matchmakers, were none the less active players in the process – a fact which belies a simplistic analysis of women as victims of such negotiations. Women used their own social relations and knowledge to advance their own goals through matchmaking. One such goal was increasing contact with their own relatives by encouraging close kin such as siblings to marry into the same family as they had.

The active role of women in working to build kin support through marriage negotiations was apparent when word came from another town that a match made for a sister of one of my camp neighbours had been called off. Following this news my neighbour worked hard to find her sister a new prospect in Galway in the hopes that this would bring her sister to join her in the city. When two of her brothers arrived for a visit, she told them to approach her own husband's brother and his wife to ask if they would 'give' their son in marriage. After the match was successfully negotiated between this son and her sister, my neighbour told me proudly: 'You could say I was behind it.'

Such activity on the part of older women was not, however, officially acknowledged, and even the more formalized role of male matchmakers was a discreet one. Brothers, I was told, should not appear to be 'hawking their sisters,' a comment which revealed the gendered nature of such negotiations – the reverse claim that sisters should avoid appearing to be 'hawking their brothers (or sisters)' was never suggested.

The process referred to as 'drawing down the match' was a serious and sensitive one but if successful was followed with a celebration by the parents and other close adult relatives. Following this the two sets of parents would go to the priest in order to arrange the 'paperwork' and might book a hotel for the reception. The latter arrangements were, however, often hindered by racism as Travellers were often directly refused bookings or found that they were cancelled by hotels who later discovered their Traveller identity.

In the case of arranged marriages, weddings brought together families who already considered one another to be appropriate marriage partners; thus weddings were one of few sanctioned opportunities for young men to 'see' young women and initiate marriage proceedings. One woman told me how she had advised her mother to send her unmarried sister to a wedding in the city in order to expedite a match. As another woman told me, 'one wedding draws another.'

Traveller wedding ceremonies appear to have been minor events in the past, but during the fieldwork period it was clear that a great deal of money and effort went into these events. In the case of one wedding of two young Travellers living in houses, the plans for the wedding were followed with great interest by their relatives living in the camp. Several men 'took the pledge' to stop drinking for some weeks before the wedding in order to have enough money to buy new clothes and drinks for the event.

While the church ceremony was open to all, only those more closely related to the couple were invited to the reception, where a hot meal was served and there was an open bar and live music for singing and dancing. The wedding was an occasion for a display of wealth and generosity that increased the prestige of the families involved: the size of the reception, the quality of the food, the number of wedding cakes, and the bride's and bridesmaids' dresses were discussed and compared with those of other Traveller weddings.

Weddings were said by some to be the responsibility of the bride's parents, while others described the enterprise as a joint one of 'teamwork.' One Traveller man informed me that if the young man's family appeared reluctant to share expenses they might be told: 'You're getting a women now, you should pay up.' In many cases it was the groom's parents who supplied the couple with a trailer, and women described receiving rings and neck chains from their husbands. Couples who had accumulated money from previous employment also contributed financially. One young married woman described how she had saved up enough money to pay for her own wedding dress, the bridesmaids' dresses, and the wedding cake.

Marriage practices had been the target of intervention by service workers and by the Catholic Church. In Galway City a chaplain for Travellers had been appointed to ensure, among other things, that the Church regulations on marriage were followed, and increased intervention had resulted in a number of changes, including a discouragement of both 'matchmaking' and close-kin marriages among Travellers. In the past a Church dispensation was ostensibly required for all marriages between first, second, or third cousins, but in 1983 this was reduced to first cousins only, and Travellers (who appeared to have had little difficulty receiving dispensations for close-kin marriages in the past) were beginning to experience some pressure against such unions.

During my residence in the camp, these reforms were criticized by married women. In one case, I was told of a bishop in another city who had unexpectedly refused a proposed 'match' on the grounds that it was 'too close.' The sister of the intended bride commented to me that, on the contrary, the couple were 'nothing to each other.' In fact, she added, her parents, who had made the match, knew more about the 'kindred' than the bishop did, and wouldn't take a marriage to him if it was 'too close.' The Church, she noted with frustration, was 'changing the rules every day about marriage.' She went on to say: 'People think that itinerants [i.e., Travellers] don't care who they marry and can find another one, but it's hard to find another one.' A woman listening to her story agreed and added: 'They want you to marry strangers.'

As this exchange indicated many Travellers expressed a preference for marriage with close-kin 'friends' rather than 'strangers.' Many of the women that I knew were in fact linked to their husband's people before marriage by kinship and/or affinal ties and had in such cases married 'back in.'

Of the fourteen households that spent time in the camp, three of the married couples were first cousins (those who are unequivocally termed 'friends') and two others were second cousins. Such a pattern was also found in a data set of 116 Traveller marriages which I was able to compile from genealogies and city records, where 32 of the marriages were between first cousins – a finding consistent with earlier studies (Flynn 1975; G. Gmelch 1977; Ó Nuallain and Forde 1992).[6]

Although George Gmelch argued that close-kin marriages were increasing in the context of Traveller urbanization in early-1970s Dublin, Travellers that I spoke to did not make such a link. The finding of a longer history of cousin marriages among Traveller-Gypsies in parts of England and Wales suggests the possibility that the practice may also have a deeper history in Ireland (see Okely 1983: 156–7).

Travellers were clear on the reasons for marrying 'back in.' It was claimed that when a prospective couple were 'friends' to one another, their personal qualities and those of their families were more easily ascertained. Such factors as the diligence of prospective partners, the moral reputation of the young woman, whether the young man was 'quiet,' and the personal characteristics and economic status of the respective parents and siblings were all described as important. A strong belief in the irreversibility of marriage among Travellers (as well as the lack of divorce in Ireland prior to its legalization after the 1995 referendum) meant that a primary goal of matchmaking was the creation of an enduring relationship as the basis for a successful new unit. Also important was the opportunity to create and/or strengthen ties between wider family groups.

While matches were ideally made between families that knew one another well, marriages between the most closely linked cousins were least likely. The children of two brothers who had spent long periods camped or housed close to one another, for example, were least favoured as marriage partners. Of the thirty-two first-cousin marriages found in my larger data set only five were between the children of brothers. In contrast, ten were between the children of sisters and seventeen were between the children of a brother and sister. While there was no explicit marriage rule or prohibition, a general preference for marrying lesser known cousins was expressed. One young Traveller woman living in a house commented, 'I wouldn't want to marry the cousins I grew up with – they are more like brothers.' First-cousin marriages were more common between individuals who had resided in different residential clusters and therefore were less likely to be well known to one another. Significantly, these prospective partners were often connected by ties between women – a reality which provided women, as previously mentioned, with important linking roles.

That marriages were made between kin-based groups as well as individuals was apparent in much of the commentary surrounding matchmaking. One day, when several women in the camp were discussing recent matches made in the region, an older woman expressed some surprise that two particular families were 'marrying in.' These two families, she commented, 'would never have looked at each other before.' Other Travellers also described particular kin-groupings as being 'half married into each other' or 'joined in together.' Because such groups were often identified through the idiom of patronyms or patrilines (like the 'clan' discussed above), the significance of ties between women was masked.

For example, a man living in another camp in the city once stated categorically that 'his people,' the X____s, would never marry the Y____s because they were 'blackguards, troublemakers, and beat their wives.' His wife, however, immediately contradicted him by pointing out the existence of just such a marriage in the city. His irritated response was that in this case the X____ was not really an X____ because his mother was a W____. The W____s, he pointed out, were preferred marriage partners for the Y____s, and so this marriage was really an example of marrying 'back in again.' He ended this explanation by criticizing his wife, saying, 'You see, you don't know the half of it.' The 'half' in this case was the link through a woman – something initially made invisible by the use of surnames.

The importance of links through women was also revealed when an older woman commented that the family of a new bride, the Z____s, had a 'bad name.' She was immediately contradicted by her daughter, who assured her that this was only true of the 'old ones,' and, moreover, that the bride's mother was a U____ and so the bride was really a U____. Her mother then agreed that the U____s were indeed nice people.

The reference to families marrying 'in to each other' referred to patterns of multiple marriage between kinship groupings. Often this took the form of what has been described as 'sibling exchange' (Okely 1983: 176) – two or more marriages between the members of two siblings sets. Sometimes such marriages involved double or triple weddings, but more frequently marriages linking two sibling sets were separated in time.

One reason offered for double and triple weddings was the possibility of sharing wedding expenses more equally with another family, especially in the case of a gender balanced brother–sister/sister–brother exchange. A double wedding involving a sibling exchange had produced the third cluster of families that spent time in the camp. As mentioned, this consisted of an older married couple and the trailers of their married daughter and son. These two had married another brother–sister pair a year earlier.

Data drawn from genealogies revealed that most sibling sets contained examples of sibling exchanges, with marriages of two brothers to two sisters being more common than brother–sister/sister–brother exchanges.[7] Such marriages, however, did not create exclusive exchange groupings, as each sibling set contained many other marriages and in some cases incorporated exchanges with more than one other sibling set.[8]

Exchanges between sibling groups involving marriages that were sequential rather than simultaneous could be described as examples of 'matrimonial re-linking' (Segalen 1986: 126). Matrimonial re-linking occurred between sibling groups as well as between age-mates of structurally different generations. Thus a marriage between two sibling groups might be followed by a marriage between a younger brother of the first group and the daughter of one of the siblings of the second. The result was a sequential 'exchange' wherein two brothers, instead of marrying a pair of sisters, were linked to age-mates who formed an aunt/niece pair.

A frequent explanation for simultaneous or sequential exchanges between groups was that they were a way to ensure that spouses living some distance from their 'own people' would have the support of other close kin who had 'married in' to the same group. At the same time, as Okely has argued in the case of similar exchanges found in England, sibling links were reinforced by spousal ties (1983: 179). The support provided by such marriages was described by Travellers in the camp as particularly important for women, who were more likely to be residing among their husband's people. It was seen as especially helpful if women were marrying 'strangers' and/or moving far from their own families.

Sibling exchanges were also described as a way in which individuals who were 'difficult to marry' found matches. For instance, a family 'asking for' one particular son or daughter would be told that the match could only be made if they provided a partner for another unmarried sibling at the same time. In the case of one unhappy marriage others claimed that the husband had been duped into marrying the less desirable of two sisters when at the last minute they were allegedly switched.

The children of sibling exchanges were referred to as 'double first cousins' and were considered to be like siblings. As one married man put it, with double first cousins 'you can slag your own families because you are all the one.' Consistent with this, double first cousins, unlike simple first cousins, were excluded as potential marriage partners.

Although many Travellers expressed a preference for marriage to close relatives or 'friends,' at least half of all marriages were between 'strangers.' These 'strangers,' while less closely related than 'friends,' were none the less ideally from families that were well known. This form of 'marrying out' thus transformed existing social relations into kinship and affinal bonds in the next generation and was, like close-kin marriages, a means through which both men and women worked to create or strengthen particular relationships.[9] Marriages into unrelated and un-known families were in contrast unpopular and deemed likely to result in conflict and ultimate failure.

Women and Conflict

Most couples in the camp had peaceful relationships, but disputes were not uncommon and occurred most frequently over the expenditure of income, rumours of sexual impropriety, and/or the treatment of kin. Some women expressed their displeasure with their partners by refusing to cook for them. In more serious cases women sometimes broke the windows of the family trailer and/or vehicle. Altercations between couples in the camp were public affairs and open to the intervention of other adults, who often acted to separate the couple and scolded them for 'forgetting the children.'

While intervention was usually rapid, it was not guaranteed. In the case of one married couple others were reluctant to get involved because of the reputation of the couple for being 'awkward.' In one of their disputes the wife, whose own people were in England, tried to involve her camp neighbours but was reduced to threatening her husband with her absent male kin, claiming: 'my brothers will see me fair I guarantee you.' As this suggests, while the public life of the camp offered a degree of protection of women from male violence, such support had its limits.

Women who favoured 'marrying in' suggested that marital disputes were more easily resolved when the couple were 'friends' to one another. The involvement of close kin in the creation of marriages meant that they also had an obligation to help smooth over any later tensions. One man, for example, described to me how his sister would come to him if she was having problems with her husband and ask 'why did you tell me to marry him?' He would then try to patch things up with her husband (see also G. Gmelch 1977: 132–3).

The availability of close kin who could provide support and effect marital harmony was important to some women, but others pointed to the potentially more coercive aspects of such overlapping ties. Those who were closely related to their husbands, for example, could not voice unhappiness with their partner without creating wider disruptions in residential clusters and larger kinship networks. Despite the claims of greater stability, one women emphasized to me that conflicts between closely related couples were in fact not uncommon, and added that as a result 'you are better off marrying a stranger than your own.' She was herself in a very peaceful marriage with a 'stranger.'

One way in which some women who were living with their husband's people responded to marital conflict was by returning temporarily to their parent's home. Marital separations, both short and long term, were sufficiently common that they were not taken as indications of permanent marital breakdown. In the first years of marriage such separations appeared to be almost routine as young women (and sometimes young men) returned to their natal homes until a reconciliation was worked out.

While the high rate of separation represented an important form of agency for women, their room for manœuvre was constrained by a number of factors. Those women whose parents had died or were too far away, for example, had reduced options and even those who could return 'home' rarely had parents in a position to provide long-term support. As mentioned, women's relatives were also active in encouraging reconciliations, sometimes by inviting estranged husbands to come and convince their wives to return. Long-term sheltering of women could even be criticized for prolonging marital conflicts. One of my camp neighbours assured me that she would never take in a wife – not even her own sister. Instead, she insisted to me, she would tell her to go back to her husband.

The tensions and conflicts involved in some marital relations were also present in some other affinal relationships. Several women who had married 'strangers' described strained relationships with their mothers- and sisters-in-law. One young mother noted bitterly that her mother-in-law was interested in her children but not in her. Others who had married 'out' suggested that their female affines tried to maintain strong links to sons and brothers by casting aspersions on the morality and work habits of their wives.

Such strains were said to be less evident (and certainly were less openly expressed) when first-cousin marriages created daughter- and mother-in-law relationships between those who were already aunt and niece. Relations between aunts and their nieces/daughters-in-law were considered to be smoother and more amenable to the exigencies of co-residence than other mother- and daughter-in-law relationships.

During the fieldwork period there was a dispute between a mother-in-law and her young daughter-in-law (a 'stranger') who lived next door. The young husband responded to the altercation between his mother and his wife by initially siding with his new wife and threatening to leave the camp. He made a dramatic and very public show of preparing the trailer for departure by putting away items inside and hooking it up to the van, but he was eventually talked into staying by his siblings and other relatives. His subsequent movement of his trailer about fifty feet away from that of his mother, however, marked a new social distance and reduced the possibility of future conflict by making it possible for himself and his wife to enter and leave the camp without passing by his parents' trailer.

Women were protagonists in conflicts but were also important mediators in the context of overlapping affinal and kinship ties. One of the more dramatic incidents during the fieldwork period arose when one man accused his brother-in-law of cheating at cards. When the argument came to blows children ran to tell the women, who were sitting in another trailer. The wives of both men rushed over to separate them. Both of these women had high stakes in resolving the conflict as both were married to one of the combatants and closely related to the other – as sister and niece. As this case revealed, when women succeeded in surrounding themselves with close kin they were then sometimes caught between competing loyalties to their affines and their 'own people.' The stress of the above incident led one of the women involved to declare: 'it's best to have miles between you and your own. They've [other members of her family] all followed me and I bring nothing but trouble.'

Gendered Sexuality

As previously mentioned, the 1963 Report of the Commission had praised the 'strict morality' of Traveller family life and had noted with admiration the degree of control over women and girls. My observations and experiences of camp life suggested that the 'strict morality' still evident among Travellers continued to be deeply gendered. The burden of maintaining premarital virginity and marital fidelity, for example, lay disproportionately with women. Men's sexual activity in contrast was relatively unconstrained; indeed, pre- or extra-marital sexual relations with Traveller or settled 'girlfriends' appeared to provide a degree of prestige.

The sexual double standard was deeply felt by women even as they actively reproduced standards of female morality. Two younger wives living in the camp, for example, often expressed to me their resentment of the fact that their husbands sometimes went out for evening entertainment without them. On one occasion when it had been arranged that they would accompany their husbands to the disco, the women were giddy with excitement as they prepared for the evening. The following day, however, they were despondent. Despite their success in having evaded the racist policy that 'barred' Travellers from the venue, the evening had in their view been ruined when their husbands had asked some settled women to dance. One of the women retaliated by refusing to cook for her husband in the following days.

Unlike men, unmarried and married women were expected to maintain their sexual reputations by careful avoidance of men outside of the immediate family. Avoiding 'bad talk' was a major preoccupation for unmarried women who, along with a taboo against drinking, were expected to avoid any sexual experience. Maintaining a 'good name' was important for individuals and the wider family and allegations about women's illicit sexuality were a source of some of the more serious disputes between individuals and family groups (see also W. McDonagh 1993: 24).

Women who experienced gendered restrictions on their activities also described being 'tested' by Traveller men. I was told several times how during courtship young Traveller men might pressure their fiancées to sleep with them, but that if a young woman agreed, the man would call off the wedding because the woman had demonstrated that 'she would sleep with anybody.' While courtship was recalled fondly by many women as a period of romance, it was none the less also experienced as a time of vulnerability and risk. The fragility of the relationship during the engagement period was noted by one woman who commented, 'You can't admit that you love them until you are married.'

After the wedding, women described spending a few nights in their parents' home before moving in with their husbands. Women emphasized how they were very 'shy' during this period and indicated that it was only pressure from their husbands and from their own relatives that led to their eventually acquiescing in sexual relations.

An exception to the careful relations between women and men were relations between women and their brothers-in-law of the same age, which sometimes involved an element of sexual joking. In the camp there was an overtly flirtatious relationship between one married man and his brother's wife, and another married man joked in my presence with his sister-in-law about making love. In yet another case, when a man teased his wife's brother about 'swopping wives' his wife prompted hilarity when she immediately pointed out that such a swop would not be fair because he would end up with his brother-in-law's wife (a possible sexual partner), while she would end up with her brother. Joking about sexuality was also part of married women's conversations with one another. Such talk was, however, in contrast to women's public reticence about such subjects as menstruation or pregnancy. Some women told me they were too 'ashamed' to discuss such subjects (especially in the presence of their own mothers), but that female relatives or affines privately provided crucial information and support in these areas.

Gender and the Politics of Culture

I have described in the context of domestic labour how women's practices of purity were linked to their embodiment of an ethnicized boundary between Travellers and non-Travellers. This was also evident in discussion of arranged marriages and restrictions on female sexuality, both of which were signified not only as markers of individual and familial reputation, but as sites of Traveller moral superiority and ethnic purity.

Travellers frequently contrasted 'clean' Traveller women with 'dirty' settled women through stories about how settled women would go out with several men before getting married and in so doing prostitute themselves. Settled women, it was said, performed strip teases and were swopped around by their husbands.

Travellers' ideas about the contrasting sexual morality of Traveller and settled women affected my own interactions. Women in early conversations often asked me directly whether I had had many boy-friends and whether I had slept with my husband before marriage. Shortly after my arrival in the camp, several Traveller men also asked me if I would 'go for a ride' or to 'the pictures' in front of other men and sometimes their wives.

While I was consciously careful in my dealings with men, I still experienced difficulties. A few weeks after taking up residence in the camp, one wife paced around the camp loudly shrieking and cursing her husband for spending much of the weekly dole at the pub and leaving her alone with the children in the camp. In the course of this she came and stood outside my trailer and loudly accused me of being a 'whore and prostitute' and said that I had been 'going around' her husband. Her husband had in fact been assisting me with some genealogies earlier on. Some other women quickly came over and pulled her away, assuring me that she was drunk and angry at her husband, not at me. Later, however, some of these same women came back to my trailer and expressed astonishment that I had not countered such a serious allegation by physically attacking this woman.

The purity of Traveller women was central to Travellers' own under-standings of their ethnic identity. An origin story that I heard several times from Travellers linked Traveller origins and mobility to the protec-tion of Traveller female sexual purity. The spokesperson of the Traveller Committee, Margaret Sweeney, made reference to this story in a televi-sion interview:

> [my father said] ... that the Travellers went back to the time of Cromwell when he first came into this country when he was sent in. That Travelling People didn't have the money to pay for the rent and that a lot of the landlords of those days used to take over the young daughters of the settled community. And I feel that the Travelling People had it in them that they wouldn't let this happen and rather than that happen they took to the sides of the road and they went to other counties where they wouldn't be known.

Significantly, however, Margaret Sweeney went on to tell the televi-sion interviewer that this story must be wrong because it emphasized the essential differences between Travellers and settled people instead of focusing on their commonality. Her comments could be interpreted in the context of an attempt to win support for the cause of hardstands from the 'settled community' by emphasizing the shared Irish heritage of Travellers and non-Travellers rather than emphasizing the differences between them.

The invoking of Traveller women as markers of a 'pure' Irish and Traveller identity clearly illustrates how, in the course of publicly con-testing racism and exclusion, Travellers assert an account of Traveller origins that claims both a pure Irishness and a pure femininity. Such claims represent important forms of resistance to imposed stigma while simultaneously legitimating gendered practices in the areas of work, marriage, and sexuality that can be seen as supporting male privilege.

This chapter has attempted to demonstrate something of the com-plexities of Traveller women's lives as they were forged within gendered racism and the more intimate gendered hierarchies of family and social networks. Outsiders' focus on men's work, the targeting of 'begging' for elimination, and the privatizing of domestic space and labour appeared to have contributed to an undermining of women's economic autonomy by removing them from direct access to income. While this was exacer-bated by other practices, including residential patterns that favoured ties between men, women none the less worked actively and often success-fully to promote their own and their family's interests within such constraints. They did this in part through cultivating links to other women, both kin and non-kin, and by maximizing the opportunities presented by their external identification as representatives for their families. In the case of Margaret Sweeney, the representative role was broadened beyond the family or residential cluster to become the basis for a wider challenge to anti-Travellerism and spirited defence of a collective Traveller identity and culture. The actions and understandings of Traveller women belied simplistic categorization of them as 'victims' of Traveller men and/or Traveller culture.

Chapter 7

Childhood and Youth, Racism, and the Politics of Culture

Drawing in part on work done in the area of women and gender, a re-emerging anthropology of childhood and youth has revealed how childhood and youth are sites in which the politics of racism, culture, and nation are played out and has called for greater recognition of the agency of children within these processes (Scheper-Hughes and Sargent 1998; Stephens 1995).[1] According to this literature children are salient both 'as symbolic figures and as objects of contested forms of socialisation' (Stephens 1995: 13).

I have already discussed how one of the recurring themes in the calls for control over the activities of the Travellers in the period preceding the settlement policy was the claim that state intervention was required 'for the protection of the [Traveller and non-Traveller] children.' This chapter examines more closely the positioning of Traveller children and childhood within the context of anti-Traveller racism, imposed ideologies and practices of 'modern' childhood, and the settlement program. It uses archival, biographical, and ethnographic material to reveal the lived experiences of Traveller childhood and youth and argues that attention to the cultural politics of children and youth ensures recognition of the dynamic, contingent, and contested quality of culture created within the context of inequality.

Pre-Settlement Traveller Childhoods

In the discourse of outsiders, Travellers' deviation from an increasingly dominant model of modern childhood (which placed children within the privatized sphere of sedentary nuclear families and full-time schooling) was highlighted during the period preceding the 1960s. Other aspects of a distinctive Traveller childhood, however, were suppressed in such constructions, including, for example, their involvement in work, which provided an unusual (by the standards of modern childhood) degree of economic competence and a related capacity for early family formation, albeit within unequal structures of gender and generation.

Published autobiographical accounts relating to the pre-settlement program period reveal how Traveller children were centrally involved in the maintenance of their families and wider residential clusters. From infancy Traveller children were taken along on peddling and hawking expeditions, and they became important workers in their own right at a young age (see Gmelch 1986: 95; Joyce and Farmar 1985: 5, 33, 36–7, 43–4; Maher 1972: 11–12, 24, 57–8, 72).

Johnny 'Pop' Connors, born in the 1930s, describes how as a child he worked alongside his father selling tinware, swopping horses, and collecting rags and scrap from the non-Traveller population. In addition to this he was involved in independent scrap and rag collection, hawking holy pictures, and singing for money in pubs and hotels. Hunting and fishing were also means through which he produced food for his family (Sandford 1975: 140–1, 155, 168–70). Other Traveller children combined similar activities with selling handmade flowers, gathering recyclable bottles and jars, and occasional employment as farmworkers, turf cutters, or domestic servants (Court 1985: 98–100,182; Gmelch 1986: 57, 106; Pavee Point 1992: 27–8, 84).

Older children, and especially older girls, made essential contributions to their own and neighbouring (often related) families in the area of child care and domestic labour. Nan Donohoe, born in 1919, recalled how mothers were 'lucky' if they had an older child, especially a daughter, to care for younger children (Gmelch 1986: 113), and Nan Joyce described older girls as 'never really free' due to their child care responsibilities, adding that 'since you were nine or ten you were holding the youngest child in your arms, you were sort of weighed down with them' (Joyce and Farmar 1985: 16). Bridget Murphy (born in the early 1930s) also described how from the age of ten she was washing, baking, and keeping the caravan clean while her mother was off peddling (Court 1985: 72–3; see also Pavee Point 1992: 44–5).

These published accounts suggest that, as with many other poor and/or minority populations, Traveller children's unpaid or low-paid labour was critical to the competitiveness of their respective family enterprises because it facilitated the offering of goods and services below their labour value (see Nieuwenhuys 1994; 1996). That children understood the economic significance of their work and derived a sense of competence and pride from it is evident from a number of the published accounts, including that of Sean Maher (born in 1932), who recalled: 'By the time I was eight I was an expert at making a living on the tober [road]' (Maher 1972: 14).[2]

Published descriptions revealing the economic significance of children's activities also suggest that within their respective family units Traveller children were generally subordinated to adults, and especially to adult males. In Maher's autobiographical account, for example, he describes how he was expected to work hard and to turn over any income earned to his father, who beat him when his earnings were deemed insufficient (Maher 1972: 72). Patrick Stokes, born in the 1930s, characterized the relationship between himself and his father as one of employer and employee, and attributed the retention of control over his 'wage' to the active intervention of his mother: 'I used to sell for my father then; he'd put a price on a thing and I'd sell ... we never used to keep the money but bring it back to him. Any extra you'd give him, me mother'd make a cash box and put it in for you. My mother had to guard it for you. And when it come that you had the price of a pair of boots or something like that, she'd buy it for ya' (Court 1985: 94).

While children were generally subordinated to adults, adult authority was constrained by the early achievement of economic competence and the related ability to form viable new domestic units at a young age. Although adults maintained a high degree of control over their children by arranging marriages or 'matches' at an early age, young people's potential for economic independence facilitated the possibility of teenagers' elopements (Court 1985: 118; G. Gmelch 1977; Pavee Point 1992: 28–9, 56–8).

Travellers' reliance upon the work of children and the early transition of Traveller children to economic independence occurred within the context of the weak social infrastructure of the pre-welfare state.[3] Engagement with the existing social infrastructure, such as it was, could provide much needed support, but it could also further threaten the basis of Traveller adult control and authority. As Nan Donohoe reveals in her published biography, turning to outside sources for assistance imperiled her custody over her children: 'I used to go to the convents to get bread and milk. There was no welfare like today to help you out. There was only the 'cruelty' [National Society for the Prevention of Cruelty to Children], and if you went and complained or said you had no way to keep yourself, the kids was taken from you' (Gmelch 1986: 81).

The extent of institutionalization of Traveller children is as yet un-documented. Certainly some Traveller children ended up in orphanages and industrial schools during this period (Gmelch 1986; Maher 1972), and others were continually fearful of this possibility (Joyce and Farmar 1985: 48; Pavee Point 1992: 26). It has been suggested, moreover, that some Traveller children were removed from their parents and placed in residential care on the grounds of having 'no fixed abode' (M. McDonagh and W. McDonagh 1993: 39). This claim, which postulates a broader ethnic-based policy of child removal, requires more research.

A 1930 press report referring to a court case involving a Traveller father, his children, and the National Society for the Prevention of Cruelty to Children is of interest in this regard, because it initially suggests that there was such a policy. The headline of the piece, 'Family In Camp – Can Children Get Proper Rearing? Justice Says 'No,' suggests an ethnic-based policy of removal, an interpretation that appears to be supported by the fact that the Justice is reported as stating: 'A parent residing in the open air cannot exercise proper guardianship over his children' (CT, 25 October 1930: 5). A closer examination, however, suggests that 'camping' per se was less central to the issue than other considerations such as the absence of a wife, without whom the father allegedly had 'nobody to look after the children,' and the specifics of the form of accommodation, which was described by the NSPCC inspector as 'not even a tent [just] a few sacks put together' (ibid.). The extent to which camping per se was a basis for child removal remains unclear.

In the area of schooling, despite the 1908 Children's Act, which had legislated compulsory schooling, apprehensions of Traveller children for non-attendance were not systematic. Threats of child removal for truancy were, however, used by police as a means of moving Travellers out of a given district. The use of this threat as a means of harassment is revealed in Patrick Stokes's published account of how a policeman in Northern Ireland threatened his parents with the removal of himself and his younger siblings for non-attendance, but then dropped the threat when he found a more straightforward basis for a summons of the family: their lack of a dog license (Court 1985: 106).

Despite the challenges involved in accessing an education system geared toward a sedentary population, it is apparent that some Traveller children (in addition to those who were institutionalized) received inter-mittent schooling while travelling or living in housing, and many more received religious instruction for the sacraments of First Communion and Confirmation (CI 1963: 88; Court 1985: 63, 70–1,106; Joyce and Farmar

1985: 23, 29; Maher 1972: 41; Sandford 1975: 161–8). Some retrospective accounts describe positive experiences of formal schooling, but these same accounts also reveal the lack of the system's accommodation to mobility and racist practices such as name-calling within the schoolground and classroom (Gmelch 1986: 50; Joyce and Farmar 1985: 23–4; Maher 1972: 129; Sandford 1975: 166). In the early 1960s, only 10 per cent of Traveller children between the ages of six and fourteen were recorded as being on school rolls (CI 1963: 64).

Traveller Childhood and Settlement

Invocations of childhood were part of the anti-Traveller discourse of the pre-settlement period, but they became even more evident in the formulation and implementation of the settlement program in the 1960s. The Report of the Commission on Itinerancy portrayed state intervention as a benevolent project that would have Traveller children as its primary beneficiaries. The premise that itinerancy was inherently harmful to children was based on a number of grounds, including claims that a high Traveller infant mortality rate could be attributed to living in tents, which posed 'a particular danger to the health and welfare of infants and children' (CI 1963: 44). Life in a horse-drawn caravan was also described as 'questionable' due to allegedly overcrowded sleeping arrangements (CI 1963: 41), which worked against 'ensuring undisturbed sleep for the younger children' as well as the possibility of 'school-going children doing home exercises' (CI 1963: 42).

The creation of a healthier childhood, according to the Report of the Commission, required settlement in housing. Despite the Report's acknowledgment that there was 'little apparent difference' between the health of Traveller children and 'that of the children in the corresponding income [i.e., poorer] groups of the settled population' (CI 1963: 47), itinerancy, rather than poverty, was consistently identified as the primary danger to the health of Traveller children.

Settlement was also seen as a precondition for meeting the educational needs of Traveller children. As the Commissioners stated: 'an educational policy for itinerants can only be successful if it is one which aims at catering for those who have been induced to leave the wandering life and for those who are likely to do so' (CI 1963: 69). The emphasis on settlement meant that neither health services nor schooling would be adapted to mobility.

Along with a policy of settlement and schooling, the Report advocated a reform of Traveller methods of child-rearing. Although Traveller parents were acknowledged to have 'great affection for their children' they were also said to demonstrate 'little regard for their [children's] appearance, cleanliness, health, and none for their education or future' (CI 1963: 81). Inadequate parenting was implicated in claims that younger children were 'spoiled and undisciplined' (in contrast to older children, over whom parental authority was more approvingly described as 'strict') (CI 1963: 37). Travellers' alleged 'lack of self control,' fighting, and irregular attendance at mass was also ascribed to a 'lack of education and discipline during their formative years' (CI 1963: 87). Although it was acknowledged that the children in better-off Traveller families were 'well looked after apart from the neglect of the education' (CI 1963: 81), the latter was deemed sufficient evidence of parental deficiency.

Claims regarding the putative inadequacies of Traveller parents paved the way for the identification of the state and voluntary groups as essential agents for a re-socialization of Traveller children beyond formal schooling. Such action, it was stated, was required because: 'the lack of education [of itinerant children] extends beyond the school subjects. They also lack the respect for social conventions, law and order and for the rights of property that are inculcated in the children of the normal family in the settled community by words and example in the home, school and in the community generally' (CI 1963: 65).

Despite the denigration of Traveller parents' forms of childrearing, the 1963 report explicitly rejected any suggestion that the resolution of the Traveller 'problem' lay in the removal of Traveller children from their families. The Commissioners in fact took pains to argue that Traveller children should remain in their natal families, noting that: 'Itinerants are very attached to their children and the evil social consequences and the suffering which must follow such a policy would far outweigh the "advantages" of an education imposed in such conditions with its lasting legacy of bitterness' (CI 1963: 69).

The defence of the integrity of the Traveller family in the Report was in direct response to ongoing calls for more radical measures of child removal. Such suggestions were made more than once by politicians in Galway. One local representative, for example, stated in 1965: 'There is only one solution to the itinerant problem – take their children from them.' The suggestion of child removal, although rejected by another politician, who responded, 'Don't advocate that in this country. We have not yet, thank God, reached the stage of robbing parents of their children' (CT, 2 October 1965: 1), continued to be voiced at the local and national level during the 1970s (see *CT*, 24 November 1978: 9; Dáil, Horgan, 4 December 1979: 614), revealing the tenuous status of Travellers' parental rights even in the context of strong Constitutional protection.

Child 'Saving' in Galway City

Consistent with the Report of the Commission on Itinerancy, in Galway City the settlement project was frequently promoted by its advocates as a program of Traveller 'child saving' (*CT*, 11 April 1964: 3). Traveller children were, among other things, portrayed as being in need of 'rescue' from the wretched physical living conditions associated with camping. In a letter to the editor one of the founders of the voluntary Traveller settlement committee called for rapid provision of permanent accommodation for Travellers, noting that: 'while everyone is dithering, little tinker [Traveller] children continue to shiver like animals in ditches ... What are we waiting for? A child's death – from exposure?' (*CT*, 21 February 1969: 5).

Claims made for the settlement of Traveller children at the local level relied on a construction of Traveller children as less socialized into (and therefore as less implicated in) the Traveller way of life. A 1969 Galway newspaper editorial in favour of Traveller settlement, for example, relied heavily on a construction of the differences between Traveller adults, who were already lost to itinerancy, and their 'innocent' children, who were not. The settlement policy, it was argued, should be supported 'for the sake of the [Traveller] children':

> It is recognised that the [Traveller] adults cannot be integrated into the ordinary life of the community. The only hope of bringing those people into ordered ways of living is through the children. They deserve a chance. The children, however, cannot be rescued if the parents are to be molested by people of the locality where they are settled ... They are entitled to a chance ... if not for their own sake, then for the sake of the children (*CT*, 5 September 1969: 10)

In this case, the alleged redeemability of Traveller children relied on a model of childhood innocence. A similar construction is found in a speech by an advocate for Traveller settlement, who addressed a residents' association in Galway City as follows:

> We have looked for too long ... at the 'sins of the fathers' and ignored the distress of the children; forgetting that these parents were once themselves

little children; and that they have become what they are, not because they are wicked, but because they have never had the opportunity or the education to be any different. (*CT*, 16 February 1973: 7)

Here the use of the phrase 'sins of the father' resonated with other constructions of victimized Traveller women and (implicitly or explicitly) problematized Traveller men.

Part of the reforming of Traveller childrearing was predicated on the refashioning of Traveller families to ensure greater conformity with middle-class models of appropriate gender and age-based divisions of labour. As mentioned earlier, efforts were made to enlist adult males in wage labour and to discourage income-generating activities of women (especially 'begging') by replacing these with full-time home-making.

In addition to this there was an attempt to remove children from forms of productive labour in favour of schooling. That schooling would contribute to the reproduction of an appropriately generationed and gendered division of labour in the home was clear in the Report's description of the curriculum for itinerant children. 'In addition to reading, writing and arithmetic,' it was stated, there should be 'regular manual training, e.g., woodwork and elementary metalwork for boys, and knitting, needlework, simple cookery and domestic training for girls (CI 1963: 68). The construction of Traveller children's needs, then, served to naturalize and legitimize particular gendered and generationed domestic relations along with the settlement project itself.

In the late 1960s, other social movements of the period (especially the civil rights movement) augmented an existing discourse of settlement premised upon the putative 'needs' of Traveller children with a discourse of Traveller children's 'rights.' In 1969, for example, a speech of the Minister for Local Government was summarized in a press report entitled 'Taking Rights from an Itinerant Child.' The speech suggested that popular opposition to Traveller settlement constituted a denial of the inherent 'rights' of Traveller children [to settlement and schooling] (*CT*, 24 October 1969: 5).

While this reference to Traveller children's rights occurred in the context of a liberal discourse of inclusiveness, invocations of Traveller children's 'rights' were also found in calls for more coercive control over Traveller adults. Galway county council, for example, unanimously proposed that the national government pass legislation (described as a 'children's civil rights charter') that 'would make the itinerant child's right to education "superior" [*sic*] to that of his parents to wander around the country as they please' (*CT*, 26 September 1969: 16). Here the provision of children's rights was presented as justification for a selective weakening of the Constitutional protection of Traveller parental rights.

Other references linked Traveller child-saving through settlement to a broader process of nation-building. One Galway letter to the editor, for example, described the task of 'rehabilitating' the Travellers through their children as 'doing the work of the Founders of the State who rose in 1916' (CT, 11 April 1964: 3), while another letter-writer invoked reference to the 1916 Proclamation when he called upon politicians to support Traveller settlement because of their obligation to 'cherish all the children of the nation equally' (CT, 10 October 1975: 8; see also CT, 11 November 1977: 8).

Traveller Children 'At Risk'

The 1979 International Year of the Child and the 1980 Report of the Task Force on Child Care Services gave impetus to an expansion and professionalization of child services in Ireland. Traveller children were targeted by child professionals through being included within the emerging category of children 'at risk.' Those children defined as being 'at risk' in Ireland tended to be those who deviated from hegemonic middle-class constructions of appropriate family structures and gender and age-based roles.[4] Consistent with other 'at risk' discourses, the labelling of Traveller children focused on individual and family-related deficits rather than the structural causes of Traveller children's divergence from the model of 'proper' childhood (see Swadener and Lubeck 1995).

The 'at risk' designation for Traveller children was associated with a shift from an earlier emphasis on assimilation through the provision of integrated housing and schooling to a newer focus on the need for professional and often segregated services. By the mid-1980s the 'at risk' label was augmented by the attribution of 'disability' to Traveller children. In 1984, for example, the Minister for Education described Traveller children as 'similar in many respects to ... other educationally retarded children,' but with even greater difficulties aggravated by 'social disabilities and other consequences of their unsettled way of life' (Dáil, Faulkner, 24 May 1984: 2083–4). Here discourses of disability and anti-Traveller racism articulated with one another to reinforce the inferiorization of both categories. Although modified by the qualifier of 'social,' the shift to a 'disabling' discourse for Traveller children reflected an emerging emphasis on allegedly organic physical causes of their inferiority. Medical research documenting physical impairments among Traveller children lent additional support to this trend and served to obscure the political causes of Traveller children's marginality.[5]

The intensification of 'at risk' discourse was apparent in the 1983 Report of the Travelling People Review Body. This report placed primary emphasis on Traveller children's 'need' for settlement and schooling, and suggested that Traveller children were inadequately socialized by their families. High fertility rates, patterns of sibling care, and parental illiteracy were identified as detrimental to child development, and earlier external intervention was advocated as a necessary antidote to the resulting 'social deprivation' (Review Body 1983: 63). As previously mentioned, the attribution was applied even to wealthier families, whose mobility impeded the 'continuity of education for their children' (Review Body 1983: 46–7).

Among other recommendations, the report called for increased provision of special pre-schools for Traveller children. Such pre-schools were promoted as a means of overcoming the disadvantages allegedly associated with Traveller childhood:

Because of the social deprivation of traveller children ... early education is of paramount importance. The young traveller child needs love, security, consistent treatment by adults, even before the most basic progress can be made in acquiring an adequate vocabulary, in socialising and in learning through play ... They nearly all need at least a year in a pre-school if they are not to remain in need of remedial education throughout their school years. (Review Body 1983: 64)

The suggestion that Traveller adults denied their children 'love, security, [and] consistent treatment' represented a more fundamental assault on adult Traveller competence than was found in the 1963 report. The passage cited above included unsubstantiated assertions about the quality of Traveller children's relations within their families and wider community, patterns of adult–child relations and developmental outcomes, the importance of 'play,' and, most importantly, the necessity of formal education.

Along with the emphasis on early childhood intervention was a simultaneous call for a prolonging of Traveller childhood through the provision of education beyond the primary level. The Report problematized the fact that (as it claimed) 'the majority of [Traveller adults and children] see no purpose in attending school after the age of 12 years,' as this was the time at which '[Traveller] parents normally regard their children as adults' (Review Body 1983: 68). The extension of schooling was portrayed as necessary for pedagogical and occupational reasons, but also in order to correct an aberrant life course trajectory. The Traveller life course was to be brought into closer conformity with dominant constructions of childhood and adulthood.

The 1983 Review Body Report replaced the Commission on Itinerancy's goal of 'absorption' with a more modified 'integration' and acknowledged that some Travellers might 'retain traditions peculiar to the traveller way of life' (Review Body 1983: 6–7). Significantly, however, Traveller identity and tradition in the Report was associated with 'older travellers,' many of whom it was claimed would 'live out their lives without adapting to change' (Review Body 1983: 15). Traveller 'tradition,' by being associated with the past, was constructed as having little relevance for the younger generations. Traveller children instead continued to be deemed 'at risk' by virtue of birth into a Traveller family, where the source of 'risk' was itinerancy and alleged parental inadequacy rather than official neglect. The 'solution' to the 'problem' posed by the unkempt and unhappy looking Traveller boy featured on the cover of the 1983 report was permanent accommodation, because this was (according to the Report) a prerequisite for children's access to adequate health, educational, and welfare services (Review Body 1983: 15).[6]

That settlement (and not child welfare) remained the primary goal was revealed in the reluctance to accommodate child-related services to mobility. Families who 'choose to continue to travel' were described as having 'children with unusual needs,' for whom the 'possibility of mobile teachers' was briefly raised but not developed (Review Body 1983: 68).

The preceding discussion has revealed how constructions of Traveller children's 'needs' and occasionally 'rights' were discursively central to the project of Traveller settlement in Ireland. But it was not only Traveller childhood that was invoked in the popular and political debate over Travellers. Another category of children also appeared in these discussions – the non-Traveller children of the 'settled community.'

As discussed earlier, efforts to proceed with Traveller settlement sparked local resistance in Galway City as residents of private and public housing estates lobbied against the situating of Travellers in their neighbourhoods. Some of those who resisted Traveller settlement claimed that, like non-Traveller women, non-Traveller children were in need of adult/state protection from the 'threat' allegedly posed by the presence of Travellers. In the 1960s, for example, the chairperson of a Galway City residents' association had argued against the location of an official camping site, in part because 'the moral results of establishing such an encampment would be disastrous to our children' (*CT*, 27 September 1968: 17), and there were claims that Traveller children were being 'let run wild' and were 'sure to attack' non-Traveller children (*CT*, 11 November 1966: 1).

Such constructions of non-Traveller children as being 'at risk' intensi- fied at the local level in the 1970s and 1980s. Physical danger to settled children, for example, was said to derive from the putative lack of sanitation in unofficial Traveller camps. In a characteristic allegation it was claimed that in one housing estate non-Traveller children 'playing in the play areas [experienced] real danger from a cess-pool caused by itinerants ... using it as a toilet' (*CT*, 28 February 1975: 1).

Traveller animals (particularly horses) were also often constructed as a physical threat to non-Traveller children. A press report entitled 'Stray Horse Threat to Children' reported on how a six-month-old infant was thrown out of a go-cart by a runaway horse, an incident which prompted one city councillor to declare that 'itinerants' should be removed from the location (*CT*, 5 December 1975: 1). In the late 1980s the Galway Circuit Court granted one group of residents an injunction against the city, in part on the grounds that Galway City had failed to remove an unofficial Traveller camp with 'straying horses' that were 'a nuisance and danger- ous to children' (*CT*, 5 February 1988: 1). When the same residents were later denied the injunction by a higher court, tensions escalated, as did claims that non-Traveller children were at risk (*CT*, 19 August 1988: 3; *CT*, 21 April 1989: 11; *CT*, 28 May 1989: 1).

Along with claims about the moral and physical threats posed by the presence of Travellers were suggestions that their presence threatened non-Traveller children's ability to enact key activities associated with modern childhood, notably 'play' and school attendance. In one estate, for example, it was claimed that a green area was 'supposed to be a playground for children ... [but] the [settled] children cannot be let out on the road or onto the playground because of the horses and that is unfair' (*CT*, 23 October 1987: 11; see also *CT*, 10 July 1987: 8; *CT*, 31 July 1987: 1). Another newspaper report noted that 'school children' were 'in fear of their lives because of the threat of wild horses roaming the estate ... [which] have actually run after some of the children coming to and from school' (*CT*, 30 September 1977: 1; see also *CT*, 27 November 1981: 3).

As the preceding discussion reveals, the putative needs and rights of children were invoked by those advocating and resisting the settlement of Travellers at the local level. Usually this involved highlighting the needs of *either* Traveller children *or* settled children. In the unusual cases where both sets of children were acknowledged, their potentially conflicting claims were denied through the portrayal of Traveller children as part of the threat to 'settled' children. One tenant, for example, was reported in the press as stating: 'Our children are frequently being threatened by the young itinerants who are getting cheekier by the day' (*CT*, 23 September 1977: 1; see also *CT*, 16 September 1974: 6; *CT*, 2 July 1982: 6).

In such passages, any suggestion that Traveller and settled children might have equal claims based on their common status as children was removed as Traveller children, like street children elsewhere, were constructed as 'unrestrained and undeveloped by the ameliorating institutions of childhood' and therefore not 'at risk' but 'the risk' (Stephens 1995: 13). The 'unchildlike' qualities of these Traveller children, attributed to their socialization into a Traveller way of life, became further evidence of the illegitimacy of a Traveller way of life and need for intervention and control. The dominant model of a proper and legitimate (non-Traveller) childhood was reinforced rather than challenged by evidence of differentiation and inequality among children.

The finding that an ethnicized Traveller/non-Traveller boundary articulated with constructions of childhood resonates with Okely's (1983) findings in England. In her analysis she argues that non-Traveller-Gypsy children were constructed as particularly vulnerable to Traveller-Gypsies (as evidenced in allegations of child-stealing) as well as vice versa. According to her analysis, children on both sides of the ethnicized divide were constructed as less socialized into their respective ethnic identities and therefore as more vulnerable to inappropriate socialization by the ethnicized Other.

While the Irish texts reviewed here did not include references to child-stealing by Travellers, the construction of non-Traveller children's vulnerability and Traveller children's redeemability suggests a similar evaluation of their undeveloped ethnic socialization. The particular reference to the threat to modern childhood posed by Travellers also suggests, however, that there was more than ethnic identity at stake. It is my contention that the suggestions that Travellers were threatening non-Traveller children's health, play, and schooling reflected both anti-Traveller racism and the class-differentiated impact of a changing political economy on childhood in Ireland.

Despite the contemporary 'sanctity' of the child, Nieuwenhuys (1996) has argued that the structural conditions of post-modernity have included a relative decline in state investment in the institutions that support the domesticated and unproductive character of modern child-hood, such as free education, health care, and low-cost housing. In Ireland, a dramatic increase in unemployment during the 1980s was associated with greater risk of poverty for households with children, especially those with larger numbers of children (Callan, Nolan, and Whelan 1994: 66–7).

As discussed earlier, in Galway City a class-divided urban geography meant that the 'integration' of Travellers through housing and official sites was occurring primarily in public housing estates, and it was largely working-class adults and, even more, their children who were expected to act as agents of Traveller 'integration' into the 'settled community.' A pro-settlement discourse that promised Travellers a secure modern child-hood once settled and housed obscured the tenuous hold on such a childhood among the 'settled' working class and encouraged the view that the risk posed to their children stemmed from the presence of Travellers rather than class-based inequities exacerbated by political and economic change.

The focus on Traveller camps and/or housing as obstacles to the achievement of modern childhoods by settled children obscured the wider structural changes that were undermining the capacity of many to meet the standards of 'proper' childhood. Such a perception took on concrete expression when two long-standing Traveller camps were re-moved by the city in order to make way for the development of a sports complex, which was described as being for the use of local 'youngsters' whose families could not afford available programs and who as a result were hanging around outside a community centre and playing on the roadsides of housing estates (CT, 22 August, 1986: 6).

Researching Childhood

During the fieldwork period more than half of the national Traveller population was under the age of fifteen (*Irish Independent*, 22 August 1986: 3), a figure strikingly consistent with figures on Travellers' demog-raphy since the first count in 1944 (CI 1963: 115). In the camp the figure was two-thirds due to the preponderance of younger families. Despite occasional threats by adults that I might take them away, both girls and boys visited my trailer several times daily to chat or to simply sit silently and watch my activities. I appreciated their companionship and often asked them about daily events. They in turn offered updates and obser-vations on camp activities and inquired about my life in Canada.

I actively fostered relationships with children, and included information gleaned from my conversations with them in my fieldnotes, but remained uneasy about the propriety of using children as respondents. Like other anthropologists, I was also sceptical about the credibility of children's accounts (see Scheper-Hughes and Sargent 1998: 14).

Despite my relatively easy access to children, I was generally more interested in what adults had to say about children, and what children had to say about adults, than in what children had to say about themselves. The result was little appreciation of the opportunity provided to me at the time to explore children's active participation in and shaping of social relations and culture and to reflect more deeply upon the characteristics of their engagements with me. While I have retroactively paid more attention to the children's voices that dot my field notes much of the following discussion privileges adult perception and experience of childhood.

Having Children

Anthropological work on the cultural politics of reproduction has demonstrated the ways in which biological reproduction is not a universal naturalized 'fact of life,' but rather is shaped by wider political economies as well as unequal social relations of racism, gender, class, and age (Franklin and Ragoné 1998). Most Traveller women I knew had conceived within the first or second year of marriage and started to bear a large number of children in succession – often one a year. Early marriages ensured a long reproductive span, and genealogies that I collected from Travellers suggested that the average woman completed her reproductive career with eleven children living (see also Crawford and Gmelch 1974). The high fertility rate among Travellers was particularly striking in the context of a decline in fertility rate in the wider population, which dipped below replacement level by the late 1980s.

The importance of children was apparent in my first encounters with Traveller women. I was always asked first whether I was married, then how long I had been married, and then whether I had any children. As a married (for two years) but childless woman I inevitably received sympathetic and reassuring comments from women that there was 'plenty of time yet.' I also was the target of some public joking as well as private and serious advice about facilitating pregnancy. The former was usually from men who told me how the cold nights in the camp would facilitate sexual intimacy with my partner. From women I received more detailed information about medical and religious 'cures' for infertility drawn from acquaintances, radio and television shows, and the medical profession.

My closest relationships were with the few other married women in the camp who were also childless. Conversations with these women invariably turned to their concerns regarding their lack of conception and/or speculation about symptoms that might indicate that a pregnancy had begun. Along with information regarding various religious and medical practices, encouraging stories about other Traveller women who had conceived after many years of marriage were exchanged in these more private conversations. After five months of residence in the camp I learned that I was pregnant and shared the news with the women of the camp almost immediately. While my public declaration of the news was unusual by Traveller standards the news was graciously and happily received. I was later told that women might share such information with close acquaintances but would not discuss their pregnancies publicly until 'it showed.'

During my stay in the camp three women gave birth – in one case to twins. Newborns were showered with affection by adults and children alike and adults joked about the effect of the birth of a new sibling on the next oldest child, who was thereby displaced as the central object of attention. Such children often expressed their feelings of displacement and jealously with tantrums, but were quickly trained to defer to younger ones who had 'taken their place.' The favouring of younger children had an impact on my own interactions with children. When I imposed a 'two at a time' restriction on children visiting me in my trailer, the result was that priority of entry was always given to the youngest toddlers.

While high fertility was never officially defined as part of the 'Traveller problem' in the city or nation as a whole, and there was no family planning program specifically directed at Travellers at the time, several Traveller women living in the camp reported that they were privately encouraged by medical personnel to use contraceptives and/or, after the birth of several children, to undergo sterilization.

Fertility control was primarily associated with older women who already had large families and wanted to end their childbearing, but some younger women also mentioned that they used contraceptives for the purpose of spacing of children (having a child every other year instead of every year was mentioned as preferable) so that they could be 'reared right.' Although one older woman described how she had breastfed her babies, lactation did not provide contraceptive protection for those of reproductive age in the camp. These younger women used bottles exclu-sively, explaining that they did not breastfeed because of the lack of privacy available in their trailers.

'Taking a break' through spacing was described as relatively new and did not necessarily indicate a lower ideal family size. Younger women that I encountered continued to hope for large families, mentioning figures of ten children – a finding which contrasts with the lower 'ideal size' of six suggested by Rigal in her study of Traveller women and family planning in Dublin a couple of years later (Rigal 1993). As one younger mother told me, as soon as one child was walking, she would 'get a longing' for another.

The strength of pro-natalism and its gendered impact was well illus-trated when one of my neighbours who was 'warring' with her husband experienced a sudden and dramatic attempt at reconciliation on his part when she developed a 'weakness' that hinted that she might be preg-nant. This woman told me that she was on the pill because of medical fears about her capacity for another birth after several Caesareans. Un-like her husband, she was relieved when she discovered that she was not pregnant.

As this case suggested, the flip side of strong pro-natalism was pres-sure on women to continue to have children even at the expense of their health. Also related was the stigma associated with childlessness. As mentioned, younger married women without children were extremely concerned about the possibility of infertility, and one woman who had been married for two years recounted with great bitterness how her mother-in-law and sister-in-law had allegedly told others that she was 'wasting' her husband's life because she had not yet conceived.

One woman who had been married for many years but remained childless was socially marginalized by other women, and it was said that her husband didn't care about her because she had no children. A story was told about how when this husband went to buy a larger trailer for himself and his wife, the seller commented that he must have a big family. The husband was said to have been so 'ashamed' by the seller's comment that he refused to buy the trailer.

Sensitivity surrounding childlessness was apparent several months into my fieldwork. I had repeatedly asked for assistance from my camp neighbours with genealogies but was making little headway with men. One day an elderly man surprised me by declaring that he would tell me how many grandchildren he had and proceeded to try and name them all as I furiously took notes. In the midst of this, however, one of his married sons who was childless entered the trailer and proceeded to accuse me of getting information without paying for it. This was the most overt challenge to my research that I experienced during the field-work experience. Concerned by his reaction I abandoned my note-taking and shortly afterwards left the trailer. While the incident ended in mu-tual apologies that evening, it was a clear indication of the need for greater discretion on my part.

Child Survival

High fertility among Travellers can be partially explained by levels of neo-natal and child mortality which, although declining, remain much higher than the Irish average.[7] In the course of taking down genealogies from women I quickly learned that a gap of more than a year between the births of living children often marked such a loss. An indication of increased confidence about child survival, however, was suggested by the practice of 'spacing' and by christenings, which were described as more significant events than in the past. In one christening that I at-tended a large number of relatives and affines attended the event in which a closely related married couple 'stood for' the child. At the end each attendee placed a pound note in the baby's blanket.

Despite improved child survival rates, the still common experience of infant and child mortality ensured a pervasive sense of the precarious-ness of children's lives that was expressed in intense concern over their illnesses and potential for accidents. Children themselves spoke with me about siblings who had died, expressing sorrow and exhibiting familiar-ity with their names and death dates (even when the deaths had oc-curred before their own births or in their own infancy). At least some children also appeared to view their own early mortality as a possibility. Aware of the preference for a change in residence after a death in the home, one boy volunteered to me that he would be sure not to die in his family's trailer because then his parents would have to move. One doctor also indicated to me that Travellers had a high rate of hospital admission because when their children were ill in the night they would bring them in immediately for fear of them dying at home.

The deaths of children after infancy were the most traumatic events experienced by women and men alike. Some parents were described by others as being consumed by grief and despair by the death of a child and efforts were made not to remind them of the tragedy. In some cases bereaved parents destroyed all photos of the dead child, while in others such photos were featured in a central location. Anniversaries of children's deaths were, like the death anniversaries for adults, marked by rituals of remembrance by the immediate family and wider kinship group. Wealthier families erected large and ornate headstones to dead children in the cemetery.

One woman who had lived in a number of different locations revealed the disjuncture between her own painful experience of the death of a child and the racist perceptions of officials. When she had gone to try and get birth certificates for her ten children she had been unable to recall for the official the location of the christening of one of her children. She was unable to remember, she explained to me afterwards, because this child had been born just after the death of one of her other children and her mind 'was gone that year.' The official responded to her inability to produce the location of the christening by becoming angry and suggesting that she was fraudulently trying to get a birth certificate for a child that was not her own.

Families experiencing medical crises were surrounded by a wide group of relatives who remained closely involved on a daily level until the situation eased. The widely-shared experience of child mortality ensured that the illness of a child was intensely experienced by many beyond the immediate family.

Scholarship has been drawing attention to some genetically-linked conditions which are found in higher incidence among Travellers, and some of these were also in evidence during fieldwork. Clearly, however, the broader issue of child survival and child health was linked primarily to living conditions deriving from official neglect rather than genetic predisposition. Children of the camp suffered from preventable conditions such as chronic chest infections, scabies, fleas, and cuts, while caravan fires and traffic accidents were the cause of a disproportionate number of Traveller children's deaths in the city (as well as the country as a whole).

I was told by one physician that many of the doctors in the city excluded Travellers from their 'lists,' and many Traveller women were extremely critical of the limited and often discriminatory medical services available to them. In one case a mother described to me how she had been barred from visiting her child after she had criticized the medical personnel for the care that they were providing. Others, despite their negative experiences with the medical profession, considered the hospital to provide better support for weaker infants than the unserviced camp site, and several of the babies from the camp were hospitalized in the colder months.

Travellers utilized conventional medical facilities, but also, like many other Irish, placed strong reliance on various religious practices, such as praying, fasting, and/or consulting non-Traveller faith healers, including both lay people and clergy who were believed to possess specific 'cures.' Adults thus actively engaged in a wide range of practices to try and ensure their children's survival in the face of marginalization.

Children's Work

The high fertility rates among Travellers can be partially explained in terms of a history of infant and child mortality, but also reflected the ongoing importance of children's work within a family economy. Research conducted by the Gmelches in Dublin in the early 1970s suggested that the contributions of women *and children* had increased due to the enhanced opportunities for hawking and begging in the urban setting (G. Gmelch 1975, 1977; G. and S. Gmelch 1978). My fieldwork in the later 1980s suggested that the importance of children's work, while less than reported for Dublin, remained significant to Traveller families. Children continued to be involved in income-generating activities such as collecting items at the dump or from nearby bins, door-to-door calling, and picking winkles. Sustained contributions in these areas were most likely for older male youth, who often assisted their fathers in activities such as scrap metal collection. In the case of older girls and younger children, the more significant contributions were in the area of domestic labour (i.e., fetching water, collecting firewood, washing clothes, and shopping) and child care.

The labour of children was available not only to their own families but also to other close relatives and/or neighbours – including those like myself with no children. When I first moved into the trailer young girls immediately described how I should sweep, mop, and wash the windows and then offered to do these tasks for me. Subsequently, I followed the example of other adults in the camp when I asked children to collect water and go to the store for me. Children also acted as crucial intermediaries between families in the camp by carrying information back and forth and, as mentioned earlier, making requests for such items as firelighter, candles, and milk when households were running low (see also G. Gmelch 1977: 96).

Children's work was not unproblematized; in fact, one cluster of families living elsewhere were criticized by other Travellers for using children as 'slave labour.' Children for their part sometimes complained about some tasks – for example, picking winkles. They also, on the other hand, saw working as a means of earning income that would facilitate their individual goals. Girls mentioned buying hairclips and getting their ears pierced, while one boy stated his intention of buying a bicycle. Clearly, however, access to income through work was more likely for boys than girls, whose primary responsibilities were not income-generating.

Adult women described proudly how well they had been trained in domestic skills before marriage and how they in turn supervised girls who were taking on increased responsibilities in this area. In one case when a twelve-year-old girl was caring for her younger siblings while her mother was giving birth in the hospital, another woman told me that, while she was 'looking in' intermittently, she didn't want to do this too much for fear of undermining the young girl's confidence. The training of girls for familial responsibilities was also identified as a distinctively Traveller practice by one woman who told me that, while 'country people' (i.e., settled people) thought that formal education was more important than learning to run a house, her mother knew of a country girl who committed suicide before her intended marriage because she didn't know how to cook. Such apocryphal tales legitimated the deployment of girls' labour within the domestic sphere as a form of training for their future.

The economic value of children lay primarily in their labour, but was also augmented by state payments. Several women indicated to me that their husbands wanted more children partly for this reason. The birth of twins to a woman in the camp during the fieldwork period, for example, elicited the comment that the father was happy as there would be 'double dole.' As this case suggested, such payments often flowed to the male 'head of household' rather than the mothers who did the work of pregnancy and childcare.

During the fieldwork period there was a new bureaucratic requirement for Travellers to produce their children's birth certificates rather than the 'priest papers' from church. The requirement to produce birth certificates was difficult for families who had never applied for them and whose children were born in different jurisdictions across Ireland and the British Isles. Hardly surprising in this context were references to a trade in birth certificates, which were going for £100.

While children had a direct economic benefit to fathers in the area of transfer payments, such payments did not in and of themselves produce high fertility.[8] This was, as I have suggested, the result of various articulating forces, most notably the still high neonatal and child mortality combined with the continuing importance of children's work. The significance of these factors, however, has been downplayed in outsiders' discussions of Traveller fertility (e.g., Rigal 1993).

While children's work continued to be important within the family economy there is no doubt that increased attendance at school and youth training centres by those who could be most helpful was altering the division of labour within families. Reduced access to the labour of older children, for example, directly affected the adult workload. For married men there was the loss of older sons as assistants, while for mothers the loss of daughters meant that they had to spend more time caring for the youngest children and performing domestic labour. This latter development contributed to the stresses involved in the negotiations over child care among married women.

Child Care

An important form of children's – especially girls' – work was the care of younger children. This care went beyond responsibility for siblings to include the supervision of children from other families in the camp. One of the advantages for mothers of living in the camp was the reduced work of child care due to the collective and outdoor nature of the play space. Children worked and played largely within the confines of the camp, resulting in a reduced need for intensive active adult supervision. They also spent much of their time in multi-age groupings, which ensured ongoing care of younger children by older children, especially girls. The importance of the care provided by older children within residential clusters and wider social networks was apparent in one teenager's comment that she planned to have a lot of children, but only if there were already a lot of 'older ones to look after the younger ones.'

The collectivized life of the camp also created possibilities for support, advice, and intervention through informal 'fosterage' arrangements. Some adults described to me how, when they were children, their parents had taken on varying degrees of responsibility for the children of neighbours who were incapacitated as a result of alcoholism. Changes in the organization of work and childhood were, however, creating a shortfall in the area of childcare, especially in families with no older children, or where the older children were in school.

With men providing only minimal assistance for younger children (although they were invoked as disciplinarians for older boys and girls), women turned to girls and other women for assistance. In one case, a mother of several young children brought her teenaged sister to be a live-in care provider for a few weeks while she worked at the dump with her husband. This, however, was only a temporary solution. Wives who wanted to join their husbands in activities outside of the camp often had to try to negotiate child care arrangements with other married women, and some of these negotiations involved a degree of tension and resentment.

Care providers, for example, sometimes expressed their annoyance at the imposition of additional children, suggesting that they often had little choice in the matter. Those leaving their children, on the other hand, complained about the inferior care received – for example, that their children were 'scalded' because their diapers had remained unchanged or that their children had been inadequately supervised near roads.

One way in which child care pressures were eased and wider kinship links maintained was through the movement of children. Young children from three camp families, for instance, spent extended periods with their maternal grandparents, who were living elsewhere. This was explained as responding to the needs of the grandparents, who were described as 'lonely' because their own children had married and/or because of a recent death. In one case it was said that a child was requested by a widowed grandmother because he carried the name of her husband and one of her sons, both of whom had died. The presence of the child, it was said, brought back happy memories for her. Clearly such arrangements also provided important support for younger families, and especially for mothers experiencing intense child care pressures. The presence of a child in the maternal grandparents' home also provided a legitimate reason for women to visit distant parents more frequently and thereby maintain links with their 'own people.'

Naming

Children were important to their own families but, as I have mentioned, also played important roles in wider Traveller networks. Their position in such wider relations was marked by the practice of 'titling' or naming children after close kin. First-born children were usually named after their paternal and maternal grandparents, although women disagreed over the sequence to be followed – for example, whether the first son and first daughter should be named after the husband's father and mother, and the second son and daughter after the wife's parents, or whether the first child should be named for the husband's 'side,' the second child for the mother's 'side,' and so on. In any case, the first two boys and girls were named 'for' the four grandparents. Subsequent children were named after their parents, aunts and uncles, and sometimes great uncles and aunts on both their mother's and father's side. The pattern of naming expressed the bilateral principles of Traveller kinship.

One result of this system was that the same names were continually repeated in each generation. A child who was given the name of a grandparent, for example, shared it with uncles or aunts and with cousins who had been named after the same grandparent. One mother told me that when she named her daughter after one of her own sisters, her aunt who had the same name assumed that the child had been named after her, and thanked her for the honour.

'New' names were introduced only after the names of close relatives had been exhausted and, as a result, were most common among the youngest children of larger sibling sets. These 'new' names, however, could rapidly become very common as future children were named after these individuals.

Exceptions to the naming order occurred when 'honouring' through naming was used for other social purposes. For example, a number of women in the camp told me that they had promised to name their next boy after a young relative who had died in an accident 'as a remembrance.' Saints' names could also be given to children as thanks after a major request had been granted.

In some cases, mothers named their children after relatives, but introduced some innovation by using their children's (often untraditional) middle names in daily interactions. The limited number of given names and surnames among Travellers, however, usually required individuals to be distinguished from one another by variants for the most common given names – for example, 'Margaret,' 'Mags,' and 'Maggie,' or by generation – 'old Johnny,' 'old Nora,' or 'young Tom' or 'Tomeen.' The possessive 'our Pat' or 'our Bridget' was often used in order to indicate that the speaker was referring to their own child or sibling. Children were also often identified by reference to their father: Michael, the son of Danny, would be 'Danny's Michael' (just as married women were often identified by reference to their husbands: Eileen, the wife of Tom would be 'Tom's Eileen'). Finally, there were many colourful nicknames applied to individuals (and to married couples) to distinguish them from others with the same names. Many of these nicknames, however, were insulting and never used in front of the individuals concerned (see also Okely 1983: 174).

The State, Racism, and Child Protection

During a wedding reception attended by several adults from the camp, the hosts apparently received a message from the police that there had been a report of child abandonment. The news initially caused panic among some of the mothers, who had left their younger children in the care of older children for the duration of the festivities. When news arrived that the children were not being threatened with apprehension, however, they settled back into a public enjoyment of the party. I was later told that they believed that the report had been made by a disgruntled wedding guest and that they were determined to demonstrate that the attempt to disrupt the event had been unsuccessful.

This case, which involved outside agencies concerned with 'child protection' being drawn into internal Traveller politics, needs to be placed within the context of my earlier discussion of how the intervention of outsiders in Travellers' lives was often justified as being for the sake of the children. Aware of this dominant discourse, Travellers, and especially Traveller women, were keen to dispute the notion that they did not care for their children properly. Traveller women were in fact bitter about their vulnerability to service workers, who had the power to remove their children on alleged grounds of neglect. One woman expressed her views about the hypocrisy involved in such threats of child removal given the lack of support for Traveller children's basic needs: 'if you're not there with the children she [the social worker] will take you to court and take the children away. But if she ever did that, I would say she doesn't care about the children when she doesn't do anything with the site.'

Another woman living in a different camp expressed outrage when city officials, in an attempt to evict Travellers from the camp, threatened to imprison her neighbour and institutionalize her children if she did not leave.

> They said to the woman over there that they were going to put her to prison, they were going to put her husband to prison, and they were going to put her child into care now, if [she] didn't leave ... As far as I'm concerned, you must neglect your children for them to be taken and put into care, and that's one thing I don't see Travelling People doing is neglecting their children.

The comments made above reveal how children were central to constructions of Traveller identity and Traveller/non-Traveller boundary-making. An allegedly greater love for children was part of a Traveller identity defined in opposition to the alleged anti-child character of non-Travellers. Travellers often pointed to their larger families in support of this claim and cited news reports of crimes against children such as abuse and abandonment as confirmation of the hostility and cruelty of settled people toward children. I was frequently told that Travellers would never engage in such behaviour.

Schooling and Training Centres

I have emphasized how children were important players within their families and wider networks, but they were also involved in interactions with non-Travellers and were the primary targets of outsider intervention. The perception of settled people as cruel and uncaring toward children created a paradox for Traveller children, who were frequently in the position of dealing with settled people in shops, houses, doctor's offices, hospitals, schools, and training centres. Children were expected to overcome their fears about such encounters, and to develop the skills of interaction with settled people necessary for their own and their family's survival.

Children, however, experienced overt racism in many of these interactions. One boy, for example, explained how he had been 'barred' from the corner shop where he went regularly to get milk for his mother. The shop keeper had told him that he couldn't come back until he had cleaner clothes and didn't smell. As I discuss below, many other stories referred to similar experiences at school. Children's anxieties about such encounters may have been the source of the stories that they told me about the fearsome creatures that they believed lay outside the perimeter of the camp. Children often told me about ghosts, monsters, and 'fat,' 'naked,' or 'beardy men' that hovered nearby waiting to take them (see also Okely 1983: 168).

During the fieldwork period the most sustained program aimed at children and youth was primary schooling. By the late 1980s and 1990s this was being extended to the post-primary level. The primary schooling being promoted during field research took a number of different forms, notably the integration of Traveller children into regular schools and classrooms, special Traveller classrooms within regular schools, and completely segregated Traveller schools. None of these were adapted to geographical mobility, and accessing a sedentary school system was difficult for more mobile families. As one Traveller commented: 'It's school that is stopping the travelling.'[9]

Experiences of schooling were deeply structured by anti-Traveller racism. Several adults told of how as children they had been called names and beaten up at school. Others described trying unsuccessfully to hide in the classroom so that they would not have to go outside in the breaktime. Two women in their twenties bitterly recalled the shame of nuns treating them as though they were dirty, for example, by forcing them to take showers at the school, looking through their hair for lice, and taking away their clothes and dressing them in what they described as 'rags.'

Practices of exclusion continued in the fieldwork period. One Traveller mother who wanted her children to go to the regular school that was geographically close to the camp described how, when she first approached the school to enrol her children, she was refused. She persisted by asking the school official to contact the school that her children had been attending in another city to prove, as she said, that there were 'no complaints' about her children. The result was that her older children were admitted but they suffered harassment from other children. One girl described to me how the other children were 'bad-minded' and spit in her face. When her daughter was 'knocked down' this mother complained, but was told that the school could not control the other children's behaviour. Faced with the school's unwillingness to take action, this mother threatened to send her husband in to deal with the matter. According to the mother, the school responded by saying that if the father appeared, her children would immediately be put out of the school. The mother concluded that such an opportunity to get rid of her children was exactly 'what they wanted.' While this mother was anxious to have all of her children at the same regular school, when a younger child was ready to attend she was informed that the school was full, and this child ended up being bused across the city to a special segregated Traveller class.

Parents wanted their children to attend school in order to learn basic literacy and numeracy, as well as to make their confirmation and first holy communion. They were also aware that keeping children out of school was frowned upon by service workers. Some, however, felt that they could not afford the loss of their children's labour and were critical of what they perceived as unreasonable pressures to send children to school when they were needed at home. The interest in gaining an education on their own terms was, however, evident when my partner and I were asked if we could provide some schooling for the children within the camp itself.

Nieuwenhuys (1994, 1996) points out the potentially contradictory impact of schooling programs premised upon a model of unproductive childhood and the goal of conventional employment for poor and minority children. The result can be increased pressure as new demands to combine school work with work within the domestic and/or informal economy create a 'double day' phenomenon. In the case of Traveller children there was evidence of such a process, especially for older girls.

Schooling potentially adds to children's work loads, but, as Nieuwenhuys points out, it can also provide 'children with a space in which they [can] identify with the parameters of modern childhood,' thereby increasing the possibility of 'negotiations with elders for better clothes and food; time for school, homework, and recreation; and often payment for domestic work' (1996: 244–5). There was some evidence that Traveller children's participation in school and other Traveller-related programs such as training centres for older youth was altering in gendered ways the position of Traveller children and youth within their families, wider Traveller networks, and Irish society as a whole.

There were three training centres for Traveller youth from Galway City that were part of a broader government effort to reduce unemployment rates (see O'Hearn 1998: 110–11). These centres, especially one for older girls which was run by a well-respected nun, received very positive local press. The images of Traveller girls and young women sewing flags and other items for sale were in striking contrast to the negative images of Travellers more generally. The all-female youth training centre was also popular among Traveller parents because it provided a chance for young women to earn some money in a supervised environment. In contrast, a training centre for teenaged male Travellers that taught woodworking and metal work had been less successful in finding and keeping trainees, probably because young men had more opportunities than young women for other forms of income generation.

A third training centre for Travellers in the city was co-educational, a cause for concern among many Traveller parents in the camp, who felt that it provided too many opportunities for familiarity between male and female Travellers as well as female Travellers and non-Traveller male staff. Despite such concerns, however, it managed to attract both male and female trainees for its gardening project and a life skills program that included cooking, music, physical education, and literacy.

Training centres for Travellers instituted on the basis of their uniquely 'deprived' background, and more recently, their distinctive culture, were intended to facilitate integration through the teaching of life skills and preparation for wage work. Service providers saw the training centres and the training allowance as providing young people, and particularly young women, with a degree of independence from the domination of fathers and husbands. The allowances paid by the training centres (for both Travellers and non-Travellers) were, however, low 'sub-individual wages' (Pahl 1984: 333) that prevented individual financial autonomy, although such allowances could be significant when combined with other sources of income within a family unit. During the few weeks that I spent at the co-ed centre female trainees made it clear that, while they enjoyed the chance to earn some income and to 'get out' of the camp or house, their work there did not relieve them of their responsibilities for domestic labour within the home and thereby often created the 'double day' described by Nieuwenhuys.

Meanwhile the 'mixing' of young men and young women encouraged by the non-Traveller staff of the co-ed training centre created particular pressures for young women, who were expected to maintain their distance from young men. Once when I was working among a group of young Traveller men at the centre a young Traveller woman who came to 'rescue' me by bringing me back to a group of women was harassed by the young men, who threatened to 'put her in the maternity.'

Although there was little evidence that the training centres led to subsequent wage labour for women or men, it could be argued that they contributed to a heightened generational and ethnic identity. Youth in these centres were selected on the basis of their Traveller identity and brought together with young Travellers from across the city who were not necessarily linked through close kinship or co-residence. At the same time an intensified Traveller consciousness among Traveller youth was facilitated through national conferences organized by training centre staff and the circulation of training centre newsletters across the country.

Traveller Youth

The very creation of 'youth' as an extended period between childhood and marriage among Travellers could be seen as being produced by extended schooling, training centres, and Church-initiated reforms in the area of marriage. I have already discussed how these latter reforms undermined parental control over marriage by challenging cousin marriages. In addition to this, the reforms included the new requirement that marriages could not be performed until a course had been completed and three months had passed from the official notification of the priest. The three-month delay, which applied to all parishioners, created an unprecedented 'engagement' period among Travellers, and several older Travellers were critical of this development, arguing that the delay was the cause of the high number of matches being 'put back' or 'called-off.' The criticism suggested that the reform had served to further weaken parental control over older children.

Along with introducing an 'engagement period,' the Church was also involved in raising the lower age limit for marriage to eighteen. The new regulation was implemented for Travellers in part due to the perception that marriage ages were dropping during the 1970s (see G. Gmelch 1977: 128–30). While the Church was successful in ensuring a lower limit of eighteen, a preference for young marriages at least for girls remained strong among most parents. In one case, for example, a wedding date was set to coincide with the bride's eighteenth birthday. Parents appeared to be less concerned about ensuring early marriages for their sons; indeed, it was suggested that some mothers resisted their son's desires to marry because of the loss of access to their earnings. Few Travellers, however, remained unmarried after the age of twenty-one, and the minority that did attracted critical comments from others.

The engagement period and older age of marriage provided greater opportunity for young people to influence the selection of their partners, and they were being aided in this regard by the actions of some service providers, who sometimes colluded with young people to create delays to unwanted matches imposed by parents. In such cases, some young people were also making use of elopements or 'runaway matches.'

Elopements were not a new strategy for young Travellers, but it is possible that the opportunities for such evasion of adult authority were increasing. Certainly there were a number of such cases that occurred during the fieldwork period. In one case it was said that the couple had run away together after the young man had been refused permission to marry by the girl's parents. When the couple returned to the city after a period of absence, however, they were immediately married with the parents' support. In another case a young person had refused to marry a first cousin in a match supported by her family and eloped with a 'stranger' instead (see also G. Gmelch 1977: 127–8).

If elopements were facilitated by shifting generational relations, so, too, was more direct participation by young people and especially young men in more standard marriage negotiations. Several younger people made a point of assuring me that, unlike in the past, couples now chose their partners for themselves. One unmarried teenager in the camp told me that he would choose his 'own match' as he didn't like this 'I'll give my daughter for your son or my son for your daughter.'

The active part played by young couples in courtship already noted in the early 1970s in Dublin (G. Gmelch 1977: 127) permitted different stories to be told to different audiences. One camp neighbour, for example, told me in private that her marriage had been a 'love match,' although she insisted that it had been a 'made [arranged] match' when other Traveller women were present. Another neighbour of mine explained the apparent contradictions in such accounts by suggesting that some young people thought that they had met each other independently but in fact 'there was still a lot of movement in the background' by their respective families. Others also emphasized how, even when young men made marriage proposals directly to their intended spouse, such actions were followed up with formal matchmaking procedures.

While the extension of childhood into 'youth' may have been accompanied by a strengthening of the position of some young Travellers, it was also creating a prolonged period of dependency as family formation was delayed. These changes, as indicated, were often mediated by gender. As delayed marriage created a new period of 'youth,' for example, young women experienced heightened and lengthened adult concern regarding their moral reputations. For some young women, then, the years of sexual maturity preceding marriage were marked by intense adult surveillance and control rather than increased freedom, and this surveillance was accomplished primarily by older women. As Yuval-Davis has observed more generally, in their role as cultural reproducers older women are often offered only a limited form of social power and may use this to police proper behaviour of younger women (1997: 37).

Paradoxically, the combination of onerous domestic responsibilities and intense surveillance led some young women to actively pursue early marriage as a means of escape. One woman spoke with great nostalgia about the exhilarating release from parental control and domestic responsibility that she had experienced when she first left her natal household. The early period of marriage that preceded prolonged child bearing and rearing was identified by many women as the freest period of their lives – a time when they didn't have to 'pay any heed' to anyone except their husbands.

Within gendered and generational constraints it is clear that Traveller children and youth, through their participation in relations of work, family, and wider networks, worked to ensure their individual and family survival in the context of state and Church-imposed programs of change. Through such social relations they were involved in the active reproduction as well as the reworking of Traveller identity and culture. A focus on the actions of children and youth forces recognition of the dynamic and differentiated aspects of identity and culture, and also directs attention to the ways in which Traveller identity and culture continue to be forged through confrontations with racism. On a post-fieldwork visit to Galway City I was in a bookstore when several Traveller girls approached the store clerk asking whether there were any books on Travellers. While I had been immediately directed to such materials on my previous visits, these girls were told that there was nothing in the store for them and that they should leave. The discriminatory exclusion experienced by these literate and identity-conscious Traveller youth revealed such forces at work.

Chapter 8

Epilogue:
Racism and the Politics of
Culture into the 1990s

This study has used archival and ethnographic research to explore historical and contemporary anti-Traveller racism as well as the lived experience of Traveller identity and culture into the late 1980s.[1] Here I venture into the post-fieldwork era of the 1990s through a brief examination of two sites of official discourse from the post fieldwork period: the 1988–9 debates over The Prohibition of Incitement to Racial, Religious or National Hatred Bill and the 1995 Task Force on the Travelling Community. These two examples of political discourse can be read as examples of the ongoing struggles to define and address issues of difference and inequality in Ireland.

First, however, these texts need to be placed within the context of the shifting Irish political economy. The post-fieldwork developments cannot be detached from intensifying processes of Europeanization and globalization which have included new forms of governance and policy-making as well as Europe-wide NGO networks concerned with racism against Travellers, 'Gypsies,' and Roma (see Minority Rights Group International 1998). In Ireland globalization in the 1990s was also associated with increased investment by transnational corporations and a resulting economic boom that reversed the prolonged recession of the 1980s.

These developments were accompanied by breakthroughs in North–South relations and liberalizing social reforms that suggested newly flexible and broadened definitions of Europeanized Irishness (Hug 1999). The 1990s, however, also saw intensified expressions of 'protectionist sentiment' that in Ireland (as elsewhere in Europe) included an increasingly organized and vocal racist and anti-immigrant movement claiming to 'protect ' Irish identity and culture. Such movements have been interpreted as a reaction to the apparent erosion of democracy and the power of the nation-state associated with Europeanization (Habermas 1999: 52). The impact of such processes for differently positioned ethnicized, classed, gendered, and generationed subjects in Ireland requires much more attention. Ireland's spectacular economic growth, for example, has, as O'Hearn (1998) points out, been associated with uneven distribution and therefore greater social inequality. The question of whether Europeanized structures of power and NGO networks have created new opportunities for representation and participation for Irish Travellers or 'new mechanisms of state control, domination and exclusion needs concrete investigation (Flavel 1998: 608).

The 1989 Prohibition of Incitement to Hatred Act

Occurring just before the dramatic changes of the 1990s were the 1988–9 parliamentary debates over the Prohibition of Incitement to Racial, Religious or National Hatred Bill. This bill was presented as part of a larger process of legal reform aimed at Irish ratification of international human rights legislation, in this case, the International Covenant on Civil and Political Rights, a convention adopted by the United Nations in 1966 and signed by Ireland in 1973.[2] In the course of the debate the dominant view that Ireland was a 'homogeneous' country, and therefore relatively free of racism and intolerance, was both promoted and challenged by parliamentary senators and deputies through discussion of 'hatreds' associated with the far right, sectarian divisions, Anglo-Irish relations, and against racialized minorities, 'gays,' and especially Travelling People.

The legislation was largely uncontroversial but there was debate over a number of amendments relating to its scope and implementation. Much of the relevant discussion related to a passage in the Bill which initially defined hatred as constituting hatred 'against any group of persons on account of their colour and ethnic or national origins, as well as on grounds of their nationality, race or religion' (Seanad, Collins, 24 November 1988: 855). The Minister for Justice indicated that the original wording, and in particular, the addition of protection on the grounds of 'ethnic origins,' was designed to conform to the wording of the UN International Convention on the Elimination of all forms of Racial Discrimination, a convention which the government intended to ratify at a later date (but still had not done so at the time of writing).

Although he referred to the eventual goal of ratification of the latter Convention the Minister repeatedly emphasized that the anti-hatred legislation under discussion was not intended to address the 'general question of racial discrimination' (Seanad, Collins, 24 November 1988: 855). During the debates, however, there were attempts by both independent and opposition senators and deputies to amend the definition of hatred to more clearly include particular populations that were seen as targets of discrimination in Ireland. Despite the fact that the initial position of the Minister was that there should not be any reworking of the original wording of the legislation (Seanad, Collins, 30 November 1988: 1054), the minority government eventually responded to cross-party support for explicit protection for the Travellers by accepting a Fine Gael amendment that included protection on the basis of 'membership of the travelling community' (Dáil, Barrett, 26 April 1989: 438). Later, after an election and the formation of a new coalition government, protection on the basis of sexual orientation was also added to the legislation.[3] Having analysed the wider debate in more detail elsewhere (Helleiner 1995a), I focus here on the discussion of Travellers.

The inclusion of protection on the grounds of 'membership of the Travelling community' was the result of a sustained challenge from independents and opposition parties of the government's initial position that Anti-Hatred legislation was primarily aimed at fulfilling 'international obligations' (Seanad, Collins, 24 November 1988: 852) and had little domestic relevance for Ireland.

Underlying the original argument of the government was a theory of ethnic and race relations predicated on the prior acceptance of the ethnic and racial 'homogeneity' model of the State. The implicit proposition was that in the absence of racialized and/or ethnicized populations there was tolerance and an absence of racism. The inverse of this proposition was that the arrival of racialized populations would result in increased racism. Thus, some politicians expressed the view that the proposed legislation was appropriate because of anticipated immigration (of racialized populations) in the future.

One of the more sustained challenges to the government position came from the leader of the Workers' Party, who criticized the original wording of the Bill for reflecting a 'tendency to clap ourselves on the back and to say that we are free by an [sic] large from the racism and racist attitudes to be found in other countries' (Dáil, De Rossa, 2 March 1989: 2219). In a number of speeches this deputy challenged the dominant construction of a non-racist state by suggesting instead a more systemic intolerance. While repeating the contention that the absence of 'major racial confrontations ... is probably due to the fact that there is no significant immigration of nationals of other countries,' he suggested that attitudes toward 'travellers, blacks, coloureds or gay people' left little room for complacency (ibid.).

While De Rossa was the most trenchant critic of the tolerant state model, many other politicians involved in the debate also argued that the Bill required an amendment specifying that Travellers would be protected against incitement to hatred despite their putative shared 'race,' religion, and citizenship with other Irish. Particular reference to Travelling People, it was suggested, represented a necessary adjustment of international wording in order to fit Irish circumstances.

This is an Irish piece of legislation. This is an Irish response to our ratification of the covenant. Everybody knows that of minority groups, our exclusively Irish minority group is the travelling community and I fail to see why an Irish legislation ratifying a convention ... actually omits to mention the travelling community. (Seanad, Bulbulia, 30 November 1988: 996)

In the context of a general denial of racism and discussion of 'homogeneity' the case of the Travelling community was consistently cited as an exception requiring state action. Speaker after speaker referred to the discrimination and prejudice encountered by Travelling People, providing examples of how they were refused entry to hotels, pubs, and discos (Seanad, O'Toole, 30 November 1988: 989–92), and 'subjected to all kinds of discrimination and outrage by a number of people and institutions in Ireland such as local communities, business houses, shops, post offices, and even county council authorities' (Seanad, Fennell, 30 November 1988: 984).

Most of the discussion revolved, not around the issue of whether Travellers were the targets of incitement to hatred, but rather around the issue of their status under the legislation. In particular, it was argued, there was a possibility that they would not be covered under the racial, religious, or national provisions because their putative racial, religious, and citizenship status was the same as that of other Irish. If this was true, it was argued, then an amendment clarifying that they were to be specifically protected was required.

In these debates there was agreement on the 'indigenous' rather than 'exotic' status of Travellers and, despite parallels being drawn to their position in Ireland as 'no different to the apartheid system in South Africa' (Seanad, O'Toole, 30 November 1988: 990), discourses of 'race' were largely absent. Despite their putative Irish origins, which were variously traced to the twelfth and/or nineteenth centuries (Dáil, Flanagan, 2 March 1989: 2188; Dáil, Barrett, 26 April 1989: 253–4; Seanad, Norris, 30 November 1988: 983), politicians recognized that 'For most people in Ireland the travellers are visible, different, a threat, and are clearly identified as a different group' (Seanad, Ryan, 30 November, 1988: 1000–1).

While there was widespread agreement that the Travellers were different and that they experienced discrimination, there was uncertainty over whether they were adequately covered by the legislation's reference to protection on the basis of 'ethnic origins.' When pushed on the issue the Minister for Justice stated that this should be left to the courts to decide, but that he considered them to be protected (Seanad, Collins, 30 November 1988: 967). The degree of his ambivalence about their claim to ethnic status on the grounds of 'origins' was, however, apparent in the following statement: 'there may be certain indications but little proof of their [Traveller] origins. I could not agree to a definition now that would tie the hands of the courts and could one day turn out to be factually wrong' (Dáil, Collins, 26 April 1989: 263).

The unwillingness of the Minister to clearly state that he considered the Travellers to have separate ethnic origins was taken as evidence by the opposition that an amendment was required if the Travellers were to be guaranteed protection. A willingness to argue that Travellers *were* an ethnic group (regardless of origins) because they possessed 'a separate culture, a separate way of life and a separate language' (Dáil, Colley, 26 April 1989: 251) was a striking feature of these discussions compared to those of the past.[4] Those who were in favour of such an identification, however, revealed a certain ambiguity in their understandings of Traveller status. For example, one politician identified the Travellers as 'the greatest ethnic minority we have' (Dáil, Flanagan, 2 March 1989: 2187), but went on to suggest that they might be defined in non-ethnic terms as persons of 'substandard economic and social status' (Dáil, Flanagan, 2 March 1989: 2191).

Others suggested that 'ethnic origins' be understood to mean 'origins which have resulted in a group having common social, cultural, religious or linguistic characteristics' (Seanad, Ryan, 30 November 1988: 959), although it was acknowledged that according to such a definition 'ethnic' status would not be 'confined exclusively to the travelling people' but would include other populations such as 'Muintir na Gaeltachta [the people of the Gaelic-speaking areas] who have a sense of having common linguistic origins' (Seanad, Ryan, 30 November 1988: 959–60). The limitations of the emphasis on cultural difference outside of its construction through relations of power was strikingly evident in this extension of 'ethnicity' to a population that has remained unethnicized as a result of its identification in dominant discourse and practice with the core of the nation.

Another difficulty with cultural criteria being signifiers of ethnicity was raised by one deputy who argued that protection was needed for those who were descended from individuals who 'traditionally pursued a nomadic way of life' (Dáil, Colley, 26 April 1989: 249). This proviso was intended to deal with the situation of the housed Travellers, who were 'integrated' but still targets of 'verbal and sometimes physical abuse for the very reason that they are recognised to be apart, to be different, to be of a group called the travelling community or travellers' (Dáil, Colley, 26 April 1989: 271).

While there was an indication of greater political support for the attribution of ethnicity to Travellers the leader of the Workers' Party, who supported the goals of providing protection and ultimate equality for Travellers, expressed reservations about the 'ethnic' strategy:

> There are sections of the travelling community who argue very strongly that they are an ethnic group and if they feel, as they obviously do, that in defining themselves that way they will have a better chance of achieving equality of treatment before the law and equality of treatment in Irish society then I have no objections to this. I see problems down the road, so to speak, in that approach. Nevertheless the travellers' group are not of such huge proportions as to create major problems for Irish society if they are defined as an ethnic group. (Dáil, De Rossa, 26 April 1989: 262)

Larger concerns about labelling the Travellers as an ethnic group were apparently sufficient to make the government select a proposed amendment that sidestepped the issue altogether by simply tacking on 'membership in the Travelling community' as a basis for protection. This phrase not only invoked relations with a 'community' rather than individual characteristics, but left the issue of Traveller ethnicity unresolved. The inclusion of the amendment presented an example of reworking international legislation to reflect dominant Irish understandings of inferiorized difference.

With the passage of the amended legislation the political élite, having opened up the issue of discrimination within the Irish Republic, worked to re-establish a positive self-presentation of the Irish state in the more familiar terms of tolerance. The legislation was portrayed by those in-volved as evidence of a new pluralism that included Travellers, 'gays,' and other minorities as full members of the nation (Seanad, O'Toole, 30 November 1988: 986; Seanad, Norris, 30 November 1988: 979–80), and was praised as 'the first foundation stone on which we build the society of pluralism and tolerance we wish to have and of which the people who set up this State had a vision' (Dáil, Barnes, 15 November 1989: 601–2).

A self-congratulatory Dáil and Seanad also described the legislation as 'a valuable indicator of the fact that we are an equal intellectual and moral partner with the other countries in the European Community' (Seanad, Norris, 22 November 1989: 608), and that Ireland was not 'an illiberal conservative society' (Seanad, Ryan, 22 November 1989: 611), but rather 'a remarkably tolerant society ... without, in many cases, some of the more ugly manifestations of extremism that other societies have to deal with' (Seanad, Ryan, 22 November 1989: 613). Such statements require critical assessment in the case of Travellers.

It is clear that naming the Travelling People within this legislation marked an important development, and, indeed, similar references to 'membership of the travelling community' have been incorporated into subsequent legislation such as the republished Equal Status Bill of 1999 and proposals for a revised Irish Constitution (Government of Ireland, 1997: 37). It is also necessary to note, however, that the goals of many of the politicians involved in pressing for the amendment differed substan-tially from those of advocates for Travellers who were lobbying politi-cians for such protection. Many of the latter, for example, had made the case for Traveller protection in the language of ethnicity and cultural rights, which challenged the premises of many state programs geared at Travellers.[5]

In contrast to this, the comments of parliamentarians made it clear that their support for the inclusion of Travellers as a group to be protected was linked to the politics of implementing the state accommodation policy. As in the past, politicians described their own constituents as having 'positive attitudes towards housing the travelling people' (Dáil, Abbott, 2 March 1989: 2212–13) and doing 'more than [their] share in offering facilities to the travelling people' (Dáil, De Rossa, 2 March 1989: 2226), but criticized other politicians and their constituents for failing to deal 'with the challenges posed by the proper treatment and settlement of the travelling people' (Dáil, Abbott, 2 March 1989: 2212–13). Opposi-tion members, for example, accused Fianna Fáil politicians of backtrack-ing on plans for providing Traveller accommodation in the face of opposition from sedentary constituents (Seanad, Fennell, 30 November 1988: 984–5).

In these references to the local politics of Traveller settlement there were occasional suggestions of connections between class-based divisions and anti-Traveller protests. Thus, for example, the particular hostility of the middle classes to the provision of halting sites for Travellers was mentioned by one Senator (Seanad, Hederman, 22 November 1989: 616), while the leader of the Workers' Party linked anti-Traveller discrimination to class concerns about 'property and property rights' (Dáil, De Rossa, 2 March 1988: 2220). Any such suggestions were, however, overshadowed by the more frequent claim that 'prejudice' in Ireland was based in the psychological variables of 'ignorance and fear' rather than economic or political factors (Dáil, De Rossa, 2 March 1989: 2222–3).

The result was that politicians were able to argue that the new legislation would result in 'changing social attitudes' that would in turn lead to less resistance to the provision of accommodation for Travellers (Dáil, Fennell, 15 November 1989: 597–8). Even more explicitly, the legislation was described as facilitating the goals of settlement and integration that 'we are all trying to achieve' (Dáil, Barrett, 26 April 1989: 253), goals that were also described as essential for the 'full development of the travelling people' (Dáil, Abbott, 2 March 1989: 2214).

While one politician noted that 'Our society should be such that they can choose not to integrate' (Dáil, De Rossa, 2 March 1989: 2226–7), Traveller 'integration,' usually described in terms of housing, appeared to be the goal of most of the politicians involved in the debates. In the same speech that optimistically identified the legislation as a basis for pluralism, for example, the speaker expressed the hope that the Travellers would be 'housed and integrated with the community according to their needs and their culture' with no apparent sense of paradox (Dáil, Barnes, 15 November 1989: 602). Such statements suggest that political interest in providing protection for Travellers against incitement to hatred often had more to do with facilitating the state program of settlement than providing support for a distinctive identity and/or way of life.

This conclusion draws support from the fact that the legislation has proved to have been of little assistance in combating anti-Traveller racism. There have, in fact, been no successful prosecutions for anti-Traveller racism under the 1989 Act, despite incendiary statements by influential politicians and press reporters. In a recent case, for example, a Fine Gael councillor from Mayo who was prosecuted for his comments that '[Travellers] are able-bodied men who should be made to go out and do FAS [employment training] courses like everybody else but instead are lying out in the sun like pedigree dogs' was acquitted of the incitement to hatred charge (*Irish Times*, 2 March 1999).

The 1995 Task Force and the Politics of Culture

The debate over Incitement to Hatred legislation revealed increased use of discourses of ethnicity and culture by the political élite but, as I have suggested, remained committed to a state policy that emphasized housing and integration rather than the economic, political, or cultural rights of Travellers.

I now want to look at the later 1995 Task Force on the Travelling Community which, with representation from Traveller advocacy organizations, updated the 1963 and 1983 reports discussed earlier. In this Report there was much more consistent recognition of both anti-Traveller discrimination and Traveller identity and culture. The labels of both 'Traveller' and 'Settled' were consistently capitalized, and a model of 'interculturalism' was used to describe relations between Traveller and non-Traveller 'communities,' both of whom were portrayed as having distinct yet equally valuable cultures. That these 'communities' and 'cultures' were in fact unequally positioned vis-à-vis one another was none the less apparent in the extensive discussion of discrimination and the need for new legislation and structures to both protect Travellers and provide for their greater representation.

Traveller culture was defined in a number of ways in the document, but the discussion emphasized the ideological – for example, 'The Traveller culture lies in the values, meanings and identity that the Traveller community shares' (Task Force 1995: 71). The official recommendation under the rubric of 'culture' was vague, advising only that 'the distinct culture and identity of the Traveller community be recognized and taken into account' (Task Force 1995: 12) – phrasing that was, however, inserted into many of the more concrete recommendations in the area of policymaking and implementation.

While most of the references to Traveller culture did not involve definitions there was mention of some 'visible manifestations' of Traveller culture, notably 'Traveller nomadism, the importance of the extended family, the Traveller language, and the organization of the Traveller economy' (Task Force, 1995: 72).

Like earlier reports, the 1995 Task Force report discussed Traveller mobility primarily under the rubric of accommodation. It differed from earlier reports, however, in its almost exclusive focus on the provision of halting sites rather than housing – a focus that responded to terms of reference that had outlined the government goal of 'providing permanent serviced caravan site accommodation for all traveller families who require it by the year 2000' (Task Force 1995: 10). The report recommended the creation of a nation-wide network of both 'permanent' and 'transient' halting sites and a central Traveller Accommodation Agency to coordinate and facilitate local initiatives.

The focus on hardstands suggested more substantive recognition of Traveller mobility than earlier reports, but the degree of support for nomadism was an area of contention within the Task Force and the recommendations reflected this. While there were specific suggestions for providing improved services to nomadic families in the areas of health and education, it was also recommended that there be provision of more extensive services in the 'permanent' sites and only basic services in the 'transient' sites (the latter being intended for 'families pursuing a nomadic way of life, or visiting relatives'). This distinction suggested a more ambivalent position vis-à-vis mobility (Task Force, 1995: 53), as did the recommendation that 'Traveller families who are provided with accommodation in ... one local authority cannot expect duplicate provisions to be made by other local authorities, save where they avail of transient halting sites, for stays of short duration' (Task Force 1995: 18).

The distinction between 'permanent' and 'transient' sites, it could be argued, simply replaced the dichotomous categorizations of earlier official discourse (e.g., settled/housed versus travelling/camping) rather than responding to the realities of Travellers' usage of a variety of forms of accommodation and a variety of patterns of mobility. Significantly, as I discuss below, even these provisions prompted four members to append reservations to the report that focused on their opposition to its perceived support of nomadism.

In the area of work, the 1995 report included a much clearer acknowledgment of the existence of an ongoing Traveller economy and a call for a recognition of the economic and social value of Traveller activities such as transient trading, casual trading, recycling activities, and the keeping of horses. The discussion, however, echoed earlier reports in its emphasis on the informal self-employed activities pursued primarily by adult men and its lack of attention to the significance of other sources of income for Travellers (e.g., transfer payments, training allowances, the proceeds of begging, etc.) and the various unpaid activities performed disproportionately by women and children. The result was a skewed portrayal of the Traveller economy that, like earlier reports, briefly acknowledged the financial success of a minority of transient trading groups, but for the most part emphasized Travellers' economic marginality. This supported the recommendations for intervention in the form of formalization of informal economic activities (e.g., through licensing, the inclusion of 'limited' storage/workspace on official sites, changes in waste management, investment in recycling as part of the 'social economy,' and training in areas of traditional Traveller interest, such as horses) (Task Force 1995: 46–7). As with the 1963 and 1983 reports, moreover, despite some discussion to the contrary the 1995 Task Force continued to place more emphasis on encouraging conventional forms of wage work than supporting existing activities (Task Force 1995: 255).

While the lack of analysis of the relationship between 'culture' and 'class' among both Travellers and non-Travellers contributed to a reified construction of Traveller versus settled 'cultures' and 'communities,' an important innovation in the 1995 report was the inclusion of brief sections devoted to Traveller women and Travellers with disabilities – both of which disrupted the otherwise undifferentiated discourse of culture and identity. The former pointed to the significance of gender as a source of inequity within Irish society and among Travellers. The section mentioned Traveller women's economic roles (although these were not described) and called for a gendered collection of data and analyses of all initiatives in collaboration with Traveller women's groups, and 'culturally appropriate' attention to gendered violence and child care needs (Task Force 1995: 50).

The discussion of gender, while limited, was important because it pointed to the existence of heterogeneity and inequalities among Travellers associated not only with gender but also with age, status, and income (and, as mentioned, disability, which was discussed separately). The acknowledgment that culture was constructed within wider gendered relations of power and could be dynamic, contested, and differentiated by (at least) gender, class, and age was an important insight that was largely absent from the rest of the report.

The absence of such a perspective was apparent in the discussion of children and their relationship to Traveller culture. On the one hand the emphasis in the report on the legitimacy of Traveller culture allowed for a challenge to the earlier identification of a Traveller identity or way of life as necessarily resulting in deprivation and 'at risk' status for Traveller children (Task Force 1995: 152). On the other hand a reshaping of

Traveller childhood emerged as a primary preoccupation for the Task Force members.

This was most apparent in the discussion of education, which made up the longest section of the Task Force report. Significantly, the lower rates of school attendance among Traveller children were for the first time primarily attributed to the inadequacies of the school system (e.g., barriers of access facing mobile Traveller children and the lack of an intercultural and anti-racist curriculum) rather than the inadequacies of Travellers themselves (although the illiteracy of Traveller parents was identified as one obstacle to children's schooling) (Task Force 1995: 200). Consistent with earlier reports, however, Traveller children's low rates of school attendance were problematized and a new Traveller Education service was proposed to increase Traveller participation from pre-school to third level education (Task Force 1995: 169).

Okely has suggested that the assumption that Traveller-Gypsy children in England suffer 'deprivation' as a result of their relative lack of formal education stems from an ethnocentric devaluing of the alternative modes of learning that occur among Traveller-Gypsies, and has called for recognition of the alternative educational experiences of Gypsy children (1983: 160–4; 1997: 74–9).

Although the 1995 Task Force report identified 'role modelling' as a 'method of education within traditional Irish Traveller culture,' this source of learning was mentioned only in the context of an alleged need for formal adult education for Travellers because 'If parents experience the value of education for themselves, they will become better role models for younger Travellers and they will also value better and foster the education of their children' (Task Force 1995: 218). In this case, then, recognition of an alternative cultural mode of transmission of learning was used to support, rather than challenge, the project of formal schooling.

The promotion of intensified schooling as consistent with the report's overall call for recognition and support of Traveller identity and culture was facilitated by the lack of any discussion of Traveller children's work (and therefore the ways in which schooling might contain additional costs to families and/or increase the workload of children). Despite recognition that the 'extended family' was the basic economic unit for Travellers, as in past reports, the only reference to children's economic activities was a discussion of the need for greater control over children's begging (placed within the section on Health rather than the section on Economy). As Stephens has suggested more generally, official support of cultural diversity in childhood tends to rely on definitions of 'culture' that emphasize the 'symbolic domains' of language, values, and beliefs – i.e., those aspects of culture that can be constructed as compatible with 'national-culture programs and forms of capitalist expansion' (Stephens 1995: 38). This limited definition of culture was clearly characteristic of the discussion of childhood (as well as other aspects of Travellers' lives) in the 1995 report.

Significantly, however, even the limited recognition and support of the 'visible manifestations' of Traveller culture was a source of internal debate and, ultimately, division. In a dissenting addendum to the report four Task Force members (including three politicians from the political right) framed their objections to what they saw as support for Traveller nomadism in the larger report in terms of the putative needs of Travellers themselves and especially Traveller children. The politicians stated that they could not support the report's alleged support for a future of nomadism within the report because:

Such a lifestyle [nomadism] will always place those who participate in it at a disadvantage in terms of accessibility to health and educational services, job opportunities and general services like insurances, loans, mortgages etc. and these facts must be acknowledged by those who espouse it for themselves and *for their children*. A permanent base for young families would give the children opportunities in life very similar to those enjoyed by most *settled children* [my emphasis]. (Task Force 1995: 289)

Here the alleged interests of Traveller children (defined in terms of access to sedentary services as well as the trappings of adult middle-class life, such as 'insurances, loans, mortgages') were invoked as an argument against nomadism.

Having established the ostensible dangers of nomadism to Travellers and their children, the dissenters went on to suggest that the anti-Traveller actions of residents opposing camping Travellers in their areas were in fact based on legitimate concerns for both their property and their children. Such opposition, they claimed, reflected 'the investment made by individuals in their homes and the sacrifices that have to be made to support the investment and to give their families a better start in life' (Task Force 1995: 290).

In this passage anti-Traveller racism, class, and childhood coalesced as Traveller nomadism was constructed as a threat to both Traveller and settled middle-class childhoods, and as an ostensible concern for both sets of 'children' legitimated a denial of the Traveller right to 'culture' (defined in terms of nomadism). By attributing the ongoing risks faced by Traveller children to itinerancy, and the opportunities 'enjoyed by most settled children' to the fact that they were not nomadic, this conservative discourse legitimated anti-Traveller racism and opposed any Traveller-related initiatives beyond settlement. The invocation of naturalized children's 'needs' meanwhile obscured class-based disparities in children's 'opportunities,' and deflected attention away from the economic and political causes of these disparities by identifying camping Travellers as the pressing 'threat' to non-Traveller Irish childhood.

The texts of the 1988–9 debates and the Task Force on the Travelling Community can be read as significant steps toward the dismantling of hegemonic constructions of a monocultural and non-racist nation, but the analyses offered above emphasize the limitations of the pluralistic visions that they developed. While a growing recognition of anti-Traveller racism and commitment to greater Traveller representation in policy-making and implementation are important achievements, linking the struggle for greater equality to prior claims of Traveller culture, identity, and community brings its own challenges.

As discourses of identity and culture are taken up in dominant discourse and practice they can become reified and codified, and their production within specific histories, political economies, and struggles of class, gender, and generation obscured. The result, as has been pointed out in the case of women and children more generally (Yuval-Davis 1997; Stephens 1995), may be processes that paradoxically reproduce attributions of naturalized difference and inferiority and become sources of oppressive constraint rather than liberation. As these considerations suggest, the deployment by the Irish state (and increasingly the structures of the European Union) of discourses and practices vis-à-vis Traveller culture require ongoing critical interrogation and juxtaposition with the experiences of diverse Travellers as they continue to forge their lives within local, national, and increasingly globalized arenas structured by unequal power relations.

Notes

Introduction

1 The absence of scholarship on these issues is linked to the alleged lack of ethnicity and racism within the state; a lack variously attributed to a reaction against a history of racialized colonial subordination, the removal of the Protestant minority from the southern state through Partition, and/or a semi-peripheral economy that had, until the 1990s, yielded a pattern of emigration rather than immigration (e.g., Brown 1981: 17–18; Lee 1989: 10, 77; van Dijk 1993: 63).

2 The labels used by non-Travellers have shifted through time. In the archival sources for the period preceding the 1960s terms such as 'tinker,' 'gypsy,' 'vagrant,' 'tramp,' and 'traveller' were often used interchangeably, suggesting a much more amorphous itinerant population, with much greater fluidity at least in external identification than exists in Ireland today. It was not until the late 1950s that the multiplicity of terms began to be reduced to the encompassing term 'itinerant' adopted by the Commission on Itinerancy. By the late 1970s and early 1980s the term 'itinerant' began to be superseded by 'Traveller' or 'Travelling People,' which are used by this author.

3 McVeigh cites folk song references to the 'yellow' Gypsy or tinker as evidence of how Travellers in Ireland have been 'colourised' (1996: 13), but others have disputed such a reading (Kenny 1997: 30).

4 By 'ethnic group' they meant that Travellers: (1) were a biologically self-perpetuating group; (2) shared fundamental cultural values; and (3) had an overt unity of cultural form (that is, shared certain externally observable behavioural and material traits); (4) interacted primarily with one another (interaction with the settled community being limited largely to economic

dealings and formal institutional settings such as courts and hospitals); and
(5) defined themselves as and were considered by settled people to be a
separate group (S. Gmelch and G. Gmelch 1976: 226–7).

5 Archival sources included the major provincial weekly newspaper, the
Connacht Tribune, 1922–June 1994 (the set of Traveller-related articles re-
trieved from this source has been placed on a CD-Rom by the Cultural
Heritage Group at Pavee Point). Other weekly local papers, i.e., *Galway
Advertiser*, *Connacht Sentinel*, *Galway Observer*, as well as the national *Irish
Independent*, *Irish Times*, and *Sunday Tribune* were reviewed, though not
systematically, for the 1983–7 period. The on-line *Galway Advertiser* for 1998
to May 1999 and on-line *Irish Times* from 1996 to May 1999 were also
consulted.

   For local city policy I examined the minute books of the Galway Urban
District Council (1922–37 inclusive), the Galway Corporation (1938), and the
Galway Borough Council (1939–86 inclusive). I have also made use of the
counts of Travellers conducted by the city at varying intervals between 1975
and 1986, and limited housing files. Access to the minutes of the Galway
Itinerant Settlement Council during its early years (1967–70) was provided
by a former member of the council.

   For the development of national policy I have relied on the Irish Parliamentary Debates, focusing on the elected chamber of deputies (Dáil), and
less systematically on the Senate (Seanad) for 1922 to June 1999. For these
sources references to Travellers were located through the use of the limited
indexing system and through an examination of debates where discussion
of Travellers could be predicted. An exhaustive review of all debates, however, was not attempted. For autobiographical accounts of Traveller life, see
Court (1985); S. Gmelch (1986); Joyce and Farmar (1985); Maher (1972);
Pavee Point (1992); and Sandford (1975).

6 The original settlement was subsequently taken over by Anglo-Norman
invaders and by the end of the thirteenth century it was a walled town
dominated by Old English merchant families known as 'the tribes,' who
were exporters of hides and wool (Mac Niocaill 1984: 1, 7). The seventeenth
and eighteenth centuries were ones of turmoil. Galway's inhabitants tried to
position themselves advantageously in the shifting politics of colonialism,
and the town suffered a decline in importance.

7 Nation-wide counts of Travellers were taken in 1944, 1952, 1956, 1960, and
1961 (see Commission on Itinerancy 1963) and continued through the 1970s
to 1990s. The 1994 annual count of Travellers recorded 3,878 families within
the Republic of Ireland (Task Force 1995: 195). The advocacy organization
Pavee Point provides an estimate of approximately 30,000 Travellers within

the Republic of Ireland, 1500 in Northern Ireland and up to 15,000 elsewhere in Britain (http://homepages.iol.ie/~pavee/faq.htm).

8 These figures are based on the count of Traveller families taken by Galway City for the Traveller Health Status Study in November of 1986 (see Barry and Daly 1988). While the census-takers collected data on the basis of 'families,' I recalculated on the basis of co-residential units, most of which but not all were nuclear families. This has resulted in some reduction of the census figures.

9 Identifying details of the camp have been excluded from this description in order to maintain the privacy of those who lived there during the fieldwork period.

10 With the exception of Margaret Sweeney, who emerged as a public figure within the city and nation, I maintain privacy by not identifying individual Travellers in this study.

Chapter 1. Origins, Histories, and Anti-Traveller Racism

1 Portions of this chapter previously appeared in Helleiner 1995b.

2 Sir Henry Sidney executed many itinerants at a court session in Cork in 1575 and extracted a promise from the native lords that they would forgo their practice of retaining 'idle men' (Canny 1976: 104–5). Sidney's successor in Munster, as well as the lord deputy of Connacht, continued the executions of 'loose and masterless men' (ibid., 106, 113).

3 Since the mid-nineteenth century, the scholarly literature on European Gypsies has been dominated by a paradigm which asserts a common cultural identity for all Gypsies vis-à-vis non-Gypsies, derived, ultimately, from an allegedly common Indian origin. This particular paradigm continues to be invoked by many of those writing on European Gypsies. While the assumption that a common geographical origin has created a collective cultural identity among European Gypsies has been challenged by some researchers (Okely 1983), Piasere's claim that the 'Indian paradigm' was entering a crisis phase (1988: 105) appears to have been premature.

4 Several decades later Stewart MacAlister's work *The Secret Languages of Ireland* (1937) would challenge Kuno Meyer's argument that Shelta was an ancient Celtic language. MacAlister agreed with Kuno Meyer that the ancestors of the tinkers and other wanderers speaking cant could not have possessed the grammatical and analytical skill to have fashioned such a language, but he attributed its origin to educated victims of colonial policies – for example, those who after the dissolution of the monasteries had joined the road and mingled with other wanderers (1937: 128–9).

5 The literary use of the bohemian as a symbol of the artist was widespread during this period in Europe. Brown concluded from French material that the artistic depiction of Gypsies and other wanderers 'has less to say about "real bohemians" than it does about artists and their imagined conception of themselves and their art in relation to the established social order' (Brown 1985: 38).

6 The 1831 census recorded 1,545 male 'tinkers' and 'brassworkers' over the age of twenty. A decade later, in 1841, the recorded 'Tinkers' were reduced to 835 persons. By 1851 the numbers of 'Tinkers' was halved again to 468. Some tinkers responded to the severe conditions of the mid-nineteenth century in the same way as other Irish – through emigration. British Gypsiologists collected information from Irish tinkers living in the slums of Britain in the second half of the nineteenth century, and by the 1890s there were reports of Irish Tinkers in the northeastern United States (Arnold 1898: 217). The census figures from 1891 reveal a fourfold increase over 1851 of people 'working and dealing in tin.'

7 There are also obvious parallels between the racist constructions of Travellers and of the Jews, who were targeted in the Limerick pogrom of 1904. According to Keogh's account many of the Limerick Jews were travelling pedlars, and they were villified as usurers, killers of Christ, and threats to women (Keogh 1998: 12–16, 21), allegations which were also present in anti-Traveller discourse. The links between anti-Jewish and anti-Traveller racism at this early period and later requires further examination.

8 For nationalists such as Arthur Griffiths, for example, this was an option to be rejected despite the admitted restrictions on rural women's lives: 'Men and women in Ireland marry lacking love, and live mostly in a dull level of amity. Sometimes they do not – sometimes the woman lives in bitterness – sometimes she dies of the broken heart – *but she does not go away with the Tramp*' (as quoted in Cairns and Richards, 1987: 53–4 my emphasis).

9 This story, known as the 'nails of the Cross,' is told of and by many 'Gypsy' groups in Europe and America. Accusations of 'nail-making' were being made against Travellers as late as the 1960s (see Walsh 1971).

Chapter 2. 'Menace to the Social Order': Anti-Traveller Racism, 1922–59

1 Portions of this chapter previously appeared in Helleiner 1993, 1997, 1998a, 1998c.

2 Research in Britain has revealed the presence of Traveller-Gypsies (including Irish Travellers) in towns and cities as early as the nineteenth century

(Mayall 1988: 34–45; Okely 1983: 30–1; Sibley 1981: 77–88). Further research in Ireland may also reveal a longer history of urban presence.

3 The apparent lack of explicit discussion of Travellers in the national parliament during the 1920s and most of the 1930s suggests that the Traveller issue was relegated to local authorities. The corpus of speeches examined for the 1922–59 period consisted of oral questions relating to Travellers as well as references to Travellers found within the speeches made in the course of the estimates debates for the Minister of Justice, and debates on Local Government (Sanitary Services) Act, 1948. Further examination of other debates may yield additional references to Travellers.

4 James Dillon was a prominent figure on the national stage from the 1930s onward. He co-founded the National Centre Party in 1932, but then joined with Eoin O'Duffy to found Fine Gael (the political successor to Cumann na nGaelheal). He became vice-president of Fine Gael in 1933, was Minister for Agriculture in coalition governments from 1948 to 1951 and from 1954 to 1957, and leader of Fine Gael from 1959 to 1965 (Foster 1988: 549).

5 Patrick Cogan, a Wicklow farmer who spoke frequently against Travellers, was originally an activist with the Irish Farmers Federation. He joined Clann na Talmhan in 1943 and was deputy leader until he left in 1946 (Varley 1996).

6 Fianna Fáil had been formed as a political party in 1926 by those nationalist leaders who had opposed the Anglo-Irish Treaty of 1921 and subsequently lost the civil war of 1922–3. Six years after its formation Fianna Fáil had ousted the ruling party of Cumann na nGaeldheal on a political platform of territorial nationalism as well as economic policies of agricultural and industrial self-sufficiency. The party went on to dominate the Irish political arena, being replaced for only short periods, and always by coalitions. While the political support for Cumann na nGaeldheal during the post-independence period came from the larger farmers and manufacturers of the east and southeast, Fianna Fáil's support was centred in the west and southwest among smaller and poorer farmers, small shopkeepers, urban and rural petite bourgeoisie, and some of the urban working class (Bew and Patterson 1982: 1–3).

7 Another count which did not exclude urban areas was a census household schedule of May 1946 which included the classification of Irish families by type of residence. One of the categories listed was 'itinerant family' and 5,554 persons were recorded (Dáil, 7 May 1957: 765).

8 This Bill was unexpectedly withdrawn in 1950 because of opposition from local councils concerned that they might not be able to prosecute Travellers for camping if they did not supply sufficient sites (Noonan 1998: 158).

9 The *Connacht Tribune* reported on the case of a woman described as an 'itinerant' who was charged at Galway District Court for failing to send an eleven-year-old boy to school, but this appears to have been unusual (*CT,* 13 July 1946: 5).

10 The fact that the provincial press reporting on Travellers during this period was dominated by court cases also suggests a high degree of surveillance and harassment by the police.

Chapter 3. The Politics and Practice of Traveller Settlement Policy

1 Portions of this chapter previously appeared in Helleiner 1993.

2 The focus on sites instead of housing reflected government acceptance of the Commission on Itinerancy's recommendation that due to a housing shortage in urban areas serviced camping sites should be provided 'pending the solutions of the difficulties associated with the housing of itinerants' (Review Body 1983: 16).

3 In fact progress in the rest of the country was also slow. In 1966 the Minister admitted that he 'was not aware that any local authority has so far purchased land for the development of itinerant camps' (Dáil, Éireann, 9 February 1966: 1134). Later that year two sites were built (in County Kildare and County Limerick) but these created only eighteen parking places. There was no more provision of sites until 1968, when three more hardstands (permanent serviced camp sites) were built in Dublin City, Cork City, and Loughrea, County Galway (Review Body 1983: 131).

4 A social worker familiar with the site acknowledged the lack of supervision, the squatters, and the horses, but claimed that the site was clean and tidy, the children were going to school, weekly rents were being paid, and that it was the only city site in which the original families were 'still living happily together' (*CT,* 6 November 1970: 16). As her comment suggests, the other sites were experiencing more difficulties.

5 It is difficult to determine whether the city was only counting those who were still in their allocated dwellings and whether it counted a transfer as a new housing or not. The criteria for determining 'itinerant identity' were also not clear.

6 In 1985 it was reported that 591 houses had been constructed between 1979 and 1984, and that a further 150 were under construction. A plan to construct another 750 dwellings during the next five years was also approved (GBC, 10 June 1985). In the mid-1980s a national program of privatization provided tenants with grants toward home purchases and there was an increase in owner-occupiers in corporation-built estates in the city. This shift

reduced the tenant/non-tenant split, but class-based geographical divisions remained.

7 For more discussion of the Dublin experience, see Dublin Travellers Education and Development Group 1992; Ennis 1984; Gmelch 1989; McKeown and McGrath 1996.

Chapter 4. Travelling, Racism, and the Politics of Culture

1 Portions of this chapter previously appeared in Helleiner 1991, 1993.
2 One of the Traveller exponents of this view also acknowledged the very different histories of nomadism among different 'sub-groupings' of Travellers (M. McDonagh 1993: 13). See also R. McDonagh 1999 for a discussion of the relationship between nomadism, gender, and disability.
3 While the provision of a hardstand had been part of the original 'village' scheme this was dropped after opposition from local residents and a nearby factory owner (CT, 2 May 1980: 20).
4 Rosetta McDonald was a Traveller who was threatened with forcible eviction from Dublin County Council property where she had been camped with her husband and ten children for fourteen months. She was initially successful in obtaining an injunction against the County; however, when she was subsequently offered accommodation in one of two tigeens, the injunction was lifted. The judge had ruled that the housing authority had met its statutory obligation to McDonald through the offer of a tigeen. The case thus did not address the right to camp but rather the right to be housed.
5 The situation, however, was not necessarily better in Britain, where the 1959 Highways Act had made it an offence for a 'Gypsy' to camp on a highway and the 1960 Caravan Sites and Development Act had resulted in the closing down of many existing camping sites (Okely 1983: 106–7).
6 I reconstructed accommodation histories from the annual counts and housing lists created by the city starting in 1975. These records had a number of limitations, including the fact that they were not consistent through time – i.e., sometimes those in tigeens, flats, and houses were counted and at other times they were not. They also did not count as 'Travellers' those living in houses in the city prior to 1967, and mobility that occurred between counts was rarely recorded. The result was that the relationship between various families and the city was not fully visible. For example, some families that had lengthy associations with the city were only recorded once due to short-term visiting elsewhere and were incorrectly viewed as 'non-local' while others with more transitory relationships were inaccurately identified as

'city families.' From the available lists and surveys a file of approximately 300 co-residential family units that were recorded as having spent some time in the city was compiled. I was able to establish some basic information – the names of husband and husband's father and maiden name of husband's mother, name of wife and wife's father and maiden name of wife's mother, names of children, and occasionally age – for 120 of these units. For an additional 100 units I have only partial information, while for the remaining 80 there is little or no information as they were recorded only once during the eleven year period.

7 Between the opening of the 'village' in 1981 and the spring of 1987, forty-eight Traveller households had spent time there. Four households that had entered the group housing when it opened were still there (in some cases, however, there had been a change in tenancy within the housing scheme). Another eight had left the group housing project in order to move into a regular corporation housing estate in the city and had remained in this subsequent housing. About half of the total (twenty-three households) left the project before being allocated a house in a regular housing estate. Some of these were later recorded as living in the city, either in camps, flats, or, in some cases, back in the housing project for second and third periods of occupancy. Others, however, moved away from the city, and their subsequent accommodation pattern could not be determined. The remaining thirteen households consisted of four households that had been in the project less than three years, and nine had entered within the year.

8 A total of forty-four Traveller family units were recorded as having spent time in corporation flats between 1972 and November of 1986. Almost half of the total number of families that entered the flats (twenty-one of forty-four) had later moved into houses in regular corporation estates in the city. In at least two cases, however, Travellers had left the flats and camped for brief periods before being allocated a house. Five were still living in the flats after periods of two through nine years and eight had been there for less than a year. Ten of the families that had entered the flats in the past had left after varying periods of residence, and in most cases did not turn up again in subsequent counts.

9 I used the annual counts to reconstruct the accommodation histories for the thirty Traveller families recorded as having entered standard houses in corporation estates (many had first spent some time in the flats or tigeens) between 1967 and 1980, the first thirteen years of the implementation of a settlement policy in Galway City. By the 1986 census, eight of the thirty family units that had been housed since 1967 still had a member remaining in the original residence. In another six cases Travellers had left allocated

houses in order to move into another house in the city. If we combine these two categories we find that almost half the total (fourteen households of thirty) had stayed in housing in the city from eight to nineteen years. Another four households also remained in their allocated residences for long periods, from eight to thirteen years, but left the city shortly before the 1986 count. The remaining twelve households had left their original allocations. Seven of these, however, were recorded in 1986 as living in the city in either the group housing scheme, the flats, or another regular housing estate. The available information suggests that in many cases these units spent time living in another part of the country or in Britain before returning to the city. Five families that had left the houses they were originally allocated were not recorded as being in the city in 1986 and information on them is lacking.

10 The situation in the camp and city as a whole provided support for the view, tentatively proposed in the analysis of the 1981 national census of Travellers, that there was an association between domestic cycle and accommodation use among Travellers (Rottman, Tussing, and Wiley 1986: 27–8, 38).

11 The Traveller woman Nan Joyce had stood as an independent candidate in the 1982 national election. Margaret Sweeney stood as an independent candidate in Galway West; she did not win a seat but received 511 first preference votes, coming ahead of two other independent candidates.

12 The 'votes for itinerants' campaign in the west was linked to the work of a Dublin-based group (see Acton 1974: 157).

13 One member of the committee who downplayed mobility when speaking publicly mentioned in private that it was much easier to try and organize the camping Travellers in the winter when there was less Traveller mobility, and also acknowledged that the results of the committee's work might not be enjoyed by many of its members because some of them would later be leaving the city.

Chapter 5. Work, Class, and the Politics of Culture

1 Travellers encountered during fieldwork referred to these dealers as 'jew men.' I was unable to confirm the extent to which these urban dealers were in fact Jewish.

2 Children's allowances were introduced in Ireland on a universal basis in 1944 for third and subsequent children. In 1952 they were extended to second children and in 1963 to first children. The old-age pension was dependent upon a means test and was only for those seventy and over during this period. Margaret Sweeney suggested in one televised interview

that some Travellers were initially reluctant to take up the family allowance because of their fear that the government could then take their children away (*Hanly's People*, 12 January 1987).

3 The size of the social welfare payment was determined by the number of dependants within the family. In 1986–7 a husband and wife with four children in an urban area received £97.15 per week in unemployment assistance plus a monthly payment of £60.20 for children's allowance. For a family of ten the combined payments, averaged over four weeks, amounted to £158. 57 a week.

4 There had been efforts in the city to thwart Traveller and non-Traveller money-lenders by improving the access of poorer families to formal sources of credit. Some of the poorer families in the camp had accounts with a local credit union but it was not clear whether these had succeeded in reducing the dependence on money-lenders.

5 One well-known set of relatively wealthy Traveller 'traders' are associated with the town of Rathkeale. Others are known to be involved with long-distance travel and trade across both Britain and continental Europe.

Chapter 6. Gender, Racism, and the Politics of Culture

1 Portions of this chapter previously appeared in Helleiner 1990, 1997.

2 A much earlier sexualized portrayal of tinkers that focuses on women is Brian Merriman's 1780 poem *The Midnight Court*, in which a female character is derisively described as 'Well-fitted to rear a tinker's clan, She waggles her hips at every man' (Kennelly 1970: 100–4).

3 As Okely has pointed out for the British case, 'In the dominant society, financial support is usually considered primarily the male's duty, so the Gypsy woman out calling conceals her role as major breadwinner and often poses as an abandoned, near destitute wife and mother' (1983: 204).

4 The terms 'clan' and 'tribe' were also used to refer to particular branches of surnames. An example in Galway would be the 'Townie Tom McDonaghs.' The married sons and daughters of the late 'Townie Tom McDonagh,' were often referred to as 'Townies.' The prefix of 'Townie' allowed Travellers to distinguish between this sibling set and the many other Traveller families in the region with the McDonagh surname. 'Townie' was also applied in some contexts to the children of 'Townie Tom's' sons. In this third generation, however, the appellation was not as helpful in distinguishing among individuals. Travellers with common surnames were also distinguished from one another by attaching the names of the towns or counties that their 'older generations' had frequented. There were thus the Mountbellew

Wards, Tuam Wards, and Loughrea Wards (and Mayo McDonaghs and Roscommon McDonaghs, etc.). Such geographic terms designated broader categories of people than those based on a common father or grandfather.

5 Among the three hundred family units recorded as having spent time in the city from 1975 to 1986, and the four hundred marriages recorded in the genealogies collected from Travellers themselves, there were only twenty cases that were identified by Travellers as intermarriages. The identity of the children of such unions was determined by the social relations of the family i.e., whether they interacted primarily with other Travellers or with non-Travellers. One of my camp neighbours told me that one of her grandmothers was a 'buffer' [non-Traveller] and as a result she was sometimes teased by Travellers with the term 'half and half,' but her Traveller identity was never seriously questioned.

6 By combining census data with genealogical information collected during fieldwork I came up with 116 Traveller marriages out of a file of approximately 300 family units where I had sufficient knowledge of parentage to determine the presence or absence of first cousin relationship. Census and genealogical information on these 116 marriages revealed that 32 were between first cousins. In addition, there were two apparent uncle–niece marriages and 14 definite cases of second cousin marriages (judging from those families for which I had more information I can be certain there were many more second cousin marriages, but genealogical information is lacking). A conservative total of marriages between individuals within the second cousin range of genealogical relationship is therefore 48 out of 116 marriages.

7 My data on sibling exchange is based on genealogical information collected from Travellers during fieldwork, rather than from the annual counts. For the analysis I identified 29 sibling sets for which I had complete or almost complete information on the marriages of each member. Looking at these 29 sibling sets, I found that 21 of them contained cases of sibling exchange (i.e., more than one marriage with another sibling set). Most of the eight sets without any cases were older, a finding which raises the possibility that the practice may be becoming more common. Sibling exchanges were more likely to involve two brothers marrying two sisters than a brother and sister marrying a brother and sister. In the data set described above there were 33 separate cases of sibling exchange. Twenty of these involved two brothers marrying two sisters (40 individual marriages). Eleven involved a brother and sister marrying a sister and brother (22 individual marriages). The remaining two cases involved more than two marriages, i.e., in one case two sisters and one brother married two brothers and one sister, and in the other

case four sisters and one brother married four brothers and one sister (8 individual marriages) for a total number of 70 marriages.

8 Of the 21 sibling sets that contained sibling exchanges, most (13) had exchanged marriage partners with one other sibling set. In the case of four sibling sets, however, there had been sibling exchanges with two other sibling sets. Another three sibling sets had sibling exchanges with three other separate sibling sets. A final sibling set had sibling exchanges with four other sibling sets.

9 The significance of affinal links through spouses, siblings, and children was apparent in the ability of Travellers to list the parents and siblings of those who had 'married in' to their families. Affinal terms were used to refer to spouses' parents (father- and mother-in-law), siblings' spouses (brother- and sister-in-law), and children's spouses (son- and daughter-in-law). Other affines were identified indirectly. For instance, the spouses of one's uncles and aunts were referred to as, 'my uncle's wife,' or 'my aunt's husband.' Such affinally linked individuals, even if well known, were categorized as 'strangers' unless they were also closely related, which was often the case.

Chapter 7. Childhood and Youth, Racism, and the Politics of Culture

1 Portions of this chapter previously appeared in Helleiner 1998b, 1998c.

2 A striking example of Traveller children's capacity for economic survival when nuclear families were fragmented through the imprisonment, illness, and/or death or migration of their parents is provided by Nan Joyce's published description of how she and her older sister (aged twelve and fourteen respectively) cared for their eight younger siblings after the death of their father and during the year-long imprisonment of their mother (Joyce and Farmar 1985: 43–57).

3 During the pre-settlement period there were few state supports for Travellers, but some Travelling People used hospitals for childbirth and illness, stayed in county homes during the winter months, and gathered food, clothing, and money from individual clergy, convents, and voluntary organizations such as the Legion of Mary and Society of St Vincent de Paul (CI 1963: 48–9, 103; Maher 1972: 7–10; Court 1985: 67; Joyce and Farmar 1985: 30; S. Gmelch 1986: 48, 55–6). As mentioned earlier, Travellers were also collecting some state benefits – for example, children's allowances and old age pensions – through the use of post office addresses (CI 1963: 75).

4 The Minister responsible for child care, for example, included within his definition of children 'at risk' the 'children of single-parent families and children whose mothers have been deserted or widowed and have to find

employment because of economic necessity' (Dáil, Woods, 23 April 1980: 1875–6). In the case of Traveller children, however, it was not family structure or mothers in paid employment which put them 'at risk,' but rather itinerancy and the (allegedly related) lack of formal education. According to the Report, a lack of formal education meant that many Traveller children were 'growing up illiterate and ill-equipped to face their future' (Task Force on Child Care Services 1980: 40).

5 For medically oriented research and discourse on Travellers, see Carroll et al. 1974 and Creedon et al. 1975 as cited in Review Body 1983; Ó Nuallain and Forde 1992. For a description of living with disability as a Traveller, see R. McDonagh 1999.

6 The use of photos of Traveller-Gypsy children on the covers of British policy documents is also noted by Okely, who describes similar constructions of Traveller-Gypsy children as innocent victims of deprivation in need of rescue by outsiders (1983: 164).

7 The figures on infant mortality alone reveal a dramatic decline from an estimate of 113/1000 calculated from the 1960 census (although when only births since 1950 were included this dropped to 76/1000), which compared unfavourably with the 1961 Irish average of 30.5/1000 (although the figure for the lower income Dubliners was calculated at a more comparable 60/1000) (see CI 1963: 47, 131–6). By 1987 this had dropped to approximately 18.1/1000. The latter was, however, still more than double the Irish average of 7.4/1000. A comparable figure for lower income Irish is not provided (see Task Force on the Travelling Community 1995: 135).

8 The claim of George Gmelch (1977: 81) that an increase in payments in the mid-1970s actually reversed a shift toward family planning among Travellers in Dublin strikes me as too simplistic.

9 See Kenny (1997) for a detailed discussion of the history and politics of Traveller schooling as well as rich ethnographic material on the experiences of Traveller children and youth in the school setting.

Chapter 8. Epilogue: Racism and the Politics of Culture into the 1990s

1 Portions of this chapter previously appeared in Helleiner 1995a, 1998a.

2 To ratify this Covenant the government had to abolish the death sentence for crimes committed by persons under eighteen years of age as well as prepare legislation to prohibit incitement to hatred (Seanad, Collins, 24 November 1988: 854).

3 Amendments relating to protection on the basis of sexual orientation proposed by independents as well as by the Labour and Workers' Party were

initially rejected by the government. Before the legislation could proceed further, however, an election replaced the Fianna Fáil minority government with a Fianna Fáil–Progressive Democrat coalition and a new Minister for Justice. Following these changes, the legislation was restored with the inclusion of sexual orientation as a grounds for protection. Near the end of the debates an effort to extend the definition of hatred to include protection for women and children was made, but this attempt was unsuccessful (Dáil, Barnes, 15 November 1989: 600–3; Seanad, Jackman, 22 November 1989: 607).

4 The claim that what is known as Shelta or 'cant' or 'gammon' is a fundamental aspect of Traveller ethnicity was central to some discussions regarding the status of Travellers in the 1990s (see Dublin Travellers Education and Development Group 1992 and especially McCann et al. 1994).

5 I am referring here to the efforts of the Dublin Travellers Education and Development Group, who were actively involved in lobbying politicians for clarification of Traveller protection under the legislation.

References

Acton, Thomas. 1974. *Gypsy politics and social change*. London: Routledge and Kegan Paul.

Allen, Theodore. 1994. *The invention of the white race*. London: Verso.

Anon. 1890. Additional notes on the Irish Tinkers and their language. *Journal of the Gypsy Lore Society*, 1st ser. 2:127.

– 1908. Irish Gypsies. *Journal of the Gypsy Lore Society*, 2nd ser., 1:130.

– 1937. Meanderings: Our Irish Gypsies – the Tinkers. *Ireland's Own*, 17 April, 4.

Anthias, Floya, and Nira Yuval-Davis. 1992. *Racialised boundaries*. London: Routledge.

– 1995. Cultural racism or racist culture? Rethinking racist exclusions. *Economy and Society* 24(2):279–301.

Arensberg, Connie, and Solon Kimball. 1961 (1940). *Family and community in Ireland*. Gloucester, Mass: Peter Smith.

Arnold, Frederick. 1898. Our old poets and the Tinkers. *Journal of American Folklore* 11:210–20.

Barry, Joseph, and Leslie Daly. 1988. *The Travellers' health status study: Census of Travelling People, November 1986*. Dublin: The Health Research Board.

Beier, A.L. 1985. *Masterless men*. London: Methuen.

Bell, Diane, Pat Caplan, and Wazir Jahan Karim, eds. 1993. *Gendered fields: Women, men and ethnography*. London: Routledge.

Best, Joel, ed. 1994. *Troubling children: Studies of children and social problems*. New York: Aldine de Gruyter.

Bew, Paul, and Henry Patterson. 1982. *Seán Lemass and the making of modern Ireland, 1945–66*. Dublin: Gill and Macmillan.

Bourke, Joanna. 1993. *Husbandry to housewifery*. Oxford: Clarendon Press.

Brewer, John. 1992. Sectarianism and racism, and their parallels and differences. *Ethnic and Racial Studies* 15:352–64.

Brown, Marilyn. 1985. *Gypsies and other bohemians: The myth of the artist in nineteenth-century France*. Ann Arbor, Michigan: UMI Research Press.

Brown, Terence. 1981. *Ireland: A social and cultural history, 1922–79*. London: Fontana Press.

Burton, Frank, and Pat Carlen. 1979. *Official discourse*. London: Routledge and Kegan Paul.

Cairns, David, and Shaun Richards. 1987. 'Woman' in the discourse of Celticism: A reading of *The Shadow of the Glen*. *Canadian Journal of Irish Studies* 13:43–60.

– 1988. *Writing Ireland: Colonialism, nationalism and culture*. Manchester: Manchester University Press.

Callan, Tim, Brian Nolan, and Christopher Whelan. 1994. Who are the poor? In *Poverty and policy in Ireland*, ed. Brian Nolan and Tim Callan, 63–77. Dublin: Gill and Macmillan.

Canny, Nicholas. 1976. *The Elizabethan conquest of Ireland*. Hassocks, Sussex: Harvester Press.

Clifford, James. 1992. Travelling cultures. In *Cultural studies*, ed. Lawrence Grossberg, Cary Nelson, and Paula Treichler, 96–112, London: Routledge.

Collins, Martin. 1994. The sub-culture of poverty – a response to McCarthy. In *Irish Travellers: Culture and ethnicity*, ed. May McCann, Séamas Ó Síocháin, and Joseph Ruane, 130–3. Queen's University of Belfast: Institute of Irish Studies.

Commission on Itinerancy. 1963. *Report of the Commission on Itinerancy*. Dublin: The Stationery Office.

Court, Artelia. 1985. *Puck of the Droms*. Berkeley: University of California Press.

Corkery, Daniel. 1967 (1924). *The Hidden Ireland*. Dublin: Gill and Macmillan.

Crawford, M.H., and George Gmelch. 1974. Human biology of the Irish Tinkers: Demography, ethnohistory and genetics. *Social Biology* 21(4):321–31.

Crickley, Anastasia. 1992. Feminism and ethnicity. In *Irish Travellers: New analysis and new initiatives*, ed. Dublin Travellers Education and Development Group, 101–8. Dublin: Pavee Point Publications.

Crowley, Ethel, and Jim MacLaughlin, eds. 1997. *Under the belly of the tiger: Class, race, identity and culture in the global Ireland*. Dublin: Irish Reporter Publications.

Curtin, Chris, Pauline Jackson, and Barbara O'Connor, eds. 1987. *Gender in Irish society*. Galway: Galway University Press.

Curtin, Chris, and Tom Wilson, eds. 1989. *Ireland from below*. Galway: Galway University Press.

Curtin, Chris, Hastings Donnan, and Tom Wilson, eds. 1993. *Irish urban cultures*. Queen's University of Belfast: Institute of Irish Studies.

Curtis, Liz. 1984. *Nothing but the same old story: The roots of anti-Irish racism*. London: Information on Ireland.

Dublin Travellers Education and Development Group. 1992. *Irish Travellers: New analysis and new initiatives*. Dublin: Pavee Point Publications.

Ennis, Mervyn. 1984. Twenty years of social work. Paper presented to the Irish Association of Social Workers, 31 March–April 1.

Evanson, Eileen. 1987. Women and social security in Ireland. In *Gender in Irish society*, ed. Chris Curtin, Pauline Jackson, and Barbara O'Connor, 184–202. Galway: Galway University Press.

Ferguson, Harry, and Pat Kenny. 1995. Introduction to *On behalf of the child: Child welfare, child protection and the Child Care Act, 1991*, ed. Harry Ferguson and Pat Kenny, 1–6. Dublin: A. and A. Farmar.

Fitzpatrick, David. 1983. Irish farming families before the first world war. *Comparative Studies in Society and History* 25:339–74.

Flavel, Adrian. 1998. Introduction to *Journal of Ethnic and Migration Studies* 24(4):605–11.

Flynn, Michael. 1975. Settlement of the Travelling People. *Social Studies* 4(2):162–71.

Foster, Roy F. 1988. *Modern Ireland: 1600–1972*. London: Allen Lane.

Franklin, Sarah, and Helena Ragoné, eds. 1998. *Reproducing reproduction*. Philadelphia: University of Pennsylvania Press.

Gibbon, Peter. 1973. Arensberg and Kimball revisited. *Economy and Society* 2:478–98.

Gibbon, Peter, and Chris Curtin. 1978. The stem family in Ireland. *Comparative Studies in Society and History* 20:429–53.

Gibbons, Luke. 1996. *Transformations in Irish culture*. Cork: Cork University Press.

Gmelch, George. 1975. The effects of economic change on Irish Traveller sex roles and marriage patterns. In *Gypsies, Tinkers and other Travellers*, ed. Farnham Rehfisch, 257–69. London: Academic Press.

– 1977. *The Irish Tinkers: The urbanization of an itinerant people*. Menlo Park, California: Cummings.

Gmelch, George, and Sharon Gmelch. 1974. The itinerant settlement movement: Its policies and effects on Irish Travellers. *Studies* 68:1–16.

– 1978. Begging in Dublin. *Urban Life* 6(4):439–54.

– 1985. The cross-channel migration of Irish Travellers. *The Economic and Social Review* 16(4):287–96.

– 1987. Commercial nomadism: Occupation and mobility among Travellers in England and Wales. In *The other nomads*, ed. Aparna Rao, 133–51. Köln: Bohlau Verlag.

Gmelch, Sharon. 1975. *Tinkers and Travellers*. Dublin: O'Brien Press.

– 1977. Economic and power relations among urban Tinkers: The role of women. *Urban Anthropology* 6(3):237–47.

- 1986. *Nan: The life of a Travelling Woman.* London: Souvenir Press.
- 1989. From poverty subculture to political lobby: The Traveller rights movement in Ireland. In *Ireland from below,* ed. Chris Curtin and Tom Wilson, 301–19, Galway: Galway University Press.

Gmelch, Sharon, and George Gmelch. 1976. The emergence of an ethnic group: The Irish Tinkers. *Anthropological Quarterly* 49:225–38.

Government of Ireland. 1997. *First progress report* (of the all-party oireachtas committee on the constitution). Dublin: Stationery Office.

Greenhouse, Carol, ed. 1998. *Democracy and ethnography: Constructing identities in multicultural liberal states.* New York: State University of New York Press.

Gregory, Lady Augusta. 1970. *The wonder and supernatural plays of Lady Gregory,* ed. Ann Saddlemeyer. Gerrard's Cross: Colin Smythe.
- 1974 (1903). *Poets and dreamers.* Gerrard's Cross: Colin Smythe.

Grimes, Séamus. 1984. Educational opportunities in Galway City: Present trends and future prospects. In *Galway town and gown, 1494–1984,* ed. Diarmuid Ó Cearbhaill, 245–57. Dublin: Gill and Macmillan.

Gupta, Akhil, and James Ferguson, eds. 1997. *Anthropological locations: Boundaries and grounds of a field science.* Berkeley: University of California Press.

Habermas, Jurgen. 1999. The European nation-state and the pressures of globalization. *New Left Review* 235:46–59.

Hainsworth, Paul, ed. 1998. *Divided society: Ethnic minorities and racism in Northern Ireland.* London: Pluto Press.

Harper, Jared. 1971. 'Gypsy' research in the South. In *The not so solid south: Anthropological studies in a regional subculture,* ed. John Morland, 16–24. Athens: Southern Anthropological Society.

Helleiner, Jane. 1990. 'The Tinker's Wedding' revisited: Irish Traveller marriage. In *100 Years of Gypsy studies,* ed. Matt Salo, 77–85. Cheverly, Maryland: The Gypsy Lore Society.
- 1991. La sedentarizzazione dei Travellers Irlandesi: Retorica e realtà [The settlement of Irish Travellers: Rhetoric and reality]. *La Ricerca Folklorica* 22:67–74.
- 1993. Traveller settlement in Galway City: Politics, class, and culture. In *Irish urban cultures,* ed. Chris Curtin, Hastings Donnan, and Tom Wilson, 181–201. Queen's University of Belfast: Institute of Irish Studies.
- 1995a. Inferiorized difference and the limits of pluralism in Ireland: The 1989 Anti-hatred Act. *Canadian Journal of Irish Studies* 21(2):63–83.
- 1995b. Gypsies, Celts and Tinkers: Colonial antecedents of anti-Traveller racism in Ireland. *Ethnic and Racial Studies* 18(3):532–54.
- 1997. 'Women of the itinerant class': Gender and anti-Traveller racism in Ireland. *Women's Studies International Forum* 20(2):275–87.

- 1998a. 'Menace to the social order': Anti-Traveller discourse in the Irish parliamentary debates, 1939–59. *Canadian Journal of Irish Studies* 24(1):75–91.
- 1998b. Contested childhood: The discourse and politics of minority childhood in Ireland. *Childhood* 5(3):303–24.
- 1998c. 'For the protection of the children': The politics of minority childhood in Ireland. *Anthropological Quarterly* 71(2):51–62.

Helleiner, Jane, and Bohdan Szuchewycz. 1997. Discourses of exclusion: The Irish press and the Travelling People. In *The language and politics of exclusion: Others in discourse*, ed. Stephen Riggins, 109–30. Thousand Oaks, Calif.: Sage.

Hickman, Mary. 1998. Reconstructing deconstructing 'race': British political discourses about the Irish in Britain. *Ethnic and Racial Studies* 21(2):288–307.

Hug, Chrystel. 1999. *The politics of sexual morality in Ireland*. London: Macmillan.

Irish Folklore Commission. 1952. Tinker Questionnaire. Vols. 1255–6. Unpublished material in the archives of the Department of Folklore, University College Dublin (available on microfiche, University College, Galway.)

Jenks, Chris. 1996. *Childhood*. London: Routledge.

Joyce, Nan, and Anna Farmar. 1985. *Traveller*. Dublin: Gill and Macmillan.

Kennelly, Brendan. 1970. *Penguin book of Irish verse*. Harmondsworth, England: Penguin Books.

Kenny, Máirín. 1997. *The routes of resistance: Travellers and second-level schooling*. Aldershot: Ashgate.

Keogh, Dermot. 1998. *Jews in twentieth-century Ireland: Refugees, anti-Semitism and the holocaust*. Cork: Cork University Press.

Lee, J.J. 1989. *Ireland: 1912–1985*. Cambridge: Cambridge University Press.

Leland, Charles. 1892. What we have done. *Journal of the Gypsy Lore Society*, 1st ser., 3(4):193–9.

Lentin, Ronit. 1998. 'Irishness,' the 1937 constitution and citizenship: A gender and ethnicity view. *Irish Journal of Sociology* 8:5–24.

Lentin, Ronit, and Robbie McVeigh, eds. Forthcoming. *Racism and anti-racism in Ireland*. Dublin: Irish Academic Press.

Leonard, Madeline. 1995. Women and informal activity in Belfast. *In Irish society: Sociological perspectives*, ed. Patrick Clancy, Sheelagh Drudy, Kathleen Lynch, and Liam O'Dowd, 235–49. Dublin: Institute for Public Administration.

Lucassen, Leo Wim Willems, and Annemarie Cottar. 1998. *Gypsies and other itinerant groups: A socio-historical approach*. New York: St Martin's Press.

MacAlister, Stewart. 1937. *The secret languages of Ireland*. Cambridge: Cambridge University Press.

MacGréine, Pádraig. 1931. Irish Tinkers or 'Travellers.' *Béaloideas: Journal of the Folklore Society of Ireland* 3:170–86.

– 1932. Further notes on Tinkers' cant. *Béaloideas: Journal of the Folklore Society of Ireland* 3:290–303.
– 1934. Some notes on Tinkers and their 'cant'. *Béaloideas: Journal of the Folklore Society of Ireland* 4:259–63.
Mac Gréil, Micheál. 1996. *Prejudice in Ireland revisited*. Maynooth: Survey and Research Unit.
Mac Laughlin, Jim. 1995. *Travellers and Ireland: Whose country, whose history?* Cork: Cork University Press.
– 1996. The evolution of anti-Traveller racism in Ireland. *Race and Class* 37(3):47–63.
Mac Niocaill, Gearóid. 1984. Medieval Galway: Its origins and charter. In *Galway town and gown, 1494–1984*, ed. Diarmuid Ó Cearbhaill, 1–9. Dublin: Gill and Macmillan.
MacNeill, Eoin. 1920. *Phases of Irish history*. Dublin: M.H. Gill.
MacRitchie, David. 1889. Irish Tinkers and their language. *Journal of the Gypsy Lore Society*, 1st ser., 1:350–7.
– 1890. Additional notes on the Irish Tinkers and their language. *Journal of the Gypsy Lore Society*, 1st ser., 2:127
Madec, Mary O'Malley. 1993. The Irish Travelling woman: Mother and mermaid. In *Irish women's studies reader*, ed. Ailbhe Smythe, 214–29. Dublin: Attic Press.
Maher, Sean. 1972. (rpt. 1998). *On the road to God knows where*. Dublin: Talbot Press.
Mahon, Evelyn. 1995. From democracy to femocracy: The women's movement in the Republic of Ireland. In *Irish society: Sociological perspectives*, ed. Patrick Clancy, Sheelagh Drudy, Kathleen Lynch, and Liam O'Dowd, 675–708. Dublin: Institute for Public Administration.
Mayall, David. 1988. *Gypsy-Travellers in nineteenth-century society*. Cambridge: Cambridge University Press.
Maxwell, Constantia. 1949. *Country and town in Ireland under the Georges*. Dundalk: Dundalgan Press.
McCann, May, Séamas Ó Síocháin, and Joseph Ruane, eds. 1994. *Irish Travellers: Culture and ethnicity*. Belfast: Queen's University of Belfast.
McCann, Thomas, and Davey Joyce. Forthcoming. Anti-Traveller racism. In *Racism and anti-racism in Ireland*, ed. Ronit Lentin and Robbie McVeigh. Dublin: Irish Academic Press.
McCarthy, Patricia. 1994. The sub-culture of poverty reconsidered. In *Irish Travellers: Culture and ethnicity*, ed. May McCann, Séamas Ó Síocháin, and Joseph Ruane, 121–9. Belfast: Queen's University of Belfast.
McDonagh, Michael. 1993. Who are the Travelling People? In *Do you know us at all?* ed. John Hyland, 9–19. Dublin: Parish of the Travelling People.

– 1994. Nomadism in Irish Traveller identity. In *Irish Travellers: Culture and ethnicity*, ed. May McCann, Séamas Ó Síocháin, and Joseph Ruane, 95–109. Belfast: Queen's University of Belfast.

McDonagh, Michael, and Winnie McDonagh. 1993. Nomadism. In *Do you know us at all?* ed. John Hyland, 33–40. Dublin: Parish of the Travelling People.

McDonagh, Rosaleen. 1999. Nomadism, ethnicity and disability. *f/m* 3:30–1.

McDonagh, Winnie. 1993. A Traveller Woman's perspective. In *Do you know us at all?* ed. John Hyland, 21–36. Dublin: Parish of the Travelling People.

McGrath, Sean. 1955. Miscellaneous information on Tinkers, particularly in County Clare. Irish Folklore Commission 1439:1–30.

McKeown, Kieran, and Brid McGrath. 1996. *Accommodating Travelling People: A report*. Dublin: Crosscare.

McVeigh, Robbie. 1992. The specificity of Irish racism. *Race and Class* 33(4): 31–45

– 1996. *The racialization of Irishness: Racism and anti-racism in Ireland*. Belfast: CRD.

Meyer, Kuno. 1891. On the Irish origin and the age of Shelta. *Journal of the Gypsy Lore Society*, 1st ser., 2(5):257–65.

Miles, Robert. 1982. *Racism and migrant labour*. London: Routledge and Kegan Paul.

– 1989. *Racism*. London: Routledge.

Minority Rights Group International. 1998. *Roma/Gypsies: A European minority*. London: Minority Rights Group International.

Moore, Henrietta. 1988. *Feminism and anthropology*. Minneapolis: University of Minnesota Press.

Nash, Catherine. 1993. Remapping and renaming: New cartographies of identity, gender and landscape in Ireland. *Feminist Review* 19:39–52.

Ní Shúinéar, Sinéad. 1994. Irish Travellers, ethnicity and the origins question. In *Irish Travellers: Culture and ethnicity*, ed. May McCann, Séamas Ó Síocháin, and Joseph Ruane. Belfast: Queen's University of Belfast.

Nieuwenhuys, Olga. 1994. *Children's lifeworlds*. London: Routledge.

– 1996. The paradox of child labor and anthropology. *Annual Review of Anthropology* 25:237–51.

Noonan, Paul. 1998. Pathologisation and resistance: Travellers, nomadism and the state. In *Divided society: Ethnic minorities and racism in Northern Ireland*, ed. Paul Hainsworth, 152–83. London: Pluto Press.

Ó Cearbhaill, Diarmuid, and Mary Cawley. 1984. Galway City, a changing regional capital: Employment and population since 1966. In *Galway town and gown, 1494–1984*, ed. Diarmuid Ó Cearbhaill, 258–75. Dublin: Gill and Macmillan.

O'Brien Johnson, Toni, and David Cairns, eds. 1991. *Gender in Irish writing*. Milton Keynes: Open University Press.

O'Flaherty, Liam. 1937. *The short stories of Liam O'Flaherty*. London: Jonathan Cape.

O'Hearn, Denis. 1998. *Inside the Celtic tiger: The Irish economy and the Asian model*. London: Pluto Press.

Okely, Judith. 1975. Gypsy women: Models in conflict. In *Perceiving women*, ed. Shirley Ardener, 55–86. London: Malaby.

– 1983. *The Traveller-Gypsies*. Cambridge: Cambridge University Press.

– 1994. An anthropological perspective on Irish Travellers. In *Irish Travellers: Culture and ethnicity*, ed. May McCann, Séamas Ó Síocháin, and Joseph Ruane, 1–19. Belfast: Queen's University of Belfast.

– 1997. Non-territorial culture as the rationale for the assimilation of Gypsy children. *Childhood* 4(1):63–80.

Ong, Aihwa. 1999. *Flexible citizenship*. Durham: Duke University Press.

Ó Nuallain, S., and M. Forde. 1992. *Changing needs of Irish Travellers: Health, education and social issues*. Renmore, Galway: Woodlands Centre.

Ó Tuathaigh, Gearóid. 1972. *Ireland before the famine, 1798–1848*. Dublin: Gill, and Macmillan.

Pahl, R.E. 1984. *Divisions of labour*. Oxford: Basil Blackwell.

Pavee Point. 1992. *Traveller ways, Traveller words*. Dublin: Pavee Point.

Peace, Adrian. 1989. From Arcadia to anomie. *Critique of Anthropology* 9(1):89–111.

Piasere, Leonardo. 1988. De origine cinganorum. In *Recueil V.*, ed. P.H. Stahl, 105–26. Paris: Études et Documents Balkaniques et Méditerraneéns.

Poole, Michael. 1997. In search of ethnicity in Ireland. In *Search of Ireland: A cultural geography*, ed. Brian Graham, 128–47. London: Routledge.

Quinn, David. 1966. *The Elizabethans and the Irish*. Ithaca, N.Y.: Cornell University Press.

Raine, Kathleen, ed. 1981. Introduction to *The Celtic twilight*, by W.B. Yeats, 7–29. Gerrard's Cross: Colin Smythe.

Review Body. 1983. *Report of the Travelling People review body*. Dublin: The Stationery Office.

Rigal, Jocelyne. 1993. The emergence of fertility control among Irish Travellers. *Irish Journal of Sociology* 3:95–108.

Roseberry, William. 1989. *Anthropologies and histories: Essays in culture, history and political economy*. New Brunswick, N.J.: Rutgers University Press.

Rottman, David B., A. Dale Tussing, and Miriam M. Wiley. 1986. *The population structure and living circumstances of Irish Travellers: Results from the 1981 census of Traveller families*. Dublin: The Economic and Social Research Institute.

Sampson, John. 1890. Tinkers and their talk. *Journal of the Gypsy Lore Society*, 1st ser., 2:204–20.

Sandford, Jeremy. 1975. *Gypsies*. London: Sphere Books.

Scheper-Hughes, Nancy, and Carolyn Sargent, eds. 1998. *Small wars: The cultural politics of childhood*. Berkeley: University of California Press.

Scott, James. 1976. *The moral economy of the peasant*. New Haven: Yale University Press.

Segalen, Martine. 1986. *Historical anthropology of the family*. Cambridge: Cambridge University Press.

Sibley, David. 1981. *Outsiders in urban societies*. Oxford: Basil Blackwell.

– 1995. *Geographies of exclusion*. London: Routledge.

Silverman, Marilyn, and Philip Gulliver, eds. 1992. *Approaching the past: Historical anthropology through Irish case studies*. New York: Columbia University Press.

Smythe, Ailbhe, ed. 1993. *Irish women's studies reader*. Dublin: Attic Press.

Stephens, S., ed. 1995. *Children and the politics of culture*. Princeton: Princeton University Press.

Swadener, B., and S. Lubeck, eds. 1995. *Children and families 'at promise': Deconstructing the discourse of risk*. Albany: State University of New York Press.

Synge, John. 1924 (1904). *'The Tinker's Wedding' and other plays*. London: George Allen and Unwin.

– 1966. *Collected works*. Vol. 2. Ed. Alan Price. London: Oxford University Press.

– 1980. *In Wicklow, West Kerry and Connemara*. Dublin: O'Brien Press.

Tannan, Marian, Suzanne Smith, and Suzie Flood. 1998. *Anti-racism: An Irish perspective*. Dublin: Harmony.

Task Force on Child Care Services. 1980. *Task force on child care services: Final report to the minister for health*. Dublin: The Stationery Office.

Task Force on the Travelling Community. 1995. *Report of the task force on the Travelling community*. Dublin: Stationery Office.

Trumpener, Katie. 1992. The time of the Gypsies: A 'people without history' in the narratives of the West. *Critical Inquiry* 18:843–84.

van Dijk, Teun. 1993. *Elite discourse and racism*. Newbury Park: Sage.

– 1997. Political discourse and racism: Describing others in Western parliaments. In *The language and politics of exclusion: Others in discourse*, ed. Stephen Riggins, 31–64. Thousand Oaks, Calif.: Sage.

Varley, Tony. 1996. Farmers against nationalists: The rise and fall of Clann na Talmhan in Galway. In *Galway: History and society*, ed. Gerald Moran, Raymond Gillespie, and William Nolan, 598–622. Dublin: Geography Publications.

Walsh, Patricia. 1971. Itinerancy and poverty. M.A. thesis, University College, Dublin.

Williams, Brackette. 1989. A class act: Anthropology and the race to nation across ethnic terrain. *Annual Review of Anthropology* 18:401–44.

Wolf, Eric. 1982. *Europe and the people without history.* Berkeley: University of California Press.

Wolf, Diane, ed. 1996. *Feminist dilemmas in fieldwork.* Boulder: Westview Press.

Yuval-Davis, Nira. 1997. *Gender and nation.* London: Sage.

Index

ANTHROPOLOGICAL HORIZONS
Editor: Michael Lambek, University of Toronto

This series, begun in 1991, focuses on theoretically ethnographic works address-
ing issues of mind and body, knowledge and power, equality and inequality, the
individual and the collective. Interdisciplinary in its perspective, the series makes
a unique contribution in several other academic disciplines: women's studies,
history, philosophy, psychology, political science, and sociology.

Published to date: